FROZEN MUSIC

FROZEN MUSIC

A LITERARY EXPLORATION OF CALIFORNIA ARCHITECTURE

EDITED BY DAVID CHU

FOREWORD BY JOHN KING

HEYDAY, BERKELEY, CALIFORNIA
SANTA CLARA UNIVERSITY, SANTA CLARA, CALIFORNIA

Library of Congress Cataloging-in-Publication Data

Frozen music : a literary exploration of California architecture /
edited by David Chu ; foreword by John King.
     p. cm. — (A California legacy book)
     ISBN 978-1-59714-137-6 (pbk.)
     1. Architecture—California. 2. Architecture in literature.
I. Chu, David (David F.), 1969–
     NA730.C2F76 2010
     720.9794—dc22   2010014804

Cover Design: Lorraine Rath
Cover photograph: Disney Concert Hall, by Kansas
    Sebastian (Michael Smith)
Interior Design/Typesetting: Leigh McLellan Design
Printing and Binding: Thomson-Shore, Dexter, MI

This California Legacy book was copublished by
Santa Clara University and Heyday. Orders, inquiries, and correspondence should be addressed to:

Heyday
P. O. Box 9145, Berkeley, CA 94709
(510) 549-3564, Fax (510) 549-1889
www.heydaybooks.com

Printed in the United States of America

10 9 8 7 6 5 4 3 2 1

Heyday Books is committed to preserving ancient forests and
natural resources. We elected to print this title on 30% post
consumer recycled paper, processed chlorine free. As a result,
for this printing, we have saved:

11 Trees (40' tall and 6-8" diameter)
4 Million BTUs of Total Energy
1,058 Pounds of Greenhouse Gases
5,095 Gallons of Wastewater
309 Pounds of Solid Waste

Heyday Books made this paper choice because our printer,
Thomson-Shore, Inc., is a member of Green Press Initiative,
a nonprofit program dedicated to supporting authors, publishers, and suppliers in their efforts to reduce their use of fiber
obtained from endangered forests.

For more information, visit www.greenpressinitiative.org

Environmental impact estimates were made using the Environmental Defense
Paper Calculator. For more information visit: www.papercalculator.org.

CONTENTS

FOREWORD

JOHN KING

A STRAND THAT LINKS many of our great buildings is the architectural concept of compression and release—an arrangement of space so that as you move through it, worlds unfold. A cathedral's low foyer makes the worship space beyond feel even more vast; the banking hall's columned grandeur makes doing business with tellers down below at once intimate and charged. Far from being jarring, intense contrasts bring each side into focus all the more.

So it is with the relationship between California's built and natural terrain.

To be sure, the physical landscape around us plays the starring role: those mountains and beaches and forests and creeks are at the core of the vaunted California Dream that, elusive and infinitely variable though it might be, entices one generation after the next, with different cues for different cultures. But pause for a moment to think: would Point Reyes be so mystical, so uniquely alluring, if it weren't a convenient Eden within forty miles of San Francisco's towers and the bungalows of the Oakland hills? Similarly, the blue perfection of San Diego Bay is heightened by the Hotel del Coronado's impossibly white swirls—just as the exotic rigor of Tehachapi Pass holds your memory because of the tight-packed subdivisions that crowd in abruptly as you begin your descent into Los Angeles.

The sensations aren't all rhapsodic; forces of nature can seem especially harrowing in light of the architectural stakes: imagine San Francisco's Coit Tower snapped loose from Telegraph Hill by an earthquake, or the Spanish make-believe of Santa Barbara shaken fiercely into dust. Fire and mudslides claim Malibu homes. "Wracked by floods, droughts, and earthquakes, in terms of safety Los Angeles might just as well be perched on the simmering upper slopes of Vesuvius," wrote *The New Yorker*'s Brendan Gill, one of many outsiders who have lingered on the apocalyptic in describing what they see stretched along the Pacific Coast, "but it doesn't matter: nothing is as outrageous and everlasting as a dream."

So our structures provide shelter, yes, but also a context for understanding what California might mean. They are manifestations of the state's different facets, the forms its image has taken over time, embodiments of why people come here and the lives they strive to create. And, as this long-overdue collection shows, they're a source of inspiration for writers to describe and critique the larger social realm.

One enduring strain of Californian design—real and imagined—is utopianism, the sense here that anything is possible not just in terms of personal lifestyle, but architecturally and urbanistically as well. This is true literally in the case of Edgar Chambless, who, we're told in a florid 1914 *Sunset* profile by Milo Hastings, was a "half-blind" inventor who "built the blocks of civilization into new playhouses of the mind" by conceiving in elaborate detail the notion of a continuous house that, if it were to stretch and snake three thousand miles, could hold the state's entire population of the time. The idea initially came to Chambless on the long-gone Angel's Flight funicular in Los Angeles, Hastings recounts, and his intent is not to mock; he's intrigued by the potential of a scenario where, among other things, all necessary food could be raised within three miles of "this ultra-urban civilization of the endless house."

Far-fetched? Not in our age, when the locavore movement gains strength with each harvest. And no more so than the plastic-tubing houses of Ernest Callenbach's 1975 novel *Ecotopia,* in which families happily fashion "foam-type moldable plastic" into spaces as long or narrow or tall as desired: "the fact that walls and ceiling merge into one another can make for unease at first, yet it is snug and secure too." And Chambless's vision was a foretaste as well of the supercharged work of Zaha Hadid, winner of the 2004 Pritzker Architecture Prize, the profession's highest honor.

Besides, think of all the fanciful worlds that in California exist: the Los Angeles homes drawing inspiration from Hollywood stage sets, the picture-book bohemia of Carmel-by-the-Sea, the crazed and scavenged exuberance of Simon Rodia's Watts Towers, which, in Robert Duncan's wonderful poem "Nel mezzo del cammin di nostra vita," live as:

> the great mitred structure rising
> out of squalid suburbs where the
> mind is beaten back to the traffic, ground
> down to the drugstore…

This is a deft dismissal of all those other California buildings, the mundane and dreary and overbearing ones. Duncan addresses in passing what other writers have dwelt on: a strain of *anti*-utopianism, the conviction that things have changed and not for the better, and from here it will only get worse. Herb Caen made an art of this in the 1960s and '70s, writing column after column on "The Vertical Earthquake"—or, in the column reprinted here, the "Edifice Wrecks" of developers and politicians and how "soon all will be new, bright, shiny and soulless." At this instant, I'll wager, someone is writing or saying the very same thing.

The purpose of this anthology is not to unspool a chronological history of the state's architectural landmarks, or to present a full roster of the designers who have mattered most. There are flavorful profiles of Frank Gehry and Bernard Maybeck—two imaginative iconoclasts born sixty-seven years apart, each absurdly romantic in his own way—but no reference to San Francisco's accomplished George Kelham of the 1920s or Santa Monica's ever-provocative Thom Mayne of today. The Golden Gate Bridge is rendered in loving prose, and the restored mission of San Luis Rey—but not the Transamerica Pyramid, or the State Capitol, or the City Beautiful extravaganzas of San Diego's Balboa Park.

And that's fine: California is a different creature than Chicago or New York City, two locales where the civic identity is bound up in structural drama, skyscraping heights; "Disneyland must be regarded as the most important single piece of construction in the West in the past several decades," architect Charles Moore argued with a straight face in his classic 1964 essay "You Have to Pay for the Public Life." Moore at the time was involved in planning and designing the Californian icon of the decades to come: Sea Ranch, a landscape stretched across the remote Sonoma coast with a design that works hard to disappear, the most lauded piece of architecture there being a rambling collage of low-slung condominiums clad in weathered planks, windows angling for a view while courtyards offer outdoor space sheltered from the ever-present wind.

Sea Ranch also embodies what lies at the heart of California's most inventive architecture: the quest to create places where we can settle as close to nature as possible, life flowing indoors and out, with a minimum amount of (apparent) fuss.

Once this occurred naturally, with tribes like the Achumawi, who would share a communal winter house ("which was really a sort of cave or cellar dug out of the ground and roofed over with sod," we're told by Jaime de Angulo in this anthology's first piece). In *Ramona*, that sepia-tinged evocation of Mexican California, Helen Hunt Jackson dwells lovingly on an arched veranda from which spill vines alive with canaries and finches: "It must have been eighty feet long, at least, for the doors of five large rooms opened on it." Fast-forward from 1884 to the 1940s and we meet the California designer who probably has shaped America's built landscape more than anyone else, residential impresario Cliff May.

May's forte, like Frank Lloyd Wright's, was the single-family home; he also had Wright's flair for self-promotion, flying his own airplane and boasting of never having been a registered architect. But unlike Wright, he had no aspirations toward city making on a grander scale. May perfected the ranch house, with its breezeways and sliding doors and unencumbered rooms, adding suave drama along the way: "Rooms fold into one another and out onto terraces and enclosed patios," Brendan Gill wrote. "A true ranch-house of the nineteenth century was the main structure in a cluster of buildings that were flung up any which way.... May has perfected an apparent randomness of plan that convincingly resembles that cluster and evokes the simplicities of an earlier, more hospitable, and (we may pretend) more affectionate time." These were houses built on the premise that change happens somewhere else, that here you are in control and at ease—which is why ranch houses spread far beyond California into regions much less suited to this version of the good life. The same thing happened with the rough-hewn look of Sea Ranch, part shed and part fort, which cast its spell on anyone who wanted to go back to the land yet also be in the intellectually stylish know. "I'd drive up a rise on some dead straight Kansas highway," Moore's then-partner William Turnbull told writer David Littlejohn, "and sure enough, there it would be: another Sea Ranch condo, out in the middle of the prairie where none of that stuff made sense."

• •

In our new millennium, as a shared awareness of finite resources seems finally to be sinking in, adventurous design has moved away from individual houses for individual families. This won't come as news to anyone who has encountered the farthest-flung subdivisions in California, the ones with the highest foreclosure rates. Big-picture utopianism is back in style: the quest for sustainable design, architecture conceived with an environmental sensibility. It's a shift going on across the globe; California's particular twist is to exult in the potential of what might be. Seize the day. Change the norms.

A pioneer in this field is Sim Van der Ryn—briefly the California State Architect in the 1970s, and ever since a proponent of "green" architecture so far ahead of the curve that even now he stands well outside the mainstream. In an essay included in this volume he describes how, when competing to design the headquarters of a purveyor of solar power systems, he pulled out a watercolor kit and "spent a day on the barren site...letting the site speak to me through my eyes and hands as I sketched." What he heard would make the Achumawi and Helen Hunt Jackson happy: "Why not make the building truly invisible and adapted to the hot summers by using a sod roof, arbors to shade the south wall," and ultimately, "leave the highway behind...and enter another reality?" He got the job.

Projects like this can seem an indulgent sideshow, wide-eyed California feeling good about itself. But then you see these principles, the long pursuit of making earth and building one, play out with a $488 million budget and international acclaim in the California Academy of Sciences, designed by Italy's Renzo Piano and covered by the world's largest living roof, a terrain of indigenous wildflowers that curves up and over the attractions inside—new hillocks in Golden Gate Park. "It's a landscape that witnesses what is underneath it," Piano tells writer Karen Steen in one of the final pieces here, and with it the notion of "sustainability" gains a romantic tinge, none the less authentic for the fact that the setting is a forested park imposed upon sand dunes a century ago.

So as you read these pieces—straight profiles, science fiction, novelistic riffs, and historic surveys—don't look for a single grand story to evolve. That's not California, and it never has been. Our narrative is compression and release, high hopes and ominous fears, dutiful city building and idiosyncratic joys. Above all, buildings that represent the aspirations or perseverance of a family, a culture, a class. And if you wonder what's coming next, you aren't alone. The story has only begun.

ACKNOWLEDGMENTS

I EXPRESS MY PROFOUND appreciation to all those who assisted in the location and selection of material for this anthology. Warm thanks go to Gray Brechin, Michael Corbett, and Jim Snyder for their suggestions of both fiction and nonfiction pieces for the book. I thank Paulette Singley of Woodbury University School of Architecture for her guidance through the wide spectrum of writing on the architecture of Los Angeles. A thank-you goes to Jesse Nelson for his advice on contemporary architecture publications and Los Angeles architectural landmarks. Thanks as well to Laurie Hannah, Jarrell Jackman, and Anne Petersen at the Santa Barbara Trust for Historic Preservation for their insights into the built and natural environments of Santa Barbara. My appreciation also goes to Tim Culvahouse, editor of *arcCA* (*Architecture California*), and Lori Reed at the American Institute of Architects, California Council, for their assistance in obtaining journal articles. Thanks also to Anthea Hartig of the National Trust for Historic Preservation and to Linda Eade at the Yosemite Research Library of the National Park Service for their advice on researching particular topics.

My thanks go as well to Kate Brumage, Lillian Fleer, Jeannine Gendar, David Isaacson, Wendy Rockett, and Julian Segal, all of the Heyday staff, for their suggestions of architects, writers, subjects, articles, and stories to include in this collection. Thanks also go to Heyday intern Tim Hopkins for scanning and proofreading the selections. Tremendous thanks go to Terry Beers of Santa Clara University, editor of the California Legacy series, for his comments on the selection of pieces, and to John King, urban design writer at the *San Francisco Chronicle*, for his feedback on the selections and his superb foreword to the book.

My sincere appreciation goes to Malcolm Margolin, publisher of Heyday, for his counsel and the confidence that he placed in this project. Finally, I offer my deepest thanks to Gayle Wattawa, acquisitions editor at Heyday, for her publishing expertise, her insights into the purpose of this book, and her patient and steadfast mentoring throughout the editorial process.

JAIME DE ANGULO

Jaime de Angulo was born to Spanish parents in Paris in 1887. He first came to the United States in 1905 and settled in California around 1913. A graduate of Johns Hopkins Medical School, de Angulo worked as an army physician, cattle rancher, anthropologist, and linguist. In 1921, he stayed with the Achumawi Indians of Modoc County, California, for two months, studying their language and culture. This time is chronicled in de Angulo's collection of interviews with and stories from the Achumawi people, *Indians in Overalls*. Jaime de Angulo died in 1950.

• •

This excerpt from *Indians in Overalls* humorously portrays life in a communal winter house of the Achumawi people and makes clear the practical considerations that guided the design of the building.

from *INDIANS IN OVERALLS*

SUKMIT AND HIS MOTHER were forever quarreling, usually in Pit River, but sometimes in English for my edification. At first it worried me but after a while I paid no more attention to it than to the breeze. The old lady had been born in an old-time Indian house. She described it to me in detail, and even made me a little model of it one day with sticks and bits of mud. She was very keen at explaining to me many apparently meaningless details, which become quite important when you consider the realities of life, and the necessities of a materially primitive culture. She had been born and reared in such a culture and had an artist's eye for the significant differences. For instance she was explaining to me that there was no door in the communal winter house (which was really a sort of cave or cellar dug out of the ground and roofed over with sod)—people went in or out through the smoke-hole by climbing a stepladder set up against the center-post. But at one end of the house there was a tunnel that led out to the outside ground, like a rabbit warren. This was for purposes of ventilation, of establishing a draft of air into and through the crowded house and out through the smoke-hole. The chiefs, the important men, usually sat or lay there on their backs, smoking their stonepipes and enjoying the fresh air (forty or fifty humans including babies can make a thick atmosphere!). Now, mothers and fathers climbed the ladder with small children in their arms, or on the hip, or strapped to the cradle-board; but bigger youngsters crawled out through the rabbit warren; and the chiefs would grab them, and hug them, and tease them, as grownups do the world over. Such a description put the whole picture in focus for me. And again the old lady (who had a pornographic mind) would say: "...the smoke-hole pretty big—have to step across, grab pole—young girl take time step across show everything....Ha, ha, ha!...you white man, ha, ha, ha!..."

GEORGE VANCOUVER

George Vancouver was born in England in 1757 and joined the Royal Navy at thirteen. As a young man he sailed with Captain James Cook on the voyage leading to the discovery of Hawaii. In 1791 Vancouver commanded an expedition to explore the Pacific coast of North America, and in April of 1792 he sighted that coast near what is now Vancouver Island. He named Puget Sound as well as many other geographic features of the Pacific Northwest. Vancouver eventually traveled along the Pacific coast as far north as Alaska and as far south as San Luis Obispo. During these years, he surveyed the coast north of San Francisco Bay several times. George Vancouver returned to England in 1794 and died there in 1798.

• •

Vancouver's memoir of his expedition, *A Voyage of Discovery to the North Pacific Ocean and Round the World*, was published after his death. In this excerpt, he gives a detailed account of Presidio structures and individual Spanish dwellings in San Francisco, in addition to specifics on the conical houses of the local Indians.

from *A VOYAGE OF DISCOVERY TO THE NORTH PACIFIC OCEAN AND ROUND THE WORLD*

THE RESIDENCE OF the friars is called a Mission. We soon arrived at the Presidio, which was not more than a mile from our landing place. Its wall, which fronted the harbour, was visible from the ships; but instead of the city or town, whose lights we had so anxiously looked for on the night of our arrival, we were conducted into a spacious verdant plane, surrounded by hills on every side, excepting that which fronted the port. The only object of human industry which presented itself, was a square area, whose sides were about two hundred yards in length, enclosed by a mud wall, and resembling a pound for cattle. Above this wall the thatched roofs of their low small houses just made their appearance. On entering the Presidio, we found one of its sides still unindosed by the wall, and very indifferently fenced in by a few bushes here and there, fastened to stakes on the ground. The unfinished state of this part, afforded us an opportunity of seeing the strength of the wall, and the manner in which it was constructed. It is about fourteen feet high, and five feet in breadth, and was first formed by uprights and horizontal rafters of large timber, between which dried sods and moistened earth were pressed as close and as hard as possible; after which the whole was cased with the earth made into a fort of mud plaster, which gave it the appearance of durability, and of being sufficiently strong to protect them, with the assistance of their fire-arms, against all the force which the natives of the country might be able to collect.

The Spanish soldiers composing the garrison amounted, I understood, to thirty-five; who, with their wives, families, and a few Indian servants, composed the whole of the inhabitants. Their houses were along the wall, within the square, and their fronts uniformly extended the same distance into the area, which is a clear open space, without buildings or other interruptions. The only entrance into it, is by a large gateway; facing which, and against the centre of the opposite wall or side, is the church; which, though small, was neat in comparison to the rest of the building. This projects further into the square than the houses, and is distinguishable from the other edifices, by being white-washed with lime made from sea-shells; as there has not yet been any lime-stone or calcarous earth discovered in the neighborhood. On the left of the church, is the commandant's house, consisting, I believe, of two rooms and a closet only, which are divided by massy walls, familiar to that which encloses the square, and communicating with each other by very small doors. Between these apartments and the outward wall was an excellent poultry house and yard, which seemed pretty well stocked; and between the roof and ceilings of the rooms was a kind of lumber garret: these were all the conveniencies the habitation seemed calculated to afford. The rest of the houses, though smaller, were fashioned exactly after the same manner; and in the winter, or rainy seasons, must at the best be very uncomfortable dwellings. For though the walls are a sufficient security against the inclemency of the weather, yet the windows, which are cut in the front wall, and look into the square, are destitute of glass, or any other defence that does not at the same time exclude the light.

The apartment in the commandant's house, into which we were ushered, was about thirty feet long, fourteen feet broad, and twelve feet high; and the other room, or chamber, I judged to be of the same dimensions, excepting in its length, which appeared to be somewhat less. The floor was of the native soil raised about three feet from its original level, without being boarded, paved, or even reduced to an even surface: the roof was covered in with flags and rushes, the walls on the inside had once been white-washed; the furniture consisted of a very sparing assortment of the most indispensable articles, of the rudest fashion, and of the meanest kind; and ill accorded with the ideas we had conceived of the sumptuous manner in which the Spaniards live on this side of the globe.[...]

The next day, being Sunday, was appointed for my visiting the mission. Accompanied by Mr. Menzies and some of the officers, and our friendly Senᵣ Sal, I rode thither to dinner. Its distance from the presidio is about a league, in an eastwardly direction; our ride was rendered unpleasant by the soil being very loose and sandy, and by the road being much incommoded with low groveling bushes.

Its situation and external appearance in a great measure resembled that of the presidio; and, like its neighbourhood, the country was pleasingly diversified with hill and dale. The hills were at a greater distance from each other, and gave more extent to the plain, which is composed of a soil infinitely richer than that of the presidio, being a mixture of sand and a black vegetable mould. The pastures bore a more luxuriant herbage, and fed a greater number of sheep and cattle. The barren sandy country through which we had passed, seemed to make a natural division between the lands of the mission and those of the presidio, and extends from the shores of the port to the foot of a ridge of mountains, which border on the exterior coast, and appear to stretch in a line parallel to it. The verdure of the plain continued to a considerable height up the sides of these hills; the summits of which, though still composed chiefly of rugged rocks, produced a few trees.

The buildings of the mission formed two sides of a square only, and did not appear as if intended, at any future time, to form a perfect quadrangle like the presidio. The architecture and materials, however, seemed nearly to correspond.

On our arrival, we were received by the reverend fathers with every demonstration of cordiality, friendship, and the most genuine hospitality. We were instantly conducted to their mansion, which was situated near, and communicated with the church. The houses formed a small oblong square, the side of the church composed one end, near which were the apartments allotted to the fathers. These were constructed nearly after the manner of those at the presidio, but appeared to be more finished, better contrived, were larger, and much more cleanly. Along the walls of this interior square, were also many other apartments adapted to various purposes.[…]

[The Indians'] houses were of a conical form, about six or seven feet in diameter at the base (which is the ground), and are constructed by a number of stakes, chiefly of the willow tribe, which are driven erect into the earth in a circular manner, the upper ends of which being small and pliable are brought nearly to join at the top, in the center of the circle; and these being securely fastened, give the upper part or roof somewhat of a flattish appearance. Thinner twigs of the like species are horizontally interwoven between the uprights, forming a piece of basket work about ten or twelve feet high; at the top a small aperture is left, which allows the smoke of the fire made in the center of the hut to escape, and admits most of the light they receive: the entrance is by a small hole close to the ground, through which with difficulty one person at a time can gain admittance. The whole is covered over with a thick thatch of dried grass and rushes.[…]

Close by stood the church, which for its magnitude, architecture, and internal decorations did great credit to the constructors of it; and presented a striking contrast between the exertions of genius, and such as bare necessity is capable of suggesting. The raising and decorating this edifice appeared to have greatly attracted the attention of the fathers; and the comforts they might have provided in their own humble habitations, seemed to have been totally sacrificed to the accomplishment of this favorite object. Even their garden, an object of such material importance, had not yet acquired any great degree of cultivation, though its soil was a rich black mould, and promised an ample return for any labour that might be bestowed upon it. The whole contained about four acres, was tolerably well fenced in, and produced some fig, peach, apple, and other fruit-trees, but afforded a very scanty supply of useful vegetables; the principal part lying waste and over-run with weeds.

On our return to the convent, we found a most excellent and abundant repast provided of beef, mutton, fish, fowls, and such vegetables as their garden afforded. The attentive and hospitable behaviour of our new friends amply compensated for the homely manner in which the dinner was served; and would certainly have precluded my noticing the distressing inconvenience these valuable people labour under, in the want of almost all the common and most necessary utensils of life, had I not been taught to expect, that this colony was in a very different stage of improvement, and that its inhabitants were infinitely more comfortably circumstanced.

HELEN HUNT JACKSON

Journalist, essayist, and novelist Helen Hunt Jackson was born in Massachusetts in 1830. Already a well-known writer by the 1870s, she gained additional fame in 1881 for *A Century of Dishonor*, her challenge to the U.S. government's treatment of American Indians. The book led to Jackson's appointment to a commission charged with investigating living conditions among the Mission Indians of Southern California. This investigative work resulted in Jackson's 1884 novel, *Ramona*, set in California at the end of the Mexican era. In it Jackson continued her advocacy of the rights of Indians while creating idealized depictions of California locales. Jackson's death in 1885 in San Francisco brought her work to an untimely end.

• •

In this description from *Ramona* of an adobe house, the author celebrates the natural abundance visible from the home's expansive veranda and open layout.

from *RAMONA*

THE SEÑORA MORENO'S house was one of the best specimens to be found in California of the representative house of the half barbaric, half elegant, wholly generous and free-handed life led there by Mexican men and women of degree in the early part of this century, under the rule of the Spanish and Mexican viceroys, when the laws of the Indies were still the laws of the land, and its old name, "New Spain," was an ever-present link and stimulus to the warmest memories and the deepest patriotism of its people.

It was a picturesque life, with more of the sentiment and gayety in it, more also that was truly dramatic, more romance, than will ever be seen again on those sunny shores. The aroma of it all lingers there still; industries and inventions have not yet slain it; it will last out its century—in fact, it can never be quite lost, so long as there is left standing one such house as the Señora Moreno's.[…]

The house was of adobe, low, with a wide veranda on the three sides of the inner court, and a still broader one across the entire front, which looked to the south. These verandas, especially those on the inner court, were supplementary rooms to the house. The greater part of the family life went on in them. Nobody stayed inside the walls, except when it was necessary. All the kitchen work, except the actual cooking, was done here, in front of the kitchen doors and windows. Babies slept, were washed, sat in the dirt, and played, on the veranda. The women said their prayers, took naps, and wove their lace there. Old Juanita shelled her beans there, and threw the pods down on the tile floor; till towards night they were sometimes piled up high around her, like corn-husks at a husking. The herdsmen and shepherds smoked there, lounged there, trained their dogs there; there the young made love, and the old dozed; the benches, which ran the entire length of the walls, were worn into hollows and shone like satin; the tiled floors also were broken and sunk in places, making little wells, which filled up in times of hard rains, and were then an invaluable addition to the children's resources for amusement, and also to the comfort of the dogs, cats, and fowls, who picked about among them, taking sips from each.

The arched veranda along the front was a delightsome place. It must have been eighty feet long, at least, for the doors of five large rooms opened on it. The two westernmost rooms had been added on, and made four steps higher than the others; which gave to that end of the veranda the look of a balcony, or loggia. Here the Señora kept her flowers; great red water-jars, hand-made by the Indians of San Luis Obispo Mission, stood in close rows against the walls, and in them were always growing fine geraniums, carnations, and yellow-flowered musk. The Señora's passion for musk she had inherited from her mother. It was so strong that she sometimes wondered at it; and one day, as she sat with Father Salvierderra in the veranda, she picked a handful of the blossoms, and giving them to him, said, "I do not know why it is, but it seems to me if I were dead I could be brought to life by the smell of musk."

"It is in your blood, Señora," the old monk replied. "When I was last in your father's house in Seville, your mother sent for me to her room, and under her window was a stone balcony full of growing musk, which so filled the room with its odor that I was like to faint. But she said it cured her of diseases, and without it she fell ill. You were a baby then."

"Yes," cried the Señora, "but I recollect that balcony. I recollect being lifted up to a window, and looking down into a bed of blooming yellow flowers; but I did not know what they were. How strange!"

"No. Not strange, daughter," replied Father Salvierderra. "It would have been stranger if you had not acquired the taste, thus drawing it in with the mother's milk. It would behoove mothers to remember this far more than they do."

Besides the geraniums and carnations and musk in the red jars, there were many sorts of climbing vines—some coming from the ground, and twining around the pillars of the veranda; some growing in great bowls, swung by cords from the roof of the veranda, or set on shelves against the walls. These bowls were of gray stone, hollowed and polished shining smooth inside and out. They also had been made by the Indians, nobody knew how many ages ago, scooped and polished by the patient creatures, with only stones for tools.

Among these vines, singing from morning till night, hung the Señora's canaries and finches, half a dozen of each, all of different generations, raised by the Señora. She was never without a young bird-family on hand; and all the way from Bonaventura to Monterey, it was thought a piece of good luck to come into possession of a canary or finch of Señora Moreno's raising.

Between the veranda and the river meadows, out on which it looked, all was garden, orange grove, and almond orchard; the orange grove always green, never without snowy bloom or golden fruit; the garden never without flowers, summer or winter; and the almond orchard, in early spring, a fluttering canopy of pink and white petals, which, seen from the hills on the opposite side of the river, looked as if rosy sunrise clouds had fallen, and become tangled in the treetops. On either hand stretched away other orchards—peach, apricot, pear, apple, pomegranate; and beyond these, vineyards. Nothing was to be seen but verdure or blossom or fruit, at whatever time of year you sat on the Señora's south veranda.

A wide straight walk shaded by a trellis so knotted and twisted with grapevines that little was to be seen of the trellis wood-work, led straight down from the veranda steps, through the middle of the garden, to a little brook at the foot of it. Across this brook, in the shade of a dozen gnarled old willow-trees, were set the broad flat stone washboards on which was done all the family washing. No long dawdling, and no running away from work on the part of the maids, thus close to the eye of the Señora at the upper end of the garden; and if they had known how picturesque they looked there, kneeling on the grass, lifting the dripping linen out of the water, rubbing it back and forth on the stones, sousing it, wringing it, splashing the clear water in each other's faces, they would have been content to stay at the washing day in and day out, for there was always somebody to look on from above. Hardly a day passed that the Señora had not visitors. She was still a person of note; her house the natural resting-place for all who journeyed through the valley; and whoever came, spent all of his time, when not eating, sleeping, or walking over the place, sitting with the Señora on the sunny veranda. Few days in winter were cold enough, and in summer the day must be hot indeed to drive the Señora and her friends indoors. There stood on the veranda three carved oaken chairs, and a carved bench, also of oak, which had been brought to the Señora for safe keeping by the faithful old sacristan of San Luis Rey, at the time of the occupation of that Mission by the United States troops, soon after the conquest of California. Aghast at the sacrilegious acts of the soldiers, who were quartered in the very church itself, and amused themselves by making targets of the eyes and noses of the saints' statues, the sacristan, stealthily, day by day and night after night, bore out of the church all that he dared to remove, burying some articles in cottonwood copses, hiding others in his own poor little hovel, until he had wagon-loads of sacred treasures. Then, still more stealthily, he carried them, a few at a time, concealed in the bottom of a cart, under a load of hay or of brush, to the house of the Señora, who felt herself deeply honored by his confidence, and received everything as a sacred trust, to be given back into the hands of the Church again, whenever the Missions should be restored, of which at that time all Catholics had good hope. And so it had come about that no bedroom in the Señora's house was without a picture or a statue of a saint or of the Madonna; and some had two; and in the little chapel in the garden the altar was surrounded by a really imposing row of holy and apostolic figures, which had looked down on the splendid ceremonies of the San Luis Rey Mission, in Father Peyri's time, no more benignly than they now did on the humbler worship of the Señora's family in its diminished estate. That one had lost an eye, another an arm, that the once brilliant colors of the drapery were now faded and shabby, only enhanced the tender reverence with which the Señora knelt before them, her eyes filling with indignant tears at thought of the heretic hands which had wrought such defilement. Even the crumbling wreaths which had been placed on some of these statues' heads at the time of the last ceremonial at which they had figured in the Mission, had been brought away with them by the devout sacristan, and the Señora had replaced each one, holding it only a degree less sacred than the statue itself.

GRAY BRECHIN

Gray Brechin was born in Los Altos, California. After many years as a television producer and architecture critic, Brechin earned a Ph.D. in geography from the University of California, Berkeley. His dissertation became *Imperial San Francisco: Urban Power, Earthly Ruin*, an environmental history of San Francisco's brutal exploitation of its surroundings. Brechin has also produced, with photographer Robert Dawson, *Farewell Promised Land: Waking from the California Dream* and has received the Dorothea Lange–Paul Taylor Prize, a Bancroft Fellowship, and a Ciriacy-Wantrup Postdoctoral Fellowship. Now vice president of the National New Deal Preservation Association, Brechin is working on a new book on the legacy of the New Deal. He lives in Berkeley.

• •

In the following article from a November 1990 issue of *SF* magazine, Brechin discusses several buildings of civic significance for San Francisco while also illustrating the broader social history of the city.

PRAYERS FROM THE PAST:
EARLY SYNAGOGUES OF SAN FRANCISCO

IMAGINE STANDING ON the turret of the Mark Hopkins mansion on Nob Hill in 1878, when Eadweard Muybridge photographed his famous panorama of San Francisco from there. Except for the hills, you would have seen a typical low-rise American city whose skyline was dominated by church steeples rather than skyscrapers. You'd probably have mistaken the majestic building just a block up from Union Square for the town cathedral, but onion domes on the twin spires were a tip-off that this was something else. Easily the most magnificent religious building in town, Temple Emanu-El stood for the early prominence of German Jews in the premier city of the American West.

Few today are aware of that prominence. Most of the standard histories of San Francisco would lead you to believe the Stanfords, Floods, Phelans, and other WASPs and WASCs had built the town. Though you will find donated parks named Koshland and Stern, you'll find no streets named Sloss or Lilienthal, despite the fact that without these and the associated families of Emanu-El, culture and philanthropy in San Francisco would have been threadbare.

These were not people who sought attention with Nob Hill castles and trumpeted charities. For the most part, they kept a low profile; scandals were kept discreetly *en famille*. Their Sutter Street temple, however, stood as testimony to their collective importance in the city—a city largely free of the anti-Semitism they had experienced in the East and in Europe.

That was because Jews grew up with the country. The Gold Rush corresponded with the aborted European revolutions of 1848 and the wave of anti-Semitism which followed. Jews were among the first to arrive in the West along with the other gold-seekers. They came to a land with new opportunities thanks to the recent American conquest; as one Jewish historian, Gustav Danziger, noted in 1895, there had probably been no Jews in California before 1848 "for the very simple reason that Alta California having been once the dominion of the Rey Catolico, and the population indolently submissive to the representatives of the Church of Rome, California might in all probability have been a good place for Jews to stay away from." After the American conquest, California wasn't a Catholic state anymore and many Jews began to envision the American West as their new Palestine, San Francisco as the new Jerusalem.

While Jewish men trekked east from the Golden Gate to try their luck in the roaring camps of the Mother Lode, most soon found mining a risky business and returned to the booming cities of the lowland. Careers in finance and dry goods were a good deal less romantic than striking it rich on the Yuba River, but they offered far steadier returns. Levi Strauss, for example, made a tidy fortune supplying blue jeans to those who persisted in mining. Today's giant Seligmann Brothers banking house got its start in San Francisco. Jews were, on the whole, a respected feature of San Francisco business. The least hint of anti-Semitism in the press was usually met with a quick rebuttal by Jew or gentile.

As Protestants and Catholics were establishing their pioneer churches, Jews were organizing their synagogues. Liturgical and social differences caused an immediate schism among Jews who had been worshipping in San Francisco. In 1850, Bavarians founded the Temple Emanu-El ("God

Is With Us"), and the Poles and Englishmen founded the more conservative Sherith Israel ("Remnants of Israel"). Many other synagogues would follow, but these two remained the chief reform congregations in the city and they built the grandest houses of worship.

Members of Emanu-El were, from the start, the Hebraic aristocrats of California. They married among themselves until their genealogies resembled a map of the New York subway system. Other Jews charged them with elitism and exclusivity. When passing through Emanu-El's cemetery in Colma, one member of Sherith Israel recalled, "I felt as ill at ease among the bones of the people buried there as I had among their living bodies."

If Emanu-El was the richest congregation, it was also, from the start, the most liberal. Its rabbis advocated assimilation and modernization of ritual, while those of Sherith Israel remained more traditional. Indeed, many Jews were alarmed at the lengths to which Emanu-El congregants were willing to go. Gustav Danziger charged them with an excess of intellect that eroded religious practice: "Eight out of every ten cultured young men and women are agnostic. It may speak much for Jewish liberalism that sixty percent of the nonvoting members of the Young Men's Christian Association are Jews; but it speaks at the same time volumes against their cohesiveness and their own building up. It is certainly a destructive democracy." Eating pork was one thing, sharing Thanksgiving with the Unitarians another, but Christmas trees and Easter egg hunts were going a bit far.

Congregation Emanu-El first considered building its temple on the crest of Nob Hill. Andrew Hallidie had not yet invented the cable car, however, and the directors ultimately decided that the site was more spectacular than accessible. They sold the site and, in 1864, built their temple instead on Sutter near Powell. Described as "Gothic-Byzantine" by its English architect, Gothic emphatically had the upper hand. The structure resembled an English Perpendicular cathedral except for the Star of David motif that liberally adorned windows and masonry. Even the onion domes recalled the Bavarian churches with which the German congregants were familiar.

The synagogue that Sherith Israel built six years later and two blocks to the west of Emanu-El looked even more like a church.

It bristled with Gothic finials and pointed arches. If you missed the tiny onion domes at the tips of its spires, you could easily have mistaken it for something Lutheran.

Perhaps because its architecture was a little too reform, Sherith Israel's directors decided to build a new temple at the turn of the century a mile west of the original site. San Francisco architect Albert Pissis, who also designed the Emporium and Flood buildings, gave the congregation a Romanesque-Baroque hybrid synagogue this time. Since Sherith Israel opened at California and Webster in 1905 its great dome has dominated southern Pacific Heights and sheltered the Jewish community of the Western Addition.

Today, Sherith Israel exudes an exotic Edwardian splendor. The walls and dome of its 1,400-seat auditorium are covered with complex polychrome stencils in a remarkable state of preservation. Wainscoting and pews are made of ruddy Honduran mahogany. The temple has some of the finest stained-glass windows in the city; on the west wall, Moses delivers the Ten Commandments in Yosemite Valley. The temple also has magnificent acoustics, amply demonstrated by its pipe organ and the seraphic voices that descend from a choir gallery in the dome.

Sherith Israel moved its temple just in time to be spared the destruction of the 1906 fire. After the disaster the temple's long-reigning and widely respected rabbi, Jacob Nieto, began a nationwide movement to provide for community welfare centers connected with synagogues.

Temple Emanu-El was not as lucky as Sherith Israel and was entirely gutted in the 1906 fire. Emanu-El's congregation shared quarters with the Unitarians while its temple was reconstructed. But 15 years later, the directors voted to sell the old site and leapfrog Sherith Israel by more than a mile, building a new temple at Lake and Arguello. Timothy Pflueger's swank 450 Sutter Street, the Medical-Dental Building, now stands where Emanu-El once did.

The temple's directors chose the architectural firm of Bakewell and Brown, designers of San Francisco's City Hall, to work with Emanu-El member Sylvain Schnaittacher. The architects took their inspiration from Hagia Sophia in Istanbul, the seminal Byzantine monument that has been a mosque for so long that many forget it began as a Christian church. The directors did not want something that looked like a cathedral this time and were willing to pay handsomely for it. The cost—$1,300,000—made Emanu-El one of the most expensive temples in the world; the congregation paid cash. The temple opened with much fanfare in 1926.

For Emanu-El, Bakewell and Brown abandoned the fine classical detailing that marked their other public buildings and relied instead on simple geometry to create a building of great power and clarity. Its tan, blocky forms mount to an immense red-tile dome clearly visible across the western city. Numerous arches echo the curve of the culminating dome.

The site the directors bought was so ample that the architects incorporated an arcaded courtyard in their plan. Descriptions of Solomon's temple suggested a courtyard with a fountain; olive trees, a fig and a cedar of Lebanon recall the Middle East, though the Richmond District fog does not. Bernard Maybeck was a consultant on the project, and it is in this theatrical space with its carved lion heads and bronze lanterns that one feels the influence of Berkeley's master set-designer.

The stark geometric clarity of the exterior is carried into the temple's auditorium. Unlike Sherith Israel's ornamental abundance, Emanu-El relies on a few points of exquisite richness: the six colossal chandeliers, the contemporary stained-glass window—representing fire and water— by Mark Adams, and, above all, the freestanding Ark of the Covenant within a peaked ciborium behind the pulpit. Los Gatos craftsmen George Dennison and Richard Ingerson created the 3,000-pound bronze house of the Torah in 1927.

The doctrinal schism that created Emanu-El and Sherith Israel in 1850 was only the first, as San Francisco Jews continued to argue about how far modernization should go. When Emanu-El adopted a reform liturgy in 1864, 55 members seceded and formed a new temple called Ohabai Shalom. Like the parent congregation, it was primarily composed of Bavarians, but like Sherith Israel, it was also more conservative.

In 1895, congregation Ohabai Shalom constructed a remarkable Victorian synagogue on Bush Street near Laguna. Architect Moses Lyon concocted a farrago of styles impossible to mistake for a Christian church. The central entry has a Romanesque tympanum, the second floor features a Gothic filigree gallery cribbed from the Doge's Palace in Venice, while the twin towers originally resembled minarets with Islamic arches and fretwork crowned by bulbous onion domes. Both towers were blown down sometime before 1916. The redwood facade was scored in alternating horizontal bands to resemble rusticated and smooth masonry. Now, almost a century later, the temple of Ohabai Shalom is one of the oldest and most unusual synagogues in the West.

Unfortunately, the building outlived its congregation, which left in 1934. A group of Zen Buddhists bought the temple in 1940, and it remained a Buddhist church until the early 1960s. The Redevelopment Agency then acquired it as a prelude to its plan to level the neighborhood. Blocked by preservationists and local activists from doing so, the agency leased the building to a Japanese Go club. In 1980, a gay Jewish congregation tried to buy the building but was stymied by red tape; it moved to the Castro instead.

Decades of neglect show on Temple Ohabai Shalom. With virtually no maintenance, all vestiges of paint have long since flaked off; as the neighborhood around it has gone upscale, the Bush Street temple has gone down. It stands today as a decaying image of the Depression in the midst of contemporary affluence.

That is about to change. A nonprofit group called the Bush Street Synagogue Cultural Center has acquired an option to buy the building and has prepared plans to completely restore it. The towers will be rebuilt, and stained-glass windows were found in place, largely intact, merely boarded over. The main auditorium will be converted to a performance space for a Jewish theater company, while the rest of the building will become an exhibition space devoted to the role of Jews in early California. The plan includes a proposal to build, on the adjacent corner lot, a new three-story building to house a Holocaust center and library, and an extension of the Lehrhaus Judaica school. Spaces will be available for neighborhood use.

A new group of historians has recently begun to reveal the extraordinarily diverse people who settled the American West. As these revisionist scholars peel away the veneer of cowboys and railroad kings, they are discovering a mosaic of startling complexity. Jews, too, were significant in the building of the West, and the restoration of the Bush Street Temple will add greatly to the emerging design.

JEAN PFAELZER

Jean Pfaelzer teaches American literature, labor studies, women's studies, and feminist theory at the University of Delaware, where she is a professor of English and American studies. In addition to dozens of articles, Pfaelzer has written five books, including *The Utopian Novel in America* and *Rebecca Harding Davis and the Origins of Social Realism*. She has served as executive director of the National Labor Law Center, as a member of the Washington, D.C., Commission for Women, and as senior legislative analyst for Congressman Frank McCloskey. Pfaelzer recently completed work on a television documentary devoted to the Chinese experience in Humboldt County, California. She currently resides outside Washington, D.C.

• •

This excerpt from *Driven Out,* Pfaelzer's history of anti-Chinese violence in California, reveals how the Chinese community in nineteenth-century San Jose made creative use of architecture to maintain a presence in the city despite white hostility.

from **"THE CHINESE REWRITE THE LETTER OF THE LAW"**

in *Driven Out: The Forgotten War against Chinese Americans*

HEAT AND DESTRUCTION

IN 1883 CHINATOWN had organized its own volunteer fire department, equipped with ladders and buckets, and rehearsed its fire brigades. But at three o'clock on the afternoon of March 4, 1887, most of the Chinese had gone to a gambling house to hear the announcement of the lottery winner. No one was there to witness the arson in Ah Toy Alley, which had been set ablaze a few minutes earlier. Chinatown thought it had prepared for danger.

Most of Chinatown was destroyed, although, as the *San Jose Evening News* reported, with "superhuman efforts" the city's Alert Hose Fire Company "saved *the ground on which* Chinatown was located and prevented the spread of the fire to the surrounding buildings" (italics added). The Chinese buildings burned, it said, because the firemen found "poor hose" and "low water pressure." Even aided by the mayor and some city councilmen, the Chinese fire brigade was unable to check the flames because someone had drained the Chinese water tank. It was not by chance that during the two weeks preceding the blaze prominent white property owners in Chinatown had added heavily to their fire insurance."

The night of the fire, some of the Chinese found shelter with friends, others slept on the floors and tables of a large laundry building, and still others slept outside in its drying yard, as the newspaper put it, "enjoying the cool air after the day of heat and destruction." By the morning of March 5, all that remained of Chinatown was one brick building, a theater, where many Chinese workers had recently watched the opera *The Romance of Three Kingdoms*.

Two months later, the *San Jose Daily Herald* declared, "Chinatown is dead. It is dead forever."

The city council tried to prevent the resurrection of Chinatown in the center of town. It announced that the scorched property that abutted the new city hall would be "more valuable for other purposes," and it hoped that the new police headquarters would frighten off the Chinese. The city began to investigate the land deeds and titles in an effort to establish a claim to all the land that was occupied by Chinatown. In the ashes it found the ruins of the Mexican city center.

SAN-DOY-SAY TONG HUNG FOW

In June, two quite different Chinatowns began to rebuild. Chinese laborers gravitated toward the outskirts of town along the Guadalupe River. Mitchell Phillips, owner of the nearby San Jose Woolen Mills, built "Woolen Mills Chinatown" to keep his Chinese laborers nearby. He leased the property to a broker, Chin Shin, who in turn rented houses and beds to Chinese mill, cannery, and glove-factory workers. Chin Shin also built the Garden City Cannery there and employed hundreds of Chinese himself.

But the Chinese merchants built their Chinatown across the street from city hall. They had defeated an injunction, raised by the Home Protection Association, against their landlord John Heinlen, a sympathetic German refugee and wealthy rancher who had purchased the land in 1867. Nonetheless, the city contained its size by forbidding the use of any traditional Pueblo lands "for the benefit of any Chinese or Mongolians."

Only two weeks after the fire, merchant Quen Hing Tong signed a master lease for fifteen hundred dollars per month. Fearful of another fire, Heinlen and the Chinese merchants worked with popular architect Theodore Lenzen, who had designed many of the town's prominent mansions and the new city hall, to plan a protected enclave, surrounded by a high picket fence covered with barbed wire. All of the buildings were to be made of brick and face inward. The merchants would post signs, in English, at each entrance reading NO ADMITTANCE and PRIVATE GROUNDS, and the maze of small, unpaved, but gated streets were to be locked each night.

The city was well aware of the Chinese's defiant stance. During construction the *San Jose Daily Mercury* commented, "The place hasn't been roofed in yet, but there's no telling what may happen if the high fence and barbed wire fail to keep out objectionable visitors." At the cost of sixty thousand dollars, San-Doy-Say Tong Hung Fow—"San Jose's Chinatown"—sprang up. Both white and Chinese residents called it Heinlentown or Heinlenville. Schools, restaurants, and shops opened, and a new temple, Ng Shing Gung, was decorated with silk hangings and equipped with incense burners, and the finest bells outside of Canton. San-Doy-Say Tong Hung Fow again became a spiritual and cultural center for the Chinese throughout the Santa Clara Valley. Historian Connie Young Yu, whose grandparents lived there, recalls that the walls gave Chinese families a great deal of safety: "Children could play in the streets. No ruffians on horseback were liable to ride down the main street and drag Chinese by queues as they once had in the past."

The only way in or out was through barred gates that were closed by a white watchman every night. As soon as fences and signs were torn down by white citizens, they would be "rebuilt and replaced as before," and yet another sign, NO THOROUGHFARE, would be nailed to the posts. Under trespass common law, the Chinese, as legal tenants, could control who came into Chinatown.

Yet the gates and barriers did not stop whites from entering Chinatown with the intent of driving out its residents. During the tense summer of 1891, local papers stirred up stories of gang warfare between the two Chinatowns. The police launched a series of raids and made mass arrests in Heinlenville for holding lottery and fan-tan games. Although there were no witnesses, the Chinese defendants were sentenced to two weeks in jail and fined fifteen dollars each, solely for being present when fan-tan games were played.

Rumors—for example, that Chinese butchers were selling pork affected with hog cholera—damaged Chinese businesses. Outside Chinatown, Chinese pedestrians were jumped and beaten on the streets, and a Chinese farmworker, Sing Lee, was slashed across the face while he was picking fruit. Ah Ling, a longtime ranch hand, was murdered walking into town. But no arrests were made. One landlord raised a Chinese man's rent for one room from $6.50 per month to $250. On a summer night in July, white police officers encouraged Chinese residents to set off fireworks and then immediately arrested them for violating a new city ordinance.

But of particular concern was the mysterious appearance of a small special police force. Heinlen and the Chinese merchants monitored the ubiquitous officers and noted their every movement. Chinese sentries were posted night and day across Chinatown, and on the slightest suspicion of anything "unfavorable," they notified one another with secret signals.

QUEN HING TONG V. CITY OF SAN JOSE

In the early fall of 1891, disgusted that the "police" showed no signs of letting up, the Chinese sued San Jose. In *Quen Hing Tong v. City of San Jose*, Quen accused the city, the chief of police, Richard Stewart, and the three "special police officers," James Darcey, Joseph Byrne, and W. H. Brown, of "conspiring together" and "intending to injure" him, to make all his Chinese tenants "uncomfortable" and their property worthless. Without warrant or right, the three "officers" daily entered Chinatown, "terrorizing the tenants and driving away the customers" and "intimidating and overawing customers" by threats and by the constant exhibition of their "stars, or badges of office."

These three special officers, claimed Quen, were also violating city codes that required all patrol officers to wear uniforms. Quen submitted affidavits from ten Chinese men who stated that because of the presence of Darcey, Byrne, and Brown, they were two months behind in the rents and owed two thousand dollars.

With this suit, Quen declared that the loss was greater than a few thousand dollars: Chinatown itself was at risk. Because the mayor had hired this irregular police force, Chinese people were being driven out of San Jose. The injunction would protect the Chinese from huge and incalculable losses—of displaced families and business, of battery and assault, and of forced relocation.

The Chinese were trying to avoid the fate of their brethren from Eureka. They understood the goal of the police intrusion into Chinatown, and they took preemptive legal action to prevent being driven out. They could have demanded large sums of money, but that might have acknowledged the inevitability of expulsion. By seeking injunctive relief, they signified that they wanted to stay. Implicitly, they also spoke for many who had been forced or burned out.[…]

THE VERDICTS

Initially, the Chinese were victorious. On August 18, 1891, judge James H. Beatty of the Ninth Circuit granted Quen's request for preliminary injunctions against the city of San Jose, Police Chief Richard Stewart, and James Darcey, Joseph Byrne, and W. H. Brown. He banned the three men from entering the Chinese premises except with a warrant, to make an arrest for a crime committed in their presence or for committing a felony [sic]. The judge, however, denied all claims for damages. In January 1892 the city moved to set aside the judge's decree, stating that there was no longer any action pending between the parties, implying that they had settled and that the city had backed off. One year later, in February 1893, the case was dismissed for lack of prosecution. Chinatown remained.

Quen Hing Tong v. City of San Jose reveals that the Chinese had put down roots in the community of San Jose, developed trustful commercial and personal relations with many white citizens, and sought and accepted the terms of private property. It exposes the difference between what the Chinese thought they were losing and what white officials thought they were losing. Considering the value of the leases, the vacant properties, the loss of business, and the impact of trespass and harassment, the Chinese decision to seek an injunction rather than full monetary compensation for their damages also reflects the difficulty in calculating the costs of being driven out. At its core, *Quen v. San Jose* was about the right of the Chinese to live in peace, where they chose, and remain in the community they had built and rebuilt.

Like *Wing Hing v. City of Eureka, Quen Hing Tong v. City of San Jose* turned to an expansive view of the law to repair racial injustice. It presumed that the law could be color-blind and that the courts should protect and restore the civic rights of the Chinese. The lawsuit hinged on the idea that the court would recognize the brutal facts of anti-Chinese terrorism and believe that after six fires, the Chinese needed to protect themselves with gates, barriers and fireproof brick buildings.[…]

In the 1906 earthquake that devastated San Francisco's Chinatown, Heinlenville suffered serious damage. The *San Jose Mercury* declared, "Now the time is believed to be ripe to wipe it out for once and for all." But if the Chinese of Heinlenville could withstand eight fires in ten years, they, like the Chinese of San Francisco, could survive the earthquake. Many refugees fled to families in Oakland and Marin County while Chinese merchants remodeled and expanded and the *miu* provided housing as people returned. It was clear that Heinlenville would not be destroyed. By 1912 the barred gates were opened, never to be closed again.

EDMUND WILSON

Edmund Wilson was born in 1895 in Red Bank, New Jersey, and had a prolific career as an American man of letters. Over many decades he contributed
literary reviews and essays to *Vanity Fair, The New Republic, The New Yorker,*
and *The New York Review of Books,* among other publications. His books
include the collections of literary criticism *Axel's Castle* and *The Shores of Light.*
He also wrote the nonfiction *To the Finland Station* and *The American Jitters:
A Year of the Slump,* as well as plays, fiction, memoirs, and poetry. Wilson
received the National Medal for Literature and the Presidential Medal of Freedom. He died in Talcottville, New York, in 1972.

• •

"The Jumping-Off Place" was published in 1932 in *The American Jitters,*
a collection of Wilson's writings about the Great Depression, and was
later included in *The American Earthquake.* In this piece, Wilson caustically juxtaposes the luxury and desperation he finds equally present in
San Diego during the 1930s.

"THE JUMPING-OFF PLACE"
from *The American Earthquake*

THE CORONADO BEACH HOTEL was built by the California millionaire
John Spreckels and opened in 1887. Spreckels had made his money
in Hawaiian sugar, and in 1887 the United States signed a treaty with the
Hawaiian king—a treaty which guaranteed to the Americans the exclusive
use of the harbor at Honolulu.

In the same year, the first vestibule train was put on the tracks by
George Pullman, and the revolt of the Apaches under the formidable
Geronimo, the last attempt of the Indians to assert their independence,
had been put down by the government and the Apaches penned up in
a reservation; the American Federation of Labor had just been founded,
Kansas and Nebraska were parching with a drought, and Henry George
had just run for mayor of New York and had been beaten only with difficulty by a coalition against him of the other parties; Grover Cleveland

was in the middle of his first term of office and threw the capitalists into consternation by denouncing the protective tariff, and an Interstate Commerce Act designed to curb the rapacity of the railroads was in process of being put through by the small businessmen and farmers; inquiries into the practices of the trusts were being got under way in Congress, while the Standard Oil Company, entering the drilling and pumping field, was already well embarked on the final stage of its progress; and Edward Bellamy had a huge and unexpected success with his socialist novel, *Looking Backward*, which prefigures an industrial utopia.

The Coronado Beach Hotel must represent the ultimate triumph of the dreams of the architects of the eighties. It is the most magnificent specimen extant of the American seaside hotel as it flourished on both coasts in that era; and it still has its real beauty as well as its immense magnificence. Snowy white and ornate as a wedding cake, clean, polished and trim as a ship, it is a monument by no means unworthy to dominate this last blue concave dent in the shoreline of the United States before it gives way to Mexico.

The bottom layer of an enormous rotunda is slit all around with long windows that remind one of those old-fashioned spinning toys that made strips of silhouettes seem to move, and surmounted, somewhat muffled, almost smothered by a sort of tremendous bonnet. This bonnet involves a red roof, a second layer of smaller windows and an elaborate broad red cone that resembles an inverted peg-top and itself includes two little rows of blinking dormer windows and an observation tower with a white railing around it, capped in turn by a red cone of its own, from which, on a tall white flagpole, flies an American flag. Behind this amusing rotunda extends the main body of the great hotel: a delirium, a lovely delirium, of superb red conical cupolas, of red roofs with white-lace crenellations, of a fine clothlike texture of shingles, of little steep flights of stairs that run up the outside of the building and little outside galleries with pillars that drip like wedding-cake icing, and of a wealth of felicitous dormers, irregular and protrusive, that seem organic like the budding of a sea-hydra. In the pavement of the principal entrance have been inlaid brass compass-points, and brass edges mark the broad white stairs which, between turned banister-rungs, lead up to the white doors of bedrooms embellished with bright brass knobs.

The whole building surrounds a large quadrangle, admirably planted and gardened. The grass is kept vivid and tender by slowly revolving sprays, and against it blooms a well-conceived harmony of the magenta and vermilion and crimson of begonia and salvia and coxcomb, bouquet-like bushes of rose-red hibiscus and immense clumps of purple bougainvillea that climbs on the stems of palms, tall-grown and carefully trimmed, in mounds of green fern or myrtle. The trees are all labeled with Latin names, as in a botanical garden. In the middle stands a low polygonal summerhouse, vine-embowered and covered with bark, inside which a boy is chalking up on a blackboard the latest stock-market quotations, while interested male guests sit and watch them in silence.

This courtyard has real dignity and brilliance. With its five tiers of white-railinged porches like decks, its long steep flights of steps like companionways, its red ladders and brass-tipped fire hose kept on hand on red-wheeled carts around corners, the slight endearing list of its warped floors and the thin wooden pillars that rise, at the bottom, from flagstones flush with the ground, it manages to suggest both an ocean liner and the portico of a colonial mansion. As you look out from one of the higher galleries at the tops of the exotic tame palms and at the little red ventilators spinning in the sun, you feel that you can still enjoy here a taste of the last luscious moment just before the power of American money, swollen with sudden growth, had turned its back altogether on the more human comforts and ornaments of the old non-mechanical world.

In the lobby, you walk as on turf across carpeting of the thickest and softest. There are wicker chairs; soft plush couches; panels of greenish-bluish tapestries on which ladies with round pulpy faces take their pleasance in Elysian boskage; sheets of stock-market quotations on hooks at the head of the stairs going down to the barbershop; and a masterpiece of interior decorating, elaborate and not easily named, but combining a set of mirrors covered with yellow curlicues, yellow-varnished rows of banister-rungs and an ambitious stained-glass window representing red poinsettias.

In the spacious, round and many-windowed dining room, where yellow-shaded candles light white tables, old respectable ladies and gentlemen eat interminable American-plan meals. After dinner, they sit on couches and talk quietly or quietly play cards in the card room.

You can wander through long suites of apartments—passing from time to time through darkish in-between chambers, made unlivable by closed-up grates, glossy mahogany mantels and sometimes a pair of twin vases cold as funeral urns.

Eventually reaching the rotunda, you come upon a swarming convention of the California Federation of Business and Professional Women's Clubs. (The General Federation of Women's Clubs was organized about two years after the opening of the Coronado Beach Hotel.) The business and professional women are fussing on the outskirts of the ballroom: "I've just seen Mildred, and she hasn't done anything about the corsages yet! Do you think we ought to give them to all officers or just to the incoming ones?" And in a conclave under hanging electric lamps in the shape of enormous coronets, they are solemnly reading aloud and debating, one by one, the amendments proposed to their innumerable by-laws.

From time to time the chambers of the vast hotel resound to a chorus of feminine voices, deliberate, school-girlish, insipid. They have composed an anthem of their own, to the tune of *John Brown's Body*, in connection with a fund they are trying to raise:

> Twenty thousand dollars by nineteen thirty-four!
> Twenty thousand dollars by nineteen thirty-four!
> Twenty thousand dollars by nineteen thirty-four!
> Our fund is marching on!
> Glory, Glory, Hallelujah!
> Glory, Glory, Hallelujah!
> Glory, Glory, Hallelujah!
> Our fund is marching on!

These business and professional women are not altogether sure about what they are going to do with this money after they have succeeded in raising it; but they have arranged for a speaking contest at which a speaker from each district will be given three minutes to offer suggestions on "How can the income of $20,000 be used to the greatest advantage of the Federation?"

• •

The new hotel at Agua Caliente across the border, where people go to see the Mexican races, has taken a good deal of the trade away from the Coronado Beach Hotel; but people still come from all over the country to San Diego across the bay.

The Americans still tend to move westward, and many drift southward toward the sun. San Diego is situated in the extreme southwestern corner of the United States; and since our real westward expansion has come to a standstill, it has become a kind of jumping-off place. On the West coast today, the suicide rate is twice that of the Middle-Atlantic coast, and the suicide rate of San Diego has become since 1911 the highest in the United States. Between January 1911 and January 1927, over five hundred people have killed themselves here. The population in 1930 was only about 148,000, having doubled since 1920.

For one thing, a great many sick people come to live in San Diego. The rate of illness in San Diego is 24 per cent of the population, whereas for the population of the United States the sick rate is only 6 per cent. The climate of Southern California, so widely advertised by Chambers of Commerce and Southern California Clubs, but probably rather unhealthy with its tepid enervating days and its nights that get suddenly chill, brings invalids to San Diego by the thousand. If they have money to move about and have failed to improve in the other health centers, the doctors, as a last resort, send them to San Diego, and it is not uncommon for patients to die just after being unloaded from the train. In the case of "ideational" diseases like asthma—diseases which are partly psychological—the sufferers have a tendency to keep moving away from places, under the illusion that they are leaving the disease behind. And when they have moved to San Diego, they find they are finally cornered, there is nowhere farther to go. According to the psychoanalysts, the idea of the setting sun suggests the idea of death. At any rate, of the five-hundred-odd suicides during the period of fifteen years mentioned above, 70 per cent were put down to "despondency and depression over chronic ill health."

But there are also the individuals who do not fit in in the conventional communities from which they come and who have heard that life in San Diego is freer and more relaxed. There at last their psychological bents or their peculiar sexual tastes will be recognized, allowed some latitude.

It is certain that many such people find here what they are seeking; but if they fail to, if they feel themselves too different from other people and are unable to accept life on the same terms, they may get discouraged and decide to resign. And then there are the people who are fleeing from something in their pasts they are ashamed of or something which would disgrace them in the eyes of their friends in the places where they previously lived. San Diego is not quite big enough so that the members of the middle-class groups do not all know one another and follow one another's doings with the most attentive interest. If your scandal overtakes you and breaks, your whole circle will hear about it; and if you are sensitive, you may prefer death. And then there are settlers in San Diego who are actually wanted by the law. This September the city is being searched for a gangster escaped from New York, who, in a beer-war, turned a machine-gun on some children. California has been a hideaway for gangsters in trouble elsewhere ever since Al Capone came here. And there are also the people with slender means who have been told that San Diego is cheap, but who find that it is less cheap than they thought; and the girls (married young in this part of the world) deserted by husbands or lovers; and the sailors and naval officers who have had enough of the service.

Since the depression, the rate has increased. In 1926, there were fifty-seven suicides in San Diego. During nine months of 1930, there were seventy-one; and between the beginning of January and the end of July of 1931, there have already been thirty-six. Three of these latter are set down in the coroner's record as due to "no work or money"; two to "no work"; one to "ill health, family troubles and no work"; two to "despondency over financial worries"; one to "financial worry and illness"; one to "health and failure to collect"; and one to "rent due him from tenants." The doctors say that some of the old people who were sent out to San Diego by their relatives but whose income has been recently cut off, have been killing themselves from pride rather than go to the poorhouse.

These coroner's records in San Diego are melancholy reading, indeed. You seem to see the last futile effervescence of the burst of the American adventure. Here our people, so long told to "go West" to escape from ill health and poverty, maladjustment and industrial oppression, are discovering that, having come West, their problems and diseases remain and that the ocean bars further flight. Among the sand-colored hotels and power plants, the naval outfitters and waterside cafés, the old spread-roofed California houses with their fine grain of gray or yellow clapboards—they come to the end of their resources in the empty California sun. In San Diego, brokers and bankers, architects and citrus ranchers, farmers, housewives, building contractors, salesmen of groceries and real estate, proprietors of poolrooms and music stores, marines and supply-corps lieu-tenants, machinists, auto mechanics, oil-well drillers, molders, tailors, car-penters, cooks and barbers, soft-drink merchants, teamsters, stage-drivers, longshoremen, laborers—mostly Anglo-Saxon whites, though with a cer-tain number of Danes, Swedes and Germans and a sprinkling of Chinese, Japanese, Mexicans, Negroes, Indians and Filipinos—ill, retired or down on their luck—they stuff up the cracks of their doors and quietly turn on the gas; they go into their back sheds or back kitchens and eat ant-paste or swallow Lysol; they drive their cars into dark alleys, get into the back seat and shoot themselves; they hang themselves in hotel bedrooms, take overdoses of sulphonal or barbital; they slip off to the municipal golf-links and there stab themselves with carving-knives; or they throw themselves into the bay, blue and placid, where gray battleships and cruisers guard the limits of their broad-belting nation—already reaching out in the eighties for the sugar plantations of Honolulu.

CHARLES FRANCIS SAUNDERS and J. SMEATON CHASE

Charles Francis Saunders was born in Pennsylvania in 1859. A businessman, he developed an interest in botany during middle age. After leaving the East Coast and taking up residence in Pasadena in 1906, he traveled throughout California and began researching and writing about California plant varieties, Indian uses of plants, gardening, and the history of the California missions. Over several decades he published many articles and eighteen books on these subjects. He died in 1941.

Born in London in 1864, J. Smeaton Chase came to California at the age of twenty-five. He traveled across the state on horseback for extended periods and recorded his experiences in three books: *California Desert Trails*, *California Coast Trails*, and *Yosemite Trails*. He eventually settled in Palm Springs and died in Banning in 1923.

• •

In this excerpt from their travel book, *The California Padres and Their Missions*, Saunders and Chase create a sentimental but attractive picture of Mission San Luis Rey de Francia, near Oceanside, California.

"MISSION SAN LUIS REY DE FRANCIA, AND SOMEWHAT OF THE PADRE WHO DOES NOT DIE"
from *The California Padres and Their Missions*

TRAVELERS BY RAIL, intending for San Luis Rey, leave the train at Oceanside whence the four miles to the Mission in its beautiful valley may be done as one chooses. I set out, camera on shoulder, to walk it in the sparkling freshness of a sunny morning succeeding a showery night; but soon a sociable Jewish peddler, overtaking me in a buggy, invited me to share a seat with him. At a crossroad, somewhat short of the Mission, he set me down, our ways parting there, and assuming me to be an itinerant portrait photographer, earnestly advised me to come again after the walnut-picking when everybody would be flush and I could make "a fortune of money" taking their pictures.

I had visited San Luis Rey in other years, when it was completely and frankly in ruins, save as to the church, and that with its scaling plaster and mellow color had the picturesque charm of half a ruin. So it was a shock to find that morning a smugly restored two-storied *convento* with a hard, white, cheerless front corridor unrelieved by vine or flower. The façade of the noble church, too, and the *campo santo* wall were sleekly plastered in glaring white, the decorations startlingly outlined in red. Remembering the dignified beauty of the dilapidated old edifice of ten years before, sunning itself under the sky like a Spanish hidalgo of broken fortunes in his ragged cloak, I could have cried for vexation at the sight of that spick-and-span product of plumb-line and rule. It was not until I bethought me of the mellowing influence that Time could be depended upon to exert and the fact that meantime the devastation of the elements had been stopped, that I felt reconciled to proceed farther, and touch the bell of the *convento*. A small community of Franciscans inhabit the Mission, and, responding to my ring, there shortly appeared a Brother in a brown skull-cap matching his brown robe. He was a tall man of comfortable girth, with a good-humored face and a fatherly manner; and he went about the task of showing me over the premises with the leisurely thoroughness of one who lived only for that purpose.

Passing from the corridor to the low, broad platform of square Mission tiles, or *ladrillos*, before the church door, the friar paused: "Here," said he with a smack of Germany in his accent, "the Indian band of forty pieces used to play of efenings. All this ground in front of the Mission was a plaza then. There were games and good times in the efening, after the day's work was over. This pavement looks new, but it is not. It is the original bricks; but, when we began restoring, we found them so worn we just turned them bottom up, and it makes a smooth pavement yet. Look, I want to show you"—and the Brother, stooping, put his finger on a depression in one. "You see that mark?—the print of an Indian child's foot: it stepped there, the little foot, when the tile was soft yet—so many years ago."

He unlocked the church door and we entered into the stillness and twilight of the building. It is larger, they say, than San Juan Capistrano's great church was.

"For forty-six years, from 1846 to '92," the Brother went on, "the church was abandoned, left to the owls and bats and human vandals. Isn't it a miracle that anything is left? And in the Mexican War it was bombarded by cannons to drive out some poor Indians who hung around yet after the last Missionary had died. Then came the soldiers in and camped for ten months. Ach, but it was a sorry wreck when the priests came again in 1892 and built their college across the way. Eferything that could be made use of had been carried away by people to build houses, timbers and railings and tiles—anything they had a mind to—not scrupling to rob the house of God. Yes, images of saints were chopped down, and fools hunting for buried money had dug up all the ground about the sanctuary. And the Mission lands that once stretched away north twenty, thirty miles, and away east as far as San Jacinto, they all were taken. That is what secularization meant. But let me tell you, mein friendt, as the old saying is, 'Who lives off the Pope, dies by the Pope': and the descendants of those robbers of Mission property, they do not prosper—no, no; there's a curse on their goods. But, though we haf no more much property, and the Indians are all gone, the work goes on. There are many people in the country now, and the Sisters' school across the road, they haf many scholars, and efery morning at eight o'clock is mass for them; and we haf our gardens once more and young orchards are growing, and already are vegetables for the school and ourselves both."

All this chat as we walked leisurely the length of the church, with a look, now at Padre Peyri's old adobe font with its built-in bowl of stone, now at the Indian mural adornments restored to their aboriginal red, blue, green, and yellow, and again at divers other matters now forgotten. A side chapel, octagonal in shape, projecting into the old cemetery, was of more than ordinary interest with an altar of really exquisite workmanship. Here, it seems, the mortuary services of the Indians were held; and, morning and evening, at such times, they came hither to utter their wailings and mournings.

"It was like the ancient Jews in the Bible," said the Brother. "The noise was disturbing in the main church; so the Fathers had them come here. It is good now for private devotions."

Over it a domed roof of tile and plaster was being restored by an expeditious little *fraile* in a tattered straw hat, his soiled brown gown tucked up under his girdle and two *paisanos* assisting him.

"He is a Mexican Brother," said my *fraile*; "the Americans don't know how to make a dome of tiles, like that. And now, you must go up into the bell tower for a view of the country, and that will be all."

At the top of a winding staircase I came among the bells and there was indeed a view—mile after mile of lonely *lomas*, with only here and there a cluster of blue-gum trees betokening the presence of some rancher's home. A sinuous line of yellowing willows and cottonwoods marked the course of the San Luis Rey River, seawardbound from the other side of Palomar veiled in a tender blue haze. To the northeast stretched the white crests of San Jacinto and the San Bernardino sierra—one lone ethereal snowbank, poised between heaven and earth. It was a beautiful picture of rural peace to carry away in my memory, but I did not like the Brother's sentence of finality. I had a recollection from my former visit of a particularly fine old doorway somewhere, by a flight of steps that led to the choir loft, against an outer wall, as at San Gabriel. Where was it? The big Brother looked down at me indulgently.

"You will haf to go inside the *convento* to see that, for it is now built about," he remarked. "If you were now a woman, I could not let you within the *convento*, but you are a man, and it is permitted. Come." And he led the way out of the church to the cloisters within.

"We haf not yet any place for guests," he lamented, as we walked together. "Not long ago, a gentleman and his wife they came one efening in their carriage, and I was so humiliated that we haf no room for such a family that want to camp."

Turning into an echoing inner corridor we came to a small courtyard, two sides of it new and sleek, but one, thank Heaven, still as of yore with its time-stained, broken plaster; and there, opening through it, was the side door of my memory—a doorway with simple but beautiful pillars, capitals, and mouldings, just as it was when the processions of Indians went chanting in and out in Padre Peyri's time—a lovely relic of the best in Mission architecture. The little patio was paved with big, square *ladril-los*, worn and moss-grown, and an ancient fountain, broken and waterless now, still remained in the midst. Here the Brother, having other matters to attend to, excused himself, shook my hand, and enjoined me to take any photographs I wanted, make myself at home, and leave when I was ready without further ceremony. For an hour I loitered about in quiet undisturbed, except for the scratching of a rake in the hands of a Brother at work among his roses and callas in the garden of the larger *patio* adjoining, and the occasional footfalls of some other Brother as he pattered along the inside corridors.

As I set out to depart by the door through which I had been brought, I encountered the big Brother again.

"And haf you seen all?" he inquired. "Ach, but I must show you Father Peyri's music-book."

He preceded me into a little room where a few broken old relics lay, and among them a huge hide-bound volume, some two feet square. The friar had all he wanted to do to lift it from the floor, and open it in the light of the deep window seat, that I might see. It was an excellent specimen of Mission work, with great square notes in black and red, and lettering so big and fair the blind might almost read it; and all on yellow, crinkly vellum, made, I take it, from San Luis Rey skins. It brought "Ramona" to my mind, and I could imagine Alessandro's father, old Pablo, whom the novel makes choir-master at this Mission, singing from the pages.

In point of size the Mission San Luis Rey was the king of them all, both as to the extent of its buildings and the population of its Indian village, which, at the crest of its prosperity (in 1826), numbered 2869. As for the church, if it lacked something of the magnificence of San Juan Capistrano's stone edifice in its prime, that was simply because adobe—the material used for San Luis—falls short of stone in its possibilities. Alfred Robinson, a Yankee trader who settled in California and who visited San Luis Rey in 1829, has left a graphic picture of it in his "Life in California." What he saw was typical of California Mission life generally. Of the neophytes, "some were engaged in agriculture, while others attended to the management of over 60,000 head of cattle[1]. Many were carpenters, masons, coopers, sadlers, shoemakers, weavers, etc., while the females were employed in spinning and preparing wool for their looms, which

• • •

1. Bancroft's figures, based on an examination of the official records, are, at the highest, some 28,000 cattle, 28,000 sheep, and 2,500 horses and mules. Popular estimates of Mission stock have usually been greatly exaggerated.

produced a sufficiency of blankets for their yearly consumption. Thus every one had his particular vocation, and each department its official superintendent or *alcalde*. These were subject to the supervision of one or more Spanish *mayordomos*, who were appointed by the missionary Father....The building occupies a large square of at least eighty or ninety yards each side…in the center of which a fountain constantly supplies the establishment with pure water. The front is protected by a long corridor, supported by thirty-two arches ornamented with latticed railings.... The interior is divided into apartments for the missionary and *mayordomos*, storerooms, workshops, hospitals, rooms for unmarried males and females....In the interior of the square might be seen the various trades at work....Adjoining are two large gardens, which supply the table with fruit and vegetables, and two or three large *ranchos* or farms…where the Indians are employed in cultivation, and domesticating cattle."

The founding of the Mission was in 1798, the location being then known as San Juan Capistrano el Viejo. Portolá's party had camped there on July 18, 1769, on their way north, in search of Monterey; and Padre Crespí, who has left a diary of the trip, makes this note of the matter: "We gave to this valley, which is excellent for a Mission, the name San Juan Capistrano, so that this glorious saint, who in his lifetime converted so many souls to God, would pray Heaven for the conversion of these poor Gentiles, to whom on the next morning we addressed a few words about God and Jesus Christ, heaven and hell. They seemed to comprehend somewhat." Who will say the saint did not hear? For when the Mission was eventually founded here—though named for another than him of Capistrano—it prospered from the start. The building of the great church that we now see must have been commenced very promptly, for the records state it was completed in 1802. This was a remarkable accomplishment for an infant Mission in a bare wilderness with only Indians for laborers. San Luis Rey, however, had for its architect and director one of the ablest and most energetic of all the Franciscans—Padre Antonio Peyri, whose parental rule extended from the very hour of the founding until the coming event of secularization cast its black shadow athwart the Mission doors. He had, of course, a companion friar at times; but such came and went: Peyri never left, and for years he was the only priest. For thirty-three years he threw himself self-sacrificingly, and with all the ardor of an intense nature, into the task of building up this Mission. Working and praying ceaselessly, he had success abundantly. To deliver this sacred trust of his life into the hands of a self-seeking secular government, to be dismembered and in general played ducks and drakes with, was more than his spirit could bear; and, one night in 1831, he fled secretly, never to return, abandoning the Mission to the inevitable. Tradition has it that when his neophytes learned that he had gone, five hundred of them set out in haste to overtake him and implore him to return, for he was greatly beloved; but the anxious throng reached San Diego (whither he had ridden to take ship for Mexico) only in time to receive his parting blessing as the vessel stood out to sea. Two bright Indian boys accompanied him, whom he entered in the College of the Propaganda at Rome, where they were the object of much interest.

The incontinent flight was the impulse of an overwrought heart, and Peyri lived to repent the error of it. An Indian servant who went with him used to tell that, when they reached a hilltop at the edge of the valley, the Padre turned and in his grief kneeled on the ground and prayed God to guard and keep his Mission. I wish we might know the spot where that prayer was uttered—that *ultimo suspiro*, as touching in its way as King Boabdil's "last sigh" when he turned and, from the mountain overlooking the Vega of Granada, took a parting look at his lost Alhambra.[2]

At the time of De Mofras' visit to San Luis Rey in 1841, there was in the Mission a picture representing Peyri surrounded by little Indian children, and the neophytes in their devotions would stop before it and make to it the same prayers as to the saint's image. Even then, after ten years of absence, his people had not given up hope that he would some day return to them. At the Mission's *rancho* of Las Flores, where the same

...

2. Alexander Forbes, an English merchant who met Peyri on the latter's way to Mexico, has left a pleasant sketch of him: "The excellent climate from which he had come, and his constant employment in the open air, made him look like a robust man of fifty years of age, although he was then sixty-seven; and although his general character and manners were necessarily very different from what could be expected from a mere cloistered monk, yet in his gray Franciscan habit, which he always wore, with his jolly figure, bald head and white locks, he looked the very *beau ideal* of a friar of the olden time."

traveler found a remnant of the San Luiseños living, an old Indian *alcalde* saluted him and said—

"Captain, they say you are from Spain. Did you see the king?"

"Yes," replied De Mofras.

"And Padre Antonio?"

"No, but I know he is at Barcelona."

"Don't they say he is dead?" put in another Indian.

"Señor," said the *alcalde*, turning to him reprovingly, "*este Padre no muere!*" (Sir, this Padre does not die!)

"Ach, but he was a man, that Father Peyri," the big Brother at the Mission had said to me, "and he from a university, making adobes!"

ANNE BLOOMFIELD and ARTHUR BLOOMFIELD

Anne Bloomfield was born in St. Paul, Minnesota, grew up in Cincinnati, and later moved to San Francisco. She was an architectural historian, preservationist, and consultant, as well as a longtime member of San Francisco's Landmarks Preservation Advisory Board. She prepared the nominations for many of San Francisco's historic districts, as designated by the city of San Francisco and the National Register. For fourteen years, she wrote the "Great Old Houses" column for *The New Fillmore*, a newspaper devoted to the city's Pacific Heights neighborhood. She died in 1999. After her death her husband, Arthur Bloomfield, edited her *New Fillmore* columns and compiled them into a book, *Gables and Fables*, published in 2007.

Born in 1931, Arthur Bloomfield grew up in the Presidio Heights neighborhood of San Francisco. A longtime music critic for the *San Francisco Examiner*, he also reviewed restaurants for KQED's *Focus* magazine. His books include *Fifty Years of the San Francisco Opera*, *Arthur Bloomfield's Restaurant Book*, *The Gastronomical Tourist*, and *Toscanini, Stokowski and Friends: A Guide to the Styles of the Great Historic Conductors*.

• •

In "A Coxhead Breaks the Rules," from *Gables and Fables*, Anne and Arthur Bloomfield introduce readers to an unconventional home built by British architect Ernest Coxhead. They celebrate Coxhead's creativity in the use of natural materials, one of the key characteristics of Bay Region architecture.

"A COXHEAD BREAKS THE RULES"

from *Gables and Fables: A Portrait of San Francisco's Pacific Heights*

I'S TINY. IT'S PLAIN. It's asymmetrical. It's even altered. So what, says the architectural devil's advocate, is so special about 2710 Scott Street?

Well, it's one of the truly original creations that helped spark the so-called Bay Area Tradition in architecture, an innovative path concerned with closeness to nature, natural materials, the "essence " of California (a tad vague, that, but no matter) and also involving the selective borrowing of imagery from earlier architectural styles.

The great Ernest Coxhead is the author of this 1893 house, heaped with praise in the works of two noted architectural historians, John Beach in Sally Woodbridge's *Bay Area Houses* and Richard Longstreth in *On the Edge of the World*. Coxhead, in partnership with his relatively silent, or perhaps one should say design-wise-invisible brother Almeric (such a Wagnerian name), began with only a small lot on a downhill site. And even for 1893 the budget—$4,200—was very little. But the client, fifty-year-old Charles Murdock, a boutique printer and sage from Boston, was a very interesting and challenging man to build a house for. He valued new ideas, he didn't care about show and fashion.

So Ernest Coxhead went to town and created a house that broke a lot of rules. It turned out a kind of visual Surprise Symphony, almost as jolly as Haydn at his jokiest. And now for a tour…

The dwarf-friendly entrance with its "mantelpiece" crown admits asymmetrically to a long hall almost oppressively low of ceiling: paneled in natural redwood, it's a miniature gallery from some English manor house (Coxhead was, in fact, born in England and didn't hide a certain nostalgia for a homeland look). At the end of the tunnel, so to speak, is—flash!— a skylit staircase with many turns, accented by a graceful banister also in redwood.

The staircase space is the spiral spine of what John Beach calls "a series of staggered-level platforms stacked around it," the first landing opening into the dining room, with windows overlooking the view to the east out back, and another giving onto the living room, which occupies the entire front of the house above the whimsically squashed entrance.

This interesting living room enjoys a carved fireplace in redwood and windows facing north and south. Up two more landings are two bedrooms to the rear, and still further up is the attic room with handsome dormer window which performs its solo turn on the Scott Street façade: a façade which, in its studied asymmetry, reminds Richard Longstreth of the artists' houses E. W. Godwin put up in London's Chelsea in the 1880s.

Longstreth calls the façade "a sea of shingles," a happy turn of phrase considering Coxhead's high-pitched roof with its upturned ends. A different kind of "high" can be found around the corner and down Green

Street where the Coxheads' own house, at 2421, went up some months after Charles Murdock's. With a towerlike façade sans slope it weighs in, perhaps, with a touch of German Expressionism of the dark, fairy tale sort, intended or not.

Fascinating calling cards for a new San Franciscan, these Coxhead houses. Reverse a few years and we find the talented Englishman moving rather precipitously to Los Angeles, ten or more days' journey from home, to meet a building boom head on. The promise of work for an Episcopal diocese seems to have been Coxhead's motivation, for during the period 1887-89 this "boy wonder" from Eastbourne designed the great majority of southern California's new Episcopal churches, including Pasadena's All Saints, which was demolished in 1923, and the presently altered Church of the Angels, also in Pasadena.

Word of new American architectural activity had reached England through pages of *British Architect* and other avenues. Setting up shop in L.A., the twenty-three-year-old Coxhead didn't forget his proper ecclesiastical Gothic, but he warmed meanwhile to Richardsonian Romanesque and the Shingle Style. A new colleague named Willis Polk who'd worked in the East and Midwest helped show Coxhead the way. By the time both men came to San Francisco in 1889, their different office temperaments had made for a stormy working relationship, but they remained close friends and influenced each other's work.

And back to 2710 Scott…

The original owner was no less interesting than the architect and his design. Charles Murdock had moved to San Francisco as a child and in due course became widely respected in the city's intellectual community. He counted among his friends, and clients, Bret Harte, Robert Louis Stevenson, John Muir, and the painter William Keith. He ran a small business devoted to "fine" printing, but with characteristic modesty he never used that term, simply identifying his firm as "book and job printers." They did handbills, tickets, theater programs, lawbooks, catalogues, magazines: regular commercial printing.

But Murdock, with no formal technical training in printing, was known for the outstanding taste and simplicity of his graphic design. His work, in short, had style. He printed the first stories of children's author Kate Douglas Wiggin and the first issues of the *Sierra Club Bulletin*.

His most famous "product" was *The Lark*, San Francisco's precious and impertinent little literary magazine of the 1890s, the first issue including Gelett Burgess's unforgettable

> I never saw a purple cow
> I never hope to see one.
> But I can tell you anyhow,
> I'd rather see than be one.

The Lark also showed off the talents of writers and artists Bruce Porter, Ernest Peixotto, Florence Lundborg and Newton Tharp. Murdock cheerfully indulged their outrageous demands, which included rough Chinese bamboo paper that kept breaking the metal type.

Murdock was active in the Unitarian Church and frequently attended the services led by the inspirational Joseph Worcester. Scarcely confining himself to matters artistic, Murdock was a state assemblyman in the 1880s, served on San Francisco's Board of Education in the 1890s and was a member of the reform (!) Board of Supervisors 1907–16.

Renaissance man? Looks that way.

MILO HASTINGS

Born in Kansas in 1884, Milo Hastings was a poultry farmer, inventor, journalist, and fiction writer. He wrote on a staggering variety of subjects, from animal husbandry to science fiction, and produced several pieces on urban design. He became a supporter of Edgar Chambless's concept of "Roadtown," a form of linear, connected housing designed to extend across the countryside. In later years a snack food entrepreneur and playwright, Hastings died in 1957.

• •

Milo Hastings presented one version of the Roadtown idea in this 1914 article for *Sunset*. He approaches a whimsical topic with charming earnestness.

THE CONTINUOUS HOUSE

EDGAR CHAMBLESS HAS come to San Francisco. Chambless is the Road-town man and Roadtown is a machine for making an improved variety of civilization at a reduced cost.

And this man Chambless, seventeen years ago sat on Angel's Flight in Los Angeles and wondered why the ground was bare within a stone's throw of the most expensive land of the city. He was half blind, this inventor, and books for him were closed. But his mind had eyes, and he saw many things that mere light rays cannot convey. He saw, as he sat on Angel's Flight, the relation that exists between transportation and land values. He saw the paradoxical struggle of men to find dwellings accessible to the public mart and yet isolated and hidden for the home nest—for men like birds will not mate and reproduce amid the flutter and chatter of the flock.

And Chambless played with the needs of men and built the blocks of civilization into new playhouses of the mind. When the blocks were arranged at last, the builder breathed deeply and said that it was good. He had invented Roadtown, the new plan of housing that promises to give us quick and easy access to things and to each other, and yet greater privacy for the home nest, and fellowship with the land and the live things—our companions of the ages before bricks were made.

In giving Roadtown a hearing remember that it is not a town and not a rural community. It is both. Compared with our present ideas of either it will have obvious advantages and obvious shortcomings, but take it as a whole and compare it with a modern town plus the surrounding farm territory, and then judge of Roadtown.

The Roadtown is a line of city projected through the country. This line of a city will be in the form of a continuous house. In the basement of the house are to be placed means of transporting passengers, freight, parcels and all utilities which can be carried by pipe or wire.

The first good seen in the continuous house idea is that of economy of construction. The excavating will be done with steam-shovels. The entire structure can be made of cement and part or all of the building will be poured. Mr. Edison figures he can build a seven-room cement house for $1200. In Roadtown this expense will be further reduced, not only by the elimination of one wall and the economics of repetition and continuity of construction, but by the fact that the Roadtown may all be constructed from a railroad track alongside. The great task of shifting steel molds, which is well nigh insurmountable in the individual house pouring scheme, becomes in Roadtown an easy duty for a steam crane on the railroad.

One of the essentials of Roadtown is a noiseless method of transportation. From each house a stairway will lead down into the endless basement, where the trains will run with no more disturbance to the inhabitants than is made by elevators in a hotel. It is just as feasible mechanically to make a noiseless horizontal, as a noiseless vertical car. The electric automobile running on smooth asphalt is sufficiently near the goal of silent efficiency to further prove the point.

Another stairway will lead from the Roadtown dwelling to the endless roofway above. Upon the outer edges of this roof promenade will be paths for bicycles and rubber-tired roller skates.

Another plan is to eliminate the basement, except a central trench for pipes and wires. The supporting walls would then be built well-trussed to carry a roofway sufficiently rigid for light-running motor vehicles.

No streets will be needed in Roadtown. This permits the windows and doors on both sides of the house to open into private gardens with no traffic beyond. With the heavy cement walls between the individual houses and with the traffic ways shut off from sight and sound, the Roadtown home, in spite of the actual proximity to neighbors, will give more privacy than is now attainable in village or city life.

The continuous passageway underneath the house will contain the pipes and wires which will bring into every home the conveniences that now mark the chief difference between city and country life. The more common of these are sewerage, hot and cold water, gas for cooking, telephone, steam heat (or hot water heat) and electric light.

All of the above list of utilities are now found in prosperous city homes, but every additional pipe laid into a city house means that the pavement in the street must be dug up and replaced, the sidewalk and cellar wall torn open, and the politicians well paid for a new franchise. In the Roadtown the adding of a new utility will cost but the expense of the house length of main pipe and a connection to lead through the floor into the room above.

Hence it will be practical to install in the Roadtown home a brine pipe for refrigeration, eliminating the use of ice; vacuum dusting and sweeping; distilled drinking water; carbon-dioxide gas for putting out local fires and making "fizzy" drinks; a disinfecting gas, the telegraphone or recording telephone, and the dictograph or loud speaking telephone, and electrically conveyed music.

Quite as marvelous as the utilities to be brought into the home by pipes and wires is the change which will be effected in home life by superior transportation. A parcels carrying system, not unlike that used in department stores or to carry books in large libraries, will serve central stores and the individual home. Each car will be set with a key trip which will automatically switch it into the proper house.

One of the most significant features of the Roadtown is that this perfected mechanical system of distributing solids, liquids and gases makes cooperation of all kinds more practical. This will not only apply to the marketing of farm crops and the purchase of raw supplies, but will undoubtedly extend to laundrying and cooking. It will be entirely feasible to send a daily bill of fare into each home from which prepared food may be ordered by telephone, and delivered from a central kitchen in heated or chilled receptacles, as the case may be. In like manner the dishes may be sent back to be washed, hotel fashion.

Previous schemes of cooperative cooking have failed because the common mess halls destroyed family life. In the Roadtown the actual mingling with one's neighbors will be about like that of the suburban or country town.

Mr. Chambless hopes to see Roadtown built and managed by restricted corporations, with provisions for the ownership ultimately passing to the inhabitants. Roadtown bonds paying a moderate rate of interest would be sold to the investing public. The tenant of Roadtown would be required to pay such a rental as would meet running expenses and interest, and pay off the principal in perhaps fifty years.

Is the Roadtown inhabitant to be the owner of his home? That depends on what we call ownership. The savage chief who owns an island owns it absolutely until some one takes it away from him. The man in New York or Sacramento, who owns his house and lot, owns it with the provision that the city may tax him for paving, water, sewerage and police protection; while private corporations charge him for light, heat and transportation. If he does not pay the first his house is taken away from him, and if he refuses to pay the latter, his house is useless. Clearly there are different kinds of ownership. The form of ownership worked out for Roadtown may differ from that with which we are now familiar, but the principle will be the same.

Few of us realize how little land we really use in production. On the basis of 33-foot houses and five to a family, it would take just about three thousand miles of Roadtown to house all the people of California. Parallel to this imaginary "state house" California's magnificent irrigated belt would form a strip extending but three-fifths of a mile on either side of the building. The wheat fields would form a band one-fourth of a mile wide and the alfalfa belt the same. The state's magnificent combined acreage of table, raisin and wine grapes would form a continuous vineyard 57 rods wide. The poultry, with 400 hens to the acre, could be provided for in a yard 37 feet in width. And all of these crops and all others, all improved farm land, in fact, could be placed within less than three miles of this ultra-urban civilization of the endless house.

WINTHROP SARGEANT

Winthrop Sargeant was born in 1903 in San Francisco. From the age of eighteen, he performed as a concert violinist with the San Francisco Symphony Orchestra, the New York Symphony, and the New York Philharmonic Orchestra. Sargeant gave up professional music performance in 1930 to pursue journalism. After writing for *Time* and *Life*, he became a music critic for *The New Yorker*, contributing reviews from 1949 to 1972. He wrote an incisive study of jazz, titled *Jazz: Hot and Hybrid*, composed an autobiography, *In Spite of Myself*, and translated the Bhagavad Gita from Sanskrit. Winthrop Sargeant died in 1986 in Salisbury, Connecticut.

• •

This delightful profile of and interview with Bernard Maybeck from a 1948 issue of *Life* magazine captures the highly individualistic architect's idealism, craftsmanship, and resourcefulness.

BERNARD MAYBECK

FOR 30 YEARS the citizens of San Francisco have been confronted with a problem. They cannot bear to tear down what is, by common consent, the city's most useless building. Its roof leaks, and the paint is peeling off its facade like the bark from a eucalyptus. It is now becoming increasingly likely that it will fall down of its own accord, since it is built largely of laths and plaster. It was originally erected for the Panama-Pacific International Exposition of 1915. For a while it was an art museum. During the Second World War the Army used it as a storage warehouse. Now it is an empty hulk standing forlornly by a pond near a corner of the Presidio. It is still known optimistically as the Palace of Fine Arts. The reason San Franciscans cannot bear to tear it down is simple: it is, for all its dilapidation, the most beautiful and publicly beloved building in California.

From time to time, horrified by its ruinous condition, enterprising citizens have suggested rebuilding the Palace of Fine Arts in permanent materials like stone and steel. In 1939 they did succeed in patching it up somewhat. But the cost of a complete restoration would admittedly run into millions. The plan has never materialized. It has left a wake of frustration in which many a city councilman has floundered, clutching his budget and cursing his sentimentality. The argument runs something like this: The damn building never was any good anyhow. It was dreamed up on a scale of elegance that has not been popular in architecture since the time when Louis XIV could spend a fortune on an outhouse. It is not functional. It is not a "machine for living." It has not helped relieve the housing shortage a bit. The trouble is that, as any kid can see, it is beautiful. Visiting architects have called it "the most imaginative romantic interpretation of classic conceptions ever built anywhere." Any city administration that undertook the practical job of demolishing it would face a public insurrection.

The man who is responsible for this hopeless state of civic indecision is an aging, unworried and sunny-tempered architect named Bernard Maybeck who built the building and has since almost forgotten about it. For 50 years, Maybeck has been doing and talking architecture in and around San Francisco with a volubility that has left its citizens intermittently grasping at dreams of civic grandeur. The Palace of Fine Arts is his masterpiece. It stands at the head of a list of far more permanent edifices—churches, office buildings, housing developments and homes—whose owners and inhabitants regard them with an emotion bordering on passion. Many authorities regard him as one of the greatest living church architects in America. In the international architectural world his reputation nudges Frank Lloyd Wright's. European theorists of building have long considered him one of the three or four American architects worth talking about. There is scarcely a prominent architect in San Francisco who has not at one time or another been his pupil. California architects in general regard him as the grandfather of the California style. He has pioneered more ideas in gracious California indoor-outdoor living than any other home builder in the state and has used and forgotten enough newfangled building and engineering principles to outfit a whole school of contemporary American architecture. His ideas are sometimes as drastic as only a poet's can be. He once approached the San Francisco planning board with a revised plan for their city which would have connected the Bay and Golden Gate Bridges with a magnificent tree-lined boulevard that might have been the envy of cities like Paris and Rome. It was pointed out to him that his plan would involve tearing down half of downtown San Francisco and excavating a good deal of the rest. "How can we do that?" inquired the city officials. "How?" snorted Maybeck with supreme detachment. "Never mind how. Just get it done!" The plan was politely turned down.

The refusal to demolish a quarter of a city was mildly disconcerting, but not of the sort to discourage a man like Maybeck. He combines the serene optimism of a yogi with an appearance that bears, as his friends often point out, an astonishing resemblance to Santa Claus. He is about 5 feet tall, has a long, gnomelike beard, sloping shoulders and childlike blue eyes. On his head, indoors and out, he wears a homemade, knitted tam-o'-shanter. Visitors to his modest home in Berkeley, across the bay, invariably find him in his front yard surrounded by eucalyptus trees, standing with grave absorption in front of an outdoor drafting table. Maybeck never takes off his tam-o'-shanter and, though he is 86, he practically never sits down. Brushing an occasional bee away from his water-color box and his T-square and triangles, he stands by the hour over his architectural drawings, working with a steady hand on colored floor plans and elevations that friends are fond of taking home to frame as pictures.

City housing authorities may regard Maybeck as somewhat of a revolutionary, but functionalists and other builders of boxlike dwellings and skyscrapers regard him as a very old-fashioned architect—old-fashioned not in his ideas of building, but in his basic attitude toward his craft. Maybeck has never been able to accept the idea that utility is the main function of architecture. He talks gravely and unsmirkingly about things like God and beauty. He loves to color his buildings in all the hues of the rainbow. He is not afraid of gold-leafed domes, wood carving and Gothic ornament. He has a profound reverence for the great architecture of the past and an equally profound reverence for the startling conceptions of his great contemporary, Frank Lloyd Wright ("A wonderfully gifted fellow," he muses). He thinks of a building as an intimate or magnificent scene against which human beings play real-life parts, and he believes simply that the world would be better, and its people happier, if their architectural scenery were more beautiful.

DUCKS AS ARCHITECTURE

The proof of these rather idealistic and anachronistic ideas is, of course, in Maybeck's buildings themselves. Owners of Maybeck houses have often hired more practical men to install their plumbing, but they have never altered a detail of the Maybeck touch in the shrinelike interiors and graceful facades of their homes. Unlike the works of most other architects, Maybeck's houses never look alike. His Christian Science Church in Berkeley is one of the most extraordinary and charming ecclesiastical structures in America—a curious, lacy combination of colonnades, trellises and dark, raftered interiors that seems to float airily on the surrounding shrubbery. Nobody, looking at it, would believe that the same man had designed the massive, glass-fronted Packard Agency on San Francisco's Van Ness Avenue and the intimate little Swedenborgian Church on Lyon Street. But they do not look like anybody else's buildings either. They seem to fit into their surroundings as though originated as part of the natural landscape. "One of the most amazing things about Maybeck's Palace of Fine Arts," remarked another San Francisco architect recently, "is that the ducks in the pond seem to be an integral part of the architecture." Maybeck's buildings also seem to fit the people he builds them for. For California's big Packard and radioman, Earle C. Anthony, he built a castle in Glendale, Calif. which lacks only a drawbridge to proclaim its owner a medieval baron, which is just about what Earle C. Anthony is. "Very important thing for an architect to know how to do," he explains, peering quizzically over his beard. "Now if you were a scientist, for example, I would build you something cold and uninteresting."

For himself Maybeck has built a little four-room house that nestles in the Berkeley hills with a spectacular view of San Francisco Bay. He not only designed it; he built it with his own hands, outwitting practically every problem involved in modern housing, and is convinced that any-body else can do the same thing for an outlay of a few dollars. To build it he stretched a frame of beams and wires that looked vaguely like a cage. Then he made some porous cement, coloring it pink just for the fun of it. Dipping old gunny sacks in the cement, he hung them, like clothes on a clothesline, on the horizontal wires of his frame, letting them overlap like shingles. When the cement hardened it made tough, durable, water and fireproof walls. The house is warm and comfortable and provides sufficient space for himself and his wife. "Anybody can do it himself," he notes delightedly. "All you need is old sacks, a few beams and wires and that porous cement. Say, that cement is simply corking," he goes on, recklessly tearing a chunk of it out of the side of the house and floating it in a basin of water to show how light it is. At this point Mrs. Maybeck interferes firmly. Maybeck has shown his floating cement to so many visitors that he is in danger of pulling his whole house to pieces for demonstration purposes. "It would be a wonderful thing for the Chinese," he muses. "They have so little wood to build with. And the sack-and-cement construction is really very solid," he continues, poking at the walls with a stick while Mrs. Maybeck quails. "Very solid indeed."

Maybeck possesses something that is rare enough even among architects: a purely artistic personality. He is continuously and persistently occupied with the problem of transforming his surroundings into beautiful and startling experiences. He pursues this problem with the relentless absorption of an insect building a nest, and he is less interested in the result than in the process of creating it. He can become as enthralled with the problem of constructing a shack out of old packing boxes, as with the plan of a skyscraper. He is always showing some humble, home-building neighbor a point or two about beautifying his roof or fixing his fireplace. He rarely enters a friend's home or even a public building without corralling the owner and suggesting all sorts of alterations, usually leaving his listener enthusiastically tearing his place to pieces in order to make them. Maybeck is a practical carpenter, wood carver, stonemason, bricklayer and painter as well as a planner. When he supervises a job of construction he clambers over scaffoldings and hops from beam to beam with a reckless enthusiasm that often terrifies men half his age. He architects not only buildings but everything from landscapes to kitchen utensils, including people. For years he architected all his wife's clothes, solemnly making blueprints of skirts, blouses and gowns, and turning her at least into Berkeley's most imaginatively dressed woman. He even architected his own pants, which for years became one of San Francisco's most noted sartorial institutions. He still wears them. They rise to a point beneath his beard ("It obviates the need of a vest," he explains) and are supported by built-in suspenders. They also open at the sides instead of having fly fronts ("because of modesty"). Disaster and frustration mean nothing to Maybeck. Several years ago Mrs. Maybeck left a pot of Crisco boiling on the stove while she went shopping in downtown Berkeley. When she got back she found the Maybeck home burned to the ground, with only a few charred timbers left standing. Maybeck surveyed the ruins with detachment a moment and then noticed the charred timbers. Greatly exited he disappeared and came back with a sandblasting machine. For several days he sandblasted the charcoal from the remaining wood. What a simply corking surface," he chortled, showing his neighbors the creamy, silken grain of polished wood from which a layer of charcoal had been removed. Soon he had rebuilt the house, using the burned and sanded wood for banisters, moldings and other woodwork. It is now occupied by his son's family and has what is probably the most beautiful wood-lined interior of any home in Berkeley.

It is easy to see how these exuberant and unworldly habits of thought have kept Maybeck from becoming a conventional corporation architect. He has never sought a client or a commission. Such clients as he has had have come to him, begging for his services. He has always been bored to death with the business side of architecture, and has usually hired a more systematic associate to handle the details of contracts and estimates. Technically his innovations in California home building have long attracted the attention of architectural scholars. A monograph on these technical matters by Jean Murray Bangs, wife of a California architect, is now in course of publication. He was the first man to make artistic use of California redwood. He used modern industrial materials like factory sash and barn-door type sliding panels long before they became popular with other modern architects. He designed large areas of glass for walls at a time when meet architects were clothing their buildings in dull, old-fashioned masonry. He was one of the first practitioners of what architects call "open planning"—the art of designing buildings in spreading units that can be added to when the growth of their functions demands greater space. He invented the typical California indoor-outdoor house and garden and the kitchen-living room combination way back in the 1890s.

But for all his revolutionary ideas in the uses of new materials and layouts, Maybeck has never allowed his materials to dominate the appearance of his buildings. Neither has he allowed his ideas to get codified into any formula or system that pedantic minds could convert into a theory of architectural progress. He hates fuctionalism, partly because it makes utility the exclusive goal of construction, but mainly because it is a cut-and-dried theory—and Maybeck loathes theories. When modern architecture is mentioned to him, Maybeck merely shrugs. "You mean all those boxes?" he inquires. "They haven't got anything to do with architecture. Architecture is an art."

Maybeck's somewhat uncompromising attitude reflects his partisanship in a struggle between mysticism and materialism that has become acute today in nearly every branch of thought. In architecture it is the struggle between the temple builder and the factory builder, the craftsman architect and the industrial architect, the individualist and the mass-minded man, or, as the novelist Arthur Koeser puts it, the yogi and the commissar. The odds are heavily stacked against architects like Maybeck. He is opposed by modern economics, which have made individualism in architecture a luxury that can be afforded by very few people. He is opposed by the technics of the industrial era which, more and more, tend to turn out buildings that are as uniform and indistinguishable as automobiles or refrigerators. To functionalists and other doctrinaire utilitarian architects, Maybeck is a madman, a hopeless romantic and a dreamer. Yet he has one characteristic common to all important architectural thinkers since the days of the ancient Greeks. They have all wanted to charm and astound their fellow men with buildings that are something more than masterpieces of efficiency or shelters from the weather.

WOOD CARVING AND CAR SEATS

Maybeck was born in New York City, where he lived as a child on Mac-Dougal Street near Bleecker in the heart of Greenwich Village. "Now, I understand, it is a center of infamy," he says. "But at that time it was a street of charming Colonial brick houses." His father was a German wood carver and a militant free-thinker, who plied his trade in a small shop where he worked for Manhattan's leading furniture and interior-decorating concerns. The ancestral craft that Maybeck learned in this shop had a great deal to do with his subsequent attitude toward his profession. In a sense, he has been hand-carving buildings ever since. As a young man, he was sent to Paris on a small allowance to study at the Ecole des Beaux Arts, which was then the undisputed capital of the architectural world. It is characteristic of Maybeck that he still speaks with hushed reverence of his Beaux Arts instructors. Some 40 years later that institution was confronted by an esthetic revolution that made it the symbol of architectural reaction, and your architects all over the world were heartily cursing every item in its curriculum. But Maybeck lacked the ideological slant of a revolutionary. He learned what the Beaux Arts had to teach him, which, as it turned out, was a great deal. He returned to New York, earned some money by designing an improved seat or railroad cars and moved on to Kansas City. There, as a struggling draftsman, he met Annie White, the sister of a fellow architect, and decided to marry her. When the Columbian Exposition at Chicago opened in 1893, Maybeck and Annie went to take a look at its famous classical revival architecture, built by such men as Hunt, Post, McKim, Mead and White. Again Maybeck's reaction to the Grecian columns and pediments of conservative architecture was remarkably moderate. While his great contemporary Frank Lloyd Wright took one look and roared away denouncing the whole exposition as a monstrous insult to good taste, Maybeck gazed at it with frank admiration. The admiration, as usual, had nothing to do with the theory behind the architecture. Maybeck had an equal admiration for the revolutionary architecture of Wright. He was merely judging buildings, as he had always done, on their own merits, without any regard for movements or programs of architectural reform. Later on, Maybeck used and discarded the whole vocabulary of classical ornament at will, sometimes using Greek columns, Gothic carving or baroque domes, sometimes approaching the more restrained style of Wright.

In the 1890s Maybeck moved on to San Francisco, taking Annie with him. Annie was recalcitrant about marriage. But Maybeck soon paid her a compliment from which few women could have escaped. While working as a draftsman on San Francisco's old Crocker building, he distorted the floral ornaments on its cornices until they looked like a vast series of capital As. The building still stands in downtown San Francisco, and Maybeck still chortles every time he sees it. Annie, seeing her initial spread all over what was then one of San Francisco's most important buildings, succumbed and they were married shortly afterward.

Immediately Maybeck, who already had a beard and a look of elderly sagacity, became the leader and mentor of San Francisco's younger architects. They collected at his home and listened reverently to his ideas, bringing box lunches and helping Annie do the dishes. He taught them architectural drawing as a professor at the University of California. Soon Maybeck's work became so famous locally that Phoebe Hearst, the mother of William Randolph, sent him to Europe to organize a competition for redesigning the campus of the University of California in Berkeley. Maybeck took Annie with him. On the way they stopped off at the Hearst home in Washington. "We slept in Willie's big double bed," he remembers gleefully. He also remembers his embarrassment in discovering that he had grown so fat that the pants of his only dress suit would not button in front. Always a resourceful man, Maybeck architected a red sash which he wore to cover the hiatus. The result was somewhat spectacular, but it settled the Hearst family even more firmly in the conviction that Maybeck was a great artist.

"IT GETS IN YOUR ELBOWS"

As a matter of fact, Maybeck was too much of an artist to be a good administrator. The competition for rebuilding the University of California ended in a welter of compromises and unworkable projects, and Maybeck himself finally lost interest in it. The European expedition had only a few concrete results. One of them was the birth of a son in Brussels. Characteristically, Maybeck could not bring himself to decide on a name for the baby. When they returned to Berkeley, they settled down near a family of neighbors named Wallenberg. One day Maybeck approached his 2-year-old offspring and politely inquired, "Who are you?" The first name that occurred to the infant's mind was Wallenberg. "Wallen," he said tentatively. Maybeck promptly named him Wallen Maybeck.

It was an example of many of the quizzical and unconventional Maybeck habits that got the good-natured, childlike little man a name for eccentricity all over the San Francisco Bay region. The Maybecks lived with their son and a good-looking daughter, Kerna, in a disorderly but architecturally charming home in the woods above Berkeley. They were fond of trading homes with friends for a few weeks at a time, a process which always ended up with extensive alterations in the friends' homes. The Maybecks were successively vegetarians and antivivisectionists. They developed a lifelong horror of milk and even refused to eat food made with it. Maybeck had, and still has, an equal horror of honey, which he will not allow anywhere near his house. "It gets in your elbows," he complains. The Maybecks were also mild hypochondriacs. Mrs. Maybeck's firm voice always questioned friends carefully when they telephoned suggesting a visit. "You haven't got a cold, have you? Well, I guess it's all right then." Smoking was absolutely prohibited. This prohibition was a source of so much satisfaction to Mrs. Maybeck that she was invariably disappointed when visitors did not try to smoke on the premises. It deprived her of the pleasure of forbidding it.

Today Maybeck still lives in Berkeley, though he has moved out of two neighboring homes that he has turned over to the families of his son and daughter. His most recent large-scale architectural job is the campus he has designed and built for Principia College, a Christian Science institution overlooking the Mississippi River at Elsah, Ill. Like much of Maybeck's architecture, it is a mixture of classic, romantic and modern styles, blended with charming personal taste and hidden self-effacingly among tree- and shrub-grown hills. "Christian Scientists always pay their bills," he remarks, earnestly. "Good thing for an architect to remember." In his outdoor drafting studio, shaded by a scrawny eucalyptus tree, he discusses architecture by the hour, always with a pencil in one hand so that he can illustrate his remarks with rapid little sketches that have the calligraphic swiftness of Chinese script. He never reads anything. "Mrs. Maybeck does all the reading," he explains, "I look at pictures." One of his favorite relaxations is crooning whole scenes from obscure French operas, singing coloratura soprano and bass parts with equal intrepidity and expert French diction. Occasionally, at 86, Maybeck has a spat with

Annie, who is a good deal bigger than he is. It usually ends up with his stamping his feet and hurling his blueprints all over the front yard. But these tantrums are rare.

Though he is the possessor of a number of honorary degrees and architectural prizes, Maybeck has an almost incredible obliviousness to what the world thinks of him. "You couldn't call me a success at all," he remarks, stroking his beard. For several years he has been hard at work on a mammoth plan for the rebuilding of San Francisco. Hundreds of blueprints and landscapes clutter his house, showing a magnificent city that he has invented out of his imagination, teeming with palatial buildings and tumbling through elegant boulevards down to the bay and the Golden Gate. Maybeck is quite aware that his dream city will never be realized. "The fact is," he confides, "that I'm really doing it to please my wife. It's beautiful, isn't it?"

HAROLD GILLIAM

Harold Gilliam was born in California in 1918. After learning the craft of writing with Wallace Stegner, Gilliam became a reporter with the *San Francisco Chronicle*. Beginning in 1961 and continuing for over thirty years, Gilliam wrote the weekly "This Land" column in the *Chronicle*. Through "This Land," Gilliam brought environmental concerns to the attention of Bay Area readers long before acquaintance with ecological issues became de rigueur. His many books include *Between the Devil and the Deep Blue Bay*, *The San Francisco Experience*, *Above Yosemite*, and *Above Carmel, Monterey, and Big Sur*. In 2009 he received the Peter Behr Award from the Marin Conservation League. He lives in San Francisco.

• •

In "The Glass Wall and Willis Polk," Gilliam recounts how Willis Polk combined steel and glass in the structural breakthrough of the Hallidie Building, a design decades ahead of its time. Enlivened with several anecdotes on Polk as a civic troublemaker, "The Glass Wall" also examines the architect's design for San Francisco's Ferry Building, including a tower modeled on that of a cathedral in Seville, Spain.

"THE GLASS WALL AND WILLIS POLK"
from *The San Francisco Experience*

OF ALL THE pyrotechnic personalities who blazed across the skies of San Francisco in the early years of the century—Jack London, George Sterling, Gelett Burgess, Bruce Porter, Arnold Genthe—none was more brilliant, eccentric, or talented than architect Willis Polk. And none made a more enduring contribution to American culture. Just as Jack London overturned the tables in the literary world, so Polk did in the field of architecture. His most significant work was a structure of revolutionary design that was at least forty years ahead of its time—the progenitor of all modern glass-and-steel skyscrapers.

You can see it on Sutter Street near Montgomery—a shining jewel of a building to delight the eye amid the humdrum structures of the downtown district. It is hard to believe now that Polk's building was originally greeted with shock, incredulity, and disapproval.

He designed it for a piece of income property then owned by the University of California—a site the university originally intended for a hotel. When the building was completed in 1918, it hit the city with the impact of an architectural explosion—as the irreverent designer doubtless intended. The front "curtain wall" is glass, reflecting the sky, nearby buildings, clouds, and wraiths of fog like a seven-story mirror framed in elaborate ironwork.

The building was named for another San Francisco innovator—Andrew Hallidie, a regent of the university and the inventor of the cable car. Subsequent owners, however, apparently unaware of the building's historic value, dropped the name, referring to it only as "150 Sutter," and permitted considerable violence to Polk's design in remodeling the first floor for a clothing store.

Polk had evidently not anticipated one eventuality. The building faced south, and on a warm day the sun, pouring through the glass wall, heated up the interior like an oven. The occupants—in the days before air conditioning—found it necessary to devise elaborate systems of blinds as a sun shield.

THE REDISCOVERY OF A MASTERPIECE

The glass curtain wall was a radical innovation in an era when walls were supposed to be solid and substantial. A few other American architects had experimented with glass but none had gone this far. Theoretically the glass wall had been possible ever since the Eiffel Tower in 1889 had demonstrated that a steel framework could rise to great heights and that heavy bearing walls were no longer necessary. But tradition dictated that the walls still should be massive, as if they, and not the steel frame, were holding up the building. With this structure, Polk opened the door to new and imaginative designs not bound to stone and masonry.

Yet no one went through the door. The concept was too advanced. The building was regarded as a freak, and several decades passed before architects began to catch up with it. It was rediscovered at mid-century, when big photographs of it were hung at the Harvard Graduate School of Design and in other architectural halls of fame. The first major building to follow Polk's lead was the United Nations Secretariat in New York in 1950, designed by an architectural team headed by Wallace Harrison and based on concepts of Le Corbusier. By mid-century, Polk's glass wall was an idea whose time had belatedly arrived. In New York the United Nations Building was followed by the Lever Brothers Building on Park Avenue, designed by Skidmore, Owings and Merrill, and the House of Seagram nearby, a work of Mies van der Rohe. The Lever design inspired San Francisco's second glass-walled building, Crown-Zellerbach (also by Skidmore, Owings and Merrill) on Market Street two blocks away from its ancestor on Sutter—and forty-two years later.

MAN OF THE SIXTEENTH CENTURY

The Hallidie Building had jolted even many of Polk's admirers, familiar with his tasteful designs in classic styles. Although it was a startling departure from his previous work, the innovation itself was consistent with his personal life as an unpredictable iconoclast and an implacable foe of staidness and pomposity. Some San Franciscans regarded him as a near genius with irresistible personal charm and others saw him as an intolerable egomaniac. Quite possibly he was both.

There is a story that he once stood on his head in the lobby of the St. Francis Hotel to collect on a bet. He often wore a French silk hat on Market Street, twirled a Malacca cane, and cultivated an extravagantly courtly manner. ("He belonged to the sixteenth century," said one of his friends.) But he also took great pleasure in insulting dignitaries. Legend holds that he was expelled from the august Bohemian Club for pulling a chair out from under a particularly starchy millionaire.

Although he was small in stature, he somehow was able to give the impression of looking down from a great height. On one occasion he was approached by an Eastern businessman, who wanted him to design a major building. The industrialist told the architect that he had greatly admired his work. Polk's response was an Olympian stare. "I would feel complimented," he said, "if I thought you knew anything about art." The rebuffed industrialist took his business elsewhere.

At a banquet in Tait's restaurant on O'Farrell Street, artist Charles Rollo Peters made a long-winded speech attacking architects for designing art galleries improperly. The next speaker was Polk, who immediately declared, "I have always known that there were more horses' asses than horses."

The outraged Peters rushed up onto the stage, shouting, "Willis, you called me a horse's ass!" Members of the audience intervened to prevent bloodshed.

Polk's monumental self-esteem and his propensity for antagonizing important people frequently had him in court. He once refused jury service because of his bitter antagonism to Prohibition, which he regarded as a personal affront and which he violated as conspicuously as possible. During one court battle he was called to the stand to testify as to his own character and reputation. "When it comes to originality," he affirmed, "Michelangelo had nothing on me."

THE GIRALDA TOWER

His remarkable self-assurance (or perhaps self-reassurance) may have been rooted in his early life in Kentucky and Missouri. His father, also an architect, was a disabled Civil War veteran who found it hard to earn a living, and young Willis helped to support the family from age six. When the boy was fourteen, the family moved to San Francisco, and he was apprenticed to an architect. In the early 1890s he became a designer in the office of Arthur Page Brown (no relation to Arthur Brown, Jr., the City Hall architect). Brown at that time had the job of designing San Francisco's Ferry Building to replace an outmoded earlier ferry terminal at the foot of Market Street.

When Brown was killed in a runaway horse accident in 1896, Polk, as chief designer, completed the job. Like most monumental buildings of that era, the Ferry Building was modeled after an ancient structure in Europe. The tower was an adaptation of the Giralda Tower of the Cathedral of Seville, which itself had been originally built as a Moorish minaret. Polk had never been to Seville, but he had pored through the architecture books in search of good designs—a custom of virtually all architects at a time when Americans still had little self-confidence regarding architectural design. Europe, particularly Paris, was the mecca of the arts; and after completing the Ferry Building Polk took a job in Chicago in the offices of Burnham and Root, one of the top American architectural firms of that era. There, Polk fell under the spell of Daniel Burnham, who later, with Polk's help, developed the Burnham Plan for San Francisco.

Burnham in turn was so impressed by Polk that he sent him back to San Francisco to open a branch office. Polk later set up his own firm. His largest building of that period—the tallest downtown structure at the time of the disaster of 1906—was the Merchants Exchange, center of the business life of that time. The building, at 465 California Street, restored by Polk after the fire, is now a bank office, but its great hall, where ship arrivals were once posted in the manner of Lloyds of London, still shows signs of Polk's opulent décor.

REBUILDER OF THE CITY

As the city's leading architect after the earthquake and fire of 1906, Polk redesigned and reconstructed more major buildings than any other architect. In later years, Polk asked Bonestell to draw up a composite picture of the large buildings he had worked on. The drawing was published in the newspapers with Polk's own heading: "The Man Who Rebuilt San Francisco."

The structures pictured included the Mills Building on Bush, the de Young Building at Market and Kearny, and the brand-new Hobart Building on Market at Second, then the tallest structure in the city. The detail for the Hobart Building's elaborate flaring tower was worked out by artist Chesley Bonestell, Polk's designer. When he tried to follow Polk's instructions, he noticed that the straight roof line appeared incongruous with the tower's curving side walls. He tried to convince Polk that the roof line should be curved, but his objections were unheeded. One morning after the building was finished, Polk called Bonestell into his office and complained, "I was walking down Market Street and I noticed how badly that straight line on the roof of the Hobart Building looks."

"I protested at the time we were designing it," Bonestell replied. "I told you it should be curved."

Polk, who could never admit he had been wrong, retorted, "You didn't protest hard enough!"

The same building caused other problems. The City Building Department claimed during construction that he was not properly fireproofing the building, and Polk retaliated with his usual acerbity. He placed a large sign on the Market Street fence enclosing the site, denouncing the city officials as incompetent bureaucrats and declaring in large letters that their requirements were unnecessary and ridiculous. It was during this controversy that there took place the well-known altercation between Polk and a city inspector, who accosted the architect on the site. Polk told him to talk to the construction superintendent, who at that moment was on the top of the steel framework. The official laboriously hauled himself up to the twelfth floor only to be informed by the superintendent that he was simply following the architect's design. The inspector clambered down again and strode up to Polk with blood in his eye, whereupon the architect airily declared with a wave of his cane that he did not wish to discuss the matter, hopped on a girder that was about to be raised to the upper stories, and was transported into the heavens. The dispute was settled only when Mr. Hobart, the building's owner, intervened, ordered Polk to remove the sign on the fence, and worked out a satisfactory settlement on the fireproofing.

TO REMEMBER R.L.S....

It was about this time that the disgruntled architect, fed up with bureaucratic interference, decided to become a candidate for mayor, evidently in order to run the city more to his liking. He called a press conference to announce his plans, but nobody showed up—possibly because the press refused to take his candidacy seriously. His opponent would have been the overwhelmingly popular Sunny Jim Rolph. In any case, Polk faced the facts and promptly announced that he would have nothing more to do with the sordid business of politics.

One of Polk's proudest accomplishments was restoration of the oldest and most revered building in the city—Mission Dolores. He meticulously studied the Franciscan missions and their traditions, following the original plans in every detail of construction. When it was necessary to replace some of the original tiles, he ordered them made in exactly the same way they had been fashioned by Indians under the padres. He shored up the old adobe with steel beams so inconspicuously that visitors declared they could not see what he had done on the building—a reaction he accepted as the highest compliment.

Polk also developed the original plan for the Opera House. It was under the inspiration of his design that a fund-raising campaign was held to build the nation's first municipal opera house as part of a World War I memorial. He died before the plans came to fruition, however, and the Opera House and Veterans Building were ultimately designed by Arthur Brown, Jr.

Another structure not entirely designed by Polk but bearing his influence is the Robert Louis Stevenson Memorial in Portsmouth Plaza. Polk was dining at the Palace Hotel with three companions—Bruce Porter, sculptor and architect; poet Gelett Burgess, author of the *Purple Cow* ditty; and designer Porter Garnett—when a ship arrived in the harbor with word of the death of their friend Stevenson in Samoa.

The warm presence of Robert Louis Stevenson was still felt in this city, and when his friends had recovered from the shock, they reminisced late into the night about the colorful Scot. Together they drew up plans for a Stevenson memorial, sketching their ideas on the tablecloth. So inspired was Polk that when he left the hotel he swept up the tablecloth and walked off with it. From the sketches on the tablecloth came the present Stevenson Memorial in Portsmouth Plaza. Polk designed the pedestal, with its inscription from Stevenson's *Christmas Sermon*. Above it is Bruce Porter's design of a galleon under full sail, symbol of the author's tales of adventure.

THE HOUSE ON RUSSIAN HILL

The Vallejo Street summit of Russian Hill is another location carrying the signature of Polk. As part of the beautification of the city for the Panama-Pacific International Exposition of 1915, Polk designed in the classic manner a pair of ramps leading up from Jones Street to the summit block of Vallejo. Immediately north of the ramps, on a cul-de-sac named Russian Hill Place, are three of Polk's Mediterranean style villas. The nineteenth-century redwood shingle houses on both sides of Vallejo were saved from the fire of 1906 because they were above the city's reservoirs and had their own water supply. The quake had broken the city water mains, but these houses had sufficient water in their cisterns to fight off the flames. One of them is Polk's own house. Vallejo Street ends in a classic balustrade he designed as part of the 1915 landscaping, and the house is immediately to the right at the top of the long stairs descending the steep eastern slope of the hill.

When Mrs. Virgil Williams asked Polk to design a house for her on that site, he agreed, but his price was a stiff one—the eastern one-third of the lot. This portion consisted principally of a nearly vertical slope, so Mrs. Williams consented. Polk's ingenious design combined both houses as a single building. His portion was draped down the hill for seven stories in a curious vertical room arrangement. From each room in the house Polk could look to the east and take pride in gazing on his first great triumph, the Ferry Building. The house has since been divided into several separate apartments, but much of Polk's elaborate woodwork remains. The upper room is two stories high with a broad mezzanine. Alongside the fireplace is a hidden panel which opens to a steep stairway leading to the lower stories and an outside exit. There are several explanations for the architect's "secret door." One was that that he needed a quick escape when creditors appeared. Another story maintains that he kept the secret from his wife and sometimes found it convenient to disappear suddenly. She was the former Christine Bareda, an ambassador's daughter of Spanish descent. The hot-blooded young lady and the tempestuous architect made a volcanic couple, and the neighbors told stories of seeing plates sailing through the windows of the big house and down the hillside. Despite their battles—and Polk's frequent affairs with other women—his wife was so devoted to him that she compiled clippings of every newspaper item referring to her illustrious husband, even those in which his name was merely mentioned in a list.

A SKYSCRAPER GIRALDA

So great was Polk's pride in the Ferry Building and his admiration for the Giralda Tower (on a trip to Spain he purloined a piece of its tile as a souvenir) that it became his strange ambition to reproduce the same tower on a colossal scale. Had he been successful, San Francisco would have had not one Ferry tower but two or three. He first tried to convince *Chronicle* publisher M. H. de Young to allow him to build a Giralda tower on the de Young Building at Kearny and Market when it was being redone after the fire. De Young could not be persuaded, and Polk designed for him instead an annex to the structure, which has again been rebuilt in recent years as the San Francisco Federal Savings Building.

Later he tried the same idea on the Crocker family, for whom he had designed the original Crocker Building still standing (although refaced) at 1 Montgomery Street. The Crockers liked the idea and told him to go ahead on a design. Polk built a four-foot model for a Giralda-style skyscraper eight hundred feet high, higher than the tallest buildings in the city today. Sadly for Polk, the building was so large that it would have required the entire triangular block behind the Crocker property at Market and Post; and the Mechanics Institute, owner of the building in the middle of the block, refused to sell. Polk died in 1924 without having achieved his ambition to build a skyscraper Giralda.

Probably it is just as well. It is ironic that his ambition lay in that direction rather than in carrying on in the modern style he pioneered with the Hallidie Building. Bonestell regrets that Polk did not live a few decades later. "All we did in those days was to go through the architecture books and adapt the classic styles. It is a pity that Polk, with all his great flair for the art, didn't live into the modem era, when architecture began to develop new styles to suit the times. But at least we have the Hallidie Building."

DESIGN WITH NATURE

And it is doubtless for his "glass building" on Sutter that Polk will chiefly be remembered—a thrust forward into a promised architectural land to which Polk pointed the way but himself could not enter. In one respect, however, Polk may still be ahead of the times. He designed the Hallidie Building's decorative ironwork—with curving lines and leafy frills—in the Venetian style of the Doge's Palace in Venice. In this respect, Polk was still indulging in his taste for ancient European styles. But the early years of this century were also the period of the *art nouveau*, a time when artists and architects were turning to "natural" forms in revolt against the harsh technology of industrialism—the same natural leafy shapes found on the Hallidie Building. If Polk's glass wall is now universally admired, his iron-work, including the imaginatively integrated balconies and fire escapes, is often regarded as hopelessly old-fashioned. Yet fashions change, and cycles bring back varying tastes. Our own era is again a time of cultural revolt, particularly among the young, and the results are apparent in natural styles of dress, poster art, and colorful decoration. A contemporary taste for lively décor is evident in San Francisco in the widespread restoration of old buildings remaining from a more imaginative era—such as Victorian houses, Ghirardelli Square, and Jackson Square. Polk's ironwork on the Hallidie façade, now painted a pallid green, was originally the bright blue and gold of the University of California—not precisely psychedelic but perhaps an indication of an affinity between the architect and the present avant-garde taste for brilliant color.

The current revolt against drabness and regimentation has not yet found major expression in commercial architecture. The city's new buildings, with a few exceptions, are mostly stark and unadorned; some resemble colossal filing cabinets. It may be time for architects again to look at the Hallidie Building and wonder if Polk had perhaps found the proper balance of sheer surface with playful decoration, of straight lines with flowing forms, of technological precision with curvaceous natural contours.

In early 1971 a new owner, who evidently cared nothing for the building's historic significance, proposed to tear it down and replace it with a high-rise structure. Its demolition was delayed under a city ordinance providing for a one-year moratorium on the razing of buildings designated as historic landmarks. Beyond that period, however, there were evidently no legal means to prevent its destruction. Clearly San Francisco urgently needs methods of permanently protecting its few architectural treasures.

DANIEL P. GREGORY

Daniel P. Gregory earned his Ph.D. in architectural history at the University of California, Berkeley. After working at *Sunset* magazine for twenty-seven years (the last fifteen as senior editor), he became editor in chief at Houseplans.com, a website devoted to making high-quality designs for the home available to diverse clients. The author of numerous articles and a contributor to many books on California architecture, Gregory is most recently the author of *Cliff May and the Modern Ranch House*.

• •

In "A Vivacious Landscape: Urban Visions between the Wars," Gregory describes the visual interplay of hills and skyscrapers in San Francisco during the early twentieth century. His discussion of the relationship between skyscraper and bridge forms and the mythic qualities they share sheds light on architects' intentions in building such structures as the Golden Gate Bridge and the Bay Bridge.

from "A VIVACIOUS LANDSCAPE: URBAN VISIONS BETWEEN THE WARS"

"ENTHRONED ON HILLS, San Francisco captivates the stranger who sees it from the Bay by the vivacity of its landscape long before revealing any of its intimate lures." So begins a travel booklet published by the San Francisco Chamber of Commerce in 1924. It is a telling statement.

In the 1920s and 1930s San Francisco's vivacious landscape—its hills and valleys and peninsular setting, its dramatic axial vistas across a gray-blue bay—helped stimulate new thoughts about the future city. The water-girded site served as both a physical constraint and a conceptual springboard. Newspaper editors, architects, engineers, and civic leaders believed that the San Francisco of the future would inevitably reach north and east across the Bay, forming the center of a great regional metropolis.

After World War I, San Francisco's outlook began to shift away from rebuilding and toward expansion. Faith in the future, in progress and growth, was strongly reinforced by the evidence of how far the city had already come. In the words of a newspaper editorial at the time of the city's

Diamond Jubilee celebration of 1921, "From a handful of people…we have grown in seventy-five years, to the metropolis of the Pacific Coast, the queen city of the West, to an aggregation of 600,000 people with palatial homes and magnificent public structures. The city that is is but a miniature of the city that is to be."

SUAVITIES OF OUTLINE: THE SKYSCRAPER VISION

As San Franciscans conceived momentous plans for the future of their city during the 1920s, a radical metamorphosis had already begun. The city's skyline grew dramatically during the boom years after the war. Downtown, the famous older landmarks, such as the ten-story Mills Building of 1891, the fifteen-story Ferry Building of 1898, and the eighteen-story Humboldt Bank Building of 1907, started to recede into the background as a new generation of larger and usually taller office buildings rose around them. (Immediately after the earthquake and fire in 1906 building heights had been limited to one and a half times the width of the street. This height restriction was removed in 1907.) Several unrealized skyscraper designs of the 1910s had pointed the way to a new urban scale, including Frank Lloyd Wright's unprecedented twenty-story slablike design of 1912 for the John Spreckels Building, Louis Christian Mullgardt's equally tall slab of 1916, and the more eclectic but also lofty design for another Spreckels Building by the Reid brothers.

By 1930 the downtown area sported an entirely new face. Along Market Street, the ten-story, block-long Southern Pacific Building (1917), the sixteen-story Matson Building (1924), and the adjacent seventeen-story Pacific Gas & Electric Building (1925) composed a colossal wall of resplendent, classically inspired corporate palazzi. Several blocks west and south of Market, the twenty-six story Pacific Telephone Building (1925) burst abruptly from a district of five- and ten-story buildings, its distinctive setback silhouette visible for miles.

In the financial district the change was equally evident. The twenty-two-story, mansard-roofed 111 Sutter Building (1927), the block-long, Gothic-ornamented thirty-one-story Russ Building (1927)—called "the largest building on the Pacific Coast"—and the twenty-two-story Shell Building (1929) formed an especially striking urban rampart. Closer to

Union Square, the elegantly faceted twenty-six-story 450 Sutter Building (1930) towered over all its neighbors.

The skyline was becoming more picturesque, enhanced by the newer, bigger towers with their distinctive belvederes, urn-studded cornices, and setback silhouettes meeting the sky. The statement in the Chamber of Commerce booklet of 1924 was just as applicable in later years: "Suavities of outline accent the horizons of San Francisco, where the skyscrapers take on fantasy as they pile up on hills and recede into vales." Indeed, Gabriel Moulin's famous panoramic photographs of 1927, looking west from the Bay—past the Ferry Building and up Market Street—show a wavelike effect: the towers along Market and north along Montgomery form two distinct hills of their own, adding to the rippling impression caused by the outlines of Telegraph, Nob, and Russian hills.

The perception of San Francisco as a romantic and modern city of towers came into sharper focus as architects grew less dependent upon Beaux-Arts ideals of beauty based on historical precedent and began to experiment with imagery more attuned, in their view, to the twentieth-century "Machine Age."

Several important events exerted a powerful influence on San Francisco architects during the 1920s, serving as catalysts for the discussion of an evolving modernism. The unprecedented New York zoning law of 1916 prescribed the maximum allowable building envelope for structures in particular zones and ultimately led to a new interest in setback silhouettes. The Tribune Tower competition in Chicago in 1922 provided an unusually clear-cut distinction between traditional and modern styles: the winning entry, by the New York firm of Howells and Hood, offered an exuberant adaptation of Gothic features to the tower form; runner-up Eliel Saarinen of Finland used a series of setbacks and expressed vertical lines to emphasize the building's height in a more abstract manner, which was perceived to be more modern. The Paris Exposition des Arts Décoratifs et Industriels of 1924-25 publicized the search for new ornamental forms as a way of expressing modernity.

Perhaps no other San Francisco architect was more dramatically influenced by these developments than Timothy Pflueger, partner in the firm of Miller and Pflueger. Pflueger gave San Francisco some of its most vivid images of skyscraper modernism during the 1920s and 1930s, both through his built work and through the presentation drawings he commissioned. Pflueger served as a sort of "cultural diffuser," bringing the latest sky-scraper imagery to San Francisco from Chicago and New York and thereby offering his hometown a partial view of what the modern metropolis should look like.

With his associate, architect A. A. Cantin, Pflueger was beginning to work on the commission for the Pacific Telephone Building when, according to writer Harold Gilliam, he came across Eliel Saarinen's widely published second-place entry for the Tribune Tower competition in Chicago. This scheme electrified the architectural profession with its expression of a soaring verticality simply and directly as a system of straightforward vertical piers, recessed spandrels, and setback outline. Pflueger adapted the design, wrapping it in gray speckled terra-cotta resembling Sierra granite. The chastely ornamented Pacific Telephone Building would bestow on San Francisco its first grand image of skyscraper modernism.

To give such a contemporary design the best possible chance of success with his clients, Pflueger hired the leading illustrator of the day, New York renderer and visionary architect Hugh Ferriss, to make a presentation drawing in 1924. As architectural historian Carol Willis has documented, Ferriss' 1922 drawings illustrating the four stages of the zoning envelope (an analysis of the New York zoning law of 1916) had received wide exposure.

Executed in his characteristic atmospheric style, the drawing presents the Telephone Building as a massive, glowing monolith rising out of the sidewalk and soaring into a darkening sky. Two low buildings with traditional detailing flank the new structure; in contrast to the sheer, brightly lit shaft between them, they are deeply shaded and give the drawing a heightened sense of drama by accentuating the contrast between old and new San Francisco. The city had no setback zoning ordinance comparable to New York's, so Pflueger was literally importing a setback style. Indeed, the Pacific Telephone Building had no need for setbacks to allow light and air to reach the ground because most of the adjacent buildings were no taller than ten stories.

A commission to design the Pacific Edgewater Clubhouse in 1927 (never executed) for a spectacular ocean-view site at Point Lobos, near the Cliff House, prompted Pflueger to hire Ferriss once again. The architect wanted a drawing that would help stimulate memberships and financial backing. Ferriss responded with an image that complemented his depiction of the Telephone Building. This time he concentrated on both the horizontality of the design and the ruggedness of the natural setting. The tiered, light-reflecting mass appears to have been chiseled out of the dark cliffs at its base. A crystalline geometry dominates the composition, broken only by two classically inspired arcades. The drawing illustrates an architecture of geology: a building inseparable from its site, a Manhattan mountain at the edge of the world.

By the early 1930s Pflueger was ready to experiment more freely. He wrote, "We are beginning to recognize glass as an asset, and to develop a mass in which the glass takes form." Three striking colored-pencil skyscraper studies from this period seem to illustrate these words. Each image presents the structure alone, without additional ornament of any kind, as if the architect had distilled his vision to the essential elements of steel, glass, and light. Just as the Depression curtailed most downtown building, Pflueger appeared to be reaching for a more radical, almost International Style approach.

In 1940 the WPA guide to San Francisco described Montgomery Street as "the Wall Street of the West." As "the narrow canyon between sky-scrapers…neat and austere between sheer walls of stone, glass, and terra cotta, it is visible evidence of San Francisco's financial hegemony over the far West." With the help of Pflueger and other skyscraper architects, San Francisco had acquired its own romantic, modern, Manhattanesque skyline.

When Pflueger designed a penthouse cocktail lounge for the Mark Hopkins Hotel in 1939—the Top of the Mark—all he had to do was make the walls disappear, using the skyline itself as the room's only ornamental mural: a view and a vision at the same time.

VISIONARY PRAGMATISM: PLANNING THE REGIONAL METROPOLIS

San Francisco experienced a sort of second Gold Rush during the 1920s, as a fever of "bridge-mindedness" swept the city. Support for civic beautification was combined with an aggressive boosterism to create an atmosphere of excitement and urgency about the future. Commercial rivalries with Los Angeles and other western cities heated up. Bridges, in particular, became synonymous with future growth and prosperity.

The automobile had come of age. Cadillacs and Packards gleamed in their palatial marble and glass showrooms along Van Ness Avenue. Suddenly motorists and automobile dealers wanted more and better roads, and, equally suddenly, San Francisco's splendid isolation came to be viewed less as a romantic feature than as an inconvenient anachronism. Ferryboats seemed especially old-fashioned, and they caused traffic jams by forcing motorists to wait in line on highways leading up to ferry slips. Architect Willis Polk summed up the feeling of many when he stated categorically: "San Francisco's ferry boats belong with the horse cars, the cobble stones, the cable cars, the turntable, and the old man with chin whiskers." In other words, the modern city would be the automobile city: smooth, expansive roadways spreading outward in all directions regardless of terrain.

In the spring of 1921 the San Francisco Motorcar Dealers Association purchased a series of newspaper advertisements championing the need for bridges across the Bay to provide greater ease of movement and promote further growth. The *San Francisco Bulletin* was sympathetic and asked Polk for help in envisioning a future bridge-crossed Bay.

Polk, who by the early 1920s had become perhaps San Francisco's best-known architect, maintained that the city had forsaken its most valuable asset: its splendid setting. The eagerness to grow had put that natural beauty at risk. He therefore urged the city to make a plan for the future that would incorporate a consistent policy on beautification. And what could more emphatically call attention to the water-girded setting than a series of beautiful bridges?

In a speech before the Commercial Club in January 1921, he referred to the Burnham Plan of 1905 and asked why the city should not realize some of the civic dreams outlined at that time. He stated: "We have by nature the most picturesque site of any city in the world but we are so used to it that we don't appreciate it." His point, to the assembled businessmen, was simple: "City planning is good business."

While Polk urged businessmen and civic leaders to dust off the old "City Beautiful" concepts of Daniel Burnham, he simultaneously proposed a variety of schemes for crossing the Bay. Four such schemes appear in a single visionary image published on the editorial page of the *San Francisco Bulletin* on May 24, 1921. The large bird's-eye sketch of the Bay Area shows a Gothic-towered suspension bridge—reminiscent of the Brooklyn Bridge—spanning the Golden Gate; a longer suspension span extending to Yerba Buena Island, where it joins up with a drawbridge extending from the Oakland shore; a tunnel south of the Goat Island span and parallel to it; and, south of that, a low drawbridge extending east from near Candlestick Point.

Inset at the right is a more detailed, though still impressionistic, view of the Golden Gate Bridge concept, showing the massive towers treated as great cathedral façades looming above the roadway. The headline blares, "Break Through San Francisco's Chinese Wall!" in a rather heavy-handed but graphic comparison of the Bay to the Great Wall of China, echoing the analogy used in a previous Motorcar Dealers Association advertisement. "It is not the drawing of an engineer nor merely a dream," proclaimed the *Bulletin* in the caption, "but is better than either; it shows what can and must be done to make San Francisco the city that some day is sure to be." This grand trans-Bay vision united romance and pragmatism to present San Francisco as a sort of Manhattan of the West, the beginning and the end point for all transportation lines—a modern automobile city with a sense of history.

The mania for bridge proposals reached a peak in the middle of the decade when architect Louis Christian Mullgardt offered his extraordinary scheme for a Brobdingnagian Multiple Bridge with eleven spans, each 500 feet long, linking the area south of Market Street with Alameda. In several dramatically highlighted perspective sketches—recalling to some extent the imagery of Italian Futurism—Mullgardt proposed that multiple lanes and levels of traffic be supported on massive skyscraper piers. He envisioned these piers housing a wide range of functions, economically fitted into a steel and concrete structure: "The structures would have unrestricted light and air, from all directions. They would be directly connected with State highways above; also Pacific ocean steamers and smaller craft, which moor at their base. They may be palatial hotels, or great factories."

Both the *San Francisco Chronicle* and the *San Francisco Examiner* reported on this remarkable proposal. Though most articles dwelt upon the "bridge-city" aspect, one emphasized Mullgardt's argument that such a structure would be an economical way to build new skyscrapers. Nothing came of the fantasy, however, and, according to architectural historian

Robert Judson Clark, not long afterward Mullgardt "joined the ranks of the unemployed."

Numerous more conventional proposals appeared during the mid-1920s, as consortiums sought the lucrative toll franchise. Such schemes built enthusiasm and support for bridging the Bay, priming the collective imagination for the colossal spans that would one day appear.

Bay crossings were but one component of a much larger dream, that of a great regional metropolis with San Francisco at its center. This vision had only been hinted at by such men as Polk and Mullgardt. In 1924, at the urging of Senator (former Mayor) James Duval Phelan and San Francisco's Commonwealth Club, businessman and civic leader Frederick Dohrmann organized the Regional Plan Association, which articulated this vision more fully. Although the association remained fully active only through 1927, it lasted long enough to give San Francisco some of the most radical and far-reaching urban-design proposals of the decade.

Dohrmann served as a kind of benefactor-visionary, underwriting most of the association's expenditures and tirelessly lobbying on behalf of regional-planning principles among his wide circle of business and political contacts. Dohrmann and his association took on the monumental task of making "a comprehensive plan for the development of the San Francisco Bay Counties." According to the association's statement of purpose, such a plan should help unify port and harbor development, form a coordinated system of highways and scenic boulevards, bridge the Bay, connect all parts of the Bay Area with rapid transit, develop recreational areas, develop the water supply, remove the growing menace of Bay pollution, and institute regional zoning. Like Polk, Mullgardt, and the Motor Dealers Association, the Regional Plan Association sought to assure continued growth and prosperity. No final plan was ever completed, but the Regional Plan Association did commission two nationally known planners to outline the new vision of San Francisco and the Bay Area as a single expansive metropolis of the future. Future greatness, according to Dohrmann and his planners, depended on carefully orchestrated growth and on San Francisco's leadership. As planning historian Mel Scott points out, the clear San Francisco bias may have exacerbated traditional community rivalries, thereby eroding support for a truly regional point of view.

In 1926 and 1927 "air-mindedness" reigned, prompting Dohrmann to develop his most visionary, if implausible, scheme: San Francisco should maintain its competitive edge over other Pacific ports by quickly becoming the center of commercial aviation in the Bay Area. He proposed that the city build a landing platform "from 150 to 200 feet above high water mark and about 1000 feet by 1000 feet in extent" on the Embarcadero south of the Ferry Building. According to Dohrmann, it would be close to other forms of transportation, a convenient transfer point for air mail, and would serve "as the necessary terminal depot to a large aviation field." He described his plan to Secretary of the Navy Curtis D. Wilbur, admitting the lack of precedent for such a structure, except perhaps an aircraft carrier. Dohrmann even asked Wilbur if he would let the association's engineers study firsthand the design of an aircraft carrier. The secretary heartily endorsed Dohrmann's idea for a landing platform while politely declining civilian inspection of his ships.

We may wonder today at the logic of building a landing field near the center of a dense downtown area. But it is important to understand the popular excitement that aviation, and transportation technology in general, stimulated during the 1920s. Enthusiasm simply obscured practicality. In the romantic age of airplanes and aviators, anything seemed possible, at least for the moment. The secretary of the navy himself was so enthralled that, in his reply to Dohrmann, he offered the opinion that a rotating platform, while obviously impractical, would be ideal.

Architect Lewis Hobart drew up the association's original stationary-platform scheme, including an elevated, double-deck street along the Embarcadero (to handle the assumed increase in traffic once bridges were built). The scheme became the centerpiece of a publicity pamphlet on aviation and highway planning for San Francisco published by the Regional Plan Association. Charles Lindbergh endorsed the idea shortly after his historic flight to Paris in 1927.

The publicity was short-lived. San Francisco's Board of Supervisors considered a variety of more realistic landing sites and in 1927 settled upon Mills Field near San Bruno (the present airport site), which was recommended by the airport committee because of its extensive acreage, reliable weather, and convenient access to the new Bayshore Highway.

Machine-age technology had outrun the dream, though proposals for an airport close to downtown died hard. The architectural firm of Miller and Pflueger drew up a scheme in 1927 for an airport near China Basin, south of Market Street, and the organizers of the Golden Gate International Exposition of 1939 were convinced that after the fair Treasure Island would become an important airline gateway to the Pacific.

With a plan for the future, and the ability to take advantage of commercial opportunities such as aviation, Dohrmann believed that San Francisco and its neighbors would rule the West.

During the 1930s San Francisco achieved two of its most visionary goals by bridging the Bay to the north and to the east: the Bay Bridge was dedicated in 1936 and the Golden Gate Bridge a year later. As John van der Zee, Harold Gilliam, and other writers have documented, these bridges were true visionary projects in the sense that each had been an idea or dream long before achieving reality. In two fell swoops the bridges themselves—which so radically altered the appearance of the city—seemed to transform San Francisco into the regional metropolis it had long sought to be. Reality outran the dream. As writer Felix Riesenberg put it in 1940, "The city of the day after tomorrow will, with these connecting spans, embrace all habitations on one hundred miles of harbor shores. This City of San Francisco Bay awaits the height of the Pacific Era."

The building of the bridges put San Francisco and Bay Area residents in the curious position of watching a vision take shape before their very eyes. The reality of the construction process—from pouring monolithic island piers to spinning the vast webs of cable—seemed to make the concept of bridging the Bay not more mundane but more mythic. Reports of construction setbacks, tragic accidents, and engineering triumphs mesmerized a public who could check on building progress simply by looking out a living-room window or up from the deck of a commuter ferry. The Bay became an amphitheater focusing all eyes on a thrilling urban metamorphosis.

Photographers, architects, painters, and writers recorded each emerging detail and the day-to-day activities of the bridge builders as if attempting to dispel the feeling of disbelief. In a pamphlet published in 1936 by the United States Steel Company upon completion of the Bay Bridge, one observer of its construction is quoted as saying, "I cannot believe my eyes. I cannot believe you. It just cannot be so. It's too marvelous." But, the writer continued, "it was so. The unbelievable had been accomplished. The Greatest Bridge in the world had been completed."

Peter Stackpole's famous Bay Bridge photographs record the duality with startling clarity. His images show workers matter-of-factly doing their jobs riveting, welding, or hoisting girders into place, and yet the new immensities of scale behind, above, or under them seem wholly divorced from the activity. The ordinary action appears unrelated to, and almost contradictory to, the extraordinary result.

The sheer magnitude of the task of construction—in terms of engineering complexity, organizational talent, financial commitment, and bridgeworkers' skill and daring—reinforced the visionary nature of each bridge. Simultaneous construction of two immense bridges during a time of economic cataclysm, the Depression, gave the bridges symbolic power as well. Even as they pointed to the future, they embodied a measure of victory over an adverse present.

Photographs could capture the magnificence, grandeur, and drama of the architecture and engineering, but only drawings and paintings could explain the mysteries of construction and describe the variety of forms to be assumed by the bridges. Such images could actually sharpen the vision and were often necessary to rally support from administrative bodies. A notable example is the extraordinary suite of paintings describing how the Golden Gate Bridge piers and towers were to be constructed. Undoubtedly commissioned to convince non-engineers—i.e., bridge directors—that the Golden Gate Bridge could in fact be built, these paintings were done by the prolific renderer and architect Chesley Bonestell.

A San Francisco-born artist who had studied architecture at Columbia University, Bonestell worked for Willis Polk during the planning and construction of the Panama-Pacific International Exposition, then as a renderer in New York during the 1920s. He returned to San Francisco in time to work for chief engineer Joseph Strauss on the Golden Gate Bridge.

The cutaway views of the south-pier foundation are especially remarkable. This pier presented the greatest construction challenge because of its underwater depth and the swiftness of surrounding tidal currents. In one pier painting a vast drum-shaped cofferdam rises from the ocean floor. The sunlit cutaway view reveals the many layers of defense against the force of ocean currents: an immensely thick concrete outer wall, multiple-story inspection shafts, and steel cross-braced superstructures. The figures of men are tiny but distinct, in control of and at ease with what they have created. The engineer's vision is all clarity and brilliance, an image of confidence and strength. These paintings are almost transcendentalist visions of triumph and self-reliance, as if Bonestell and Strauss are saying, like latter-day Captain Ahabs, "Look down deep and do believe!" Strauss included one of the cutaway drawings in his final report of 1937.

Bonestell also drew schemes for treating the southern approach through the Presidio. Only three of these images are known to be extant. One shows the approach off Marina Boulevard much as it was actually built. The other two show a scheme to develop the Palace of Fine Arts as a sort of San Francisco version of the Arc de Triomphe in Paris, complete with traffic circle and a broad boulevard on an axis with it (replacing what is today Beach Street).

Bonestell focused on demystifying and glorifying construction techniques, whereas architect Irving Morrow concentrated on dramatizing how the bridge would look when completed. His charcoal drawings of the towers, the roadway, and the entire span, done in 1930 and 1931, recall Hugh Ferriss in their use of shadow and light to emphasize scale and outline. Morrow, who had become deeply interested in aspects of modernism by the late 1920s and wrote on the subject for the local press, saw the bridge as a romantic expression of modern urbanism. Misty, ghostlike façades of a jagged modern skyscraper soar above a streamlined roadway suspended over a reflecting sea. In Morrow's deft hands, the Golden Gate Bridge could have fit into Ferriss' "Metropolis of Tomorrow."

Images of the Bay Bridge conveyed similar themes of engineering and architectural heroics. Though occupying a less precipitous and rugged site, Bay Bridge piers had to be sunk much deeper into the Bay floor in order to reach bedrock. One of the westernmost piers had to be sunk 220 feet to bedrock, even though the water at this point was only seventy feet deep. The great center anchorage under the western crossing reached bedrock at a depth of 205 feet.

Such feats of underwater construction were unprecedented. A widely published cutaway painting of the central anchorage shows its cellular construction and the great depths of water and mud in which it stands. Unlike the Bonestell images, however, this painting presents a more simplified view. The structure is complete, and though walls are carved out to show what is behind them, no attempt is made to capture a moment in the process of construction.

The Hoover-Young Commission, which in 1930 reported on the need for the Bay Bridge, made no specific suggestions as to architectural character, noting simply that "the final design should be such that it will conform with the scenic beauty of the San Francisco Bay." Timothy Pflueger chaired the team of three consulting architects who worked under Chief Engineer Charles Purcell and, according to his brother Milton Pflueger, argued for ornamental restraint. He concentrated on refining and simplifying bridge approaches.

The Bay Bridge acquired a more visionary quality when artists took up the question of scale. Bernard Maybeck proposed that monumental triumphal arches be built where the bridge meets the city, extending the scale of the structure into the urban fabric. His romantic reprise of "City Beautiful" imagery gave the Bay Bridge approach what was already built into the approach to the Golden Gate Bridge: a classically inspired monument (his Palace of Fine Arts) marking a major gateway to the city.

A more futuristic image of the Bay Bridge appears in a poster by Paul Forster to announce the opening ceremonies on November 12, 1936. The view is up from the Embarcadero, past a stylishly dressed crowd of spectators who are themselves looking up, past the old and friendly but diminished Ferry Building to the huge new roadway leaping over it. A rainbow arches behind. This clever juxtaposition of old and new San Francisco—in reality the bridge crosses the Embarcadero far south of the Ferry Building—provides an emphatic welcome to the new and more monumental urban scale represented by the bridge. The proximity to downtown made the Bay Bridge towers visual extensions of the city's modern skyline, capturing the spirit of Mullgardt's fanciful skyscraper-bridge from the previous decade.

ALLAN TEMKO

Allan Temko was born in New York City in 1924. After service in the Navy during World War II, he graduated from Columbia University and pursued further study at the Sorbonne and the University of California, Berkeley. He taught at the Sorbonne and wrote *Notre Dame of Paris*, the definitive architectural study of the cathedral. Temko returned to Berkeley to teach journalism and then became the architecture critic for the *San Francisco Chronicle* from 1961 until 1993. A contributor to *The New Yorker, Harper's,* and other magazines, Temko received numerous awards, including the Gold Medal of the Commonwealth Club of California, a Guggenheim Fellowship, and a Lifetime Achievement Award from the Society of Professional Journalists. He won the Pulitzer Prize in 1990 for his architecture criticism. He died in 2006.

• •

In "Bridge of Bridges," Temko celebrates the Golden Gate Bridge as a treasure comparable to the cathedrals of Europe. He combines his own insights into the bridge's design and construction with a well-informed overview of the architects, engineers, and historical circumstances responsible for its creation.

BRIDGE OF BRIDGES:
A QUANTUM LEAP INTO ARCHITECTURAL GLORY

BY NOW THE Golden Gate Bridge is recognized everywhere as a classic work of structural art. The great reddish web of steel, profiled against a panorama of hills and sky and open sea, has become as profound a symbol of its time and place as the Parthenon or Notre Dame. It's our closest equivalent to a cathedral, if only because it expresses the American will—our national ethos—with a grandeur, grace and almost mythic strength that earlier civilizations reserved for shrines.

That a technical feat should be an emblem of spiritual aspiration, comparable to religious architecture, is not so strange when the bridge is seen as a poetic conquest of space. Many medieval bridges, such as the Pont d'Avignon, were designed with chapels to celebrate the safety and beauty of the arched crossings. Famous bridge builders, such as the monk-engineer Benezet at Avignon, were sainted for their pious labors.

In that historical context, the Golden Gate Bridge must be counted a miracle. Flung up against winds and tide, shaken by earthquakes in the midst of construction, the clear span of 4,200 feet was an act of faith, at a time when people still believed in machines and the idea of progress. In the depths of the Depression, the bridge demonstrated that an amalgam of Yankee know-how, fearless enterprise and free thought could solve any problem, surmount any obstacle, with the intelligence and energy that carried the nation forward on Walt Whitman's Open Road.

The bridge thus is best seen as a community achievement at a particular moment in history. No other monument better sums up the closing phase of the industrial age, even though Rockefeller Center, Boulder Dam and the Bay Bridge—a formidable local rival with twin main spans of 2,310 feet each—were built at almost the same time.

None of those mighty projects quite matched the bravura of this bridge of bridges. The Golden Gate's main span, carrying lighter loads on its single deck, is almost as long as the Bay Bridge's pair of doubledecked suspension spans. At more than four-fifths of a mile across open water, it represented a quantum leap beyond its nearest rival, the 3,500-foot George Washington Bridge above the Hudson River, whose original single deck, of unparalleled elegance, linked New York and New Jersey in 1931. The George Washington itself had more than doubled the 1,595-foot Brooklyn Bridge, completed in 1883, which easily eclipsed all previous metal suspension spans going back to the early 19th century.

The Golden Gate capped this series of heroic accomplishments, and the wonder is how long its supremacy has lasted. Spans of more than 5,000 feet are being planned in Japan and elsewhere; and thanks to high-strength steels and other new materials and new techniques, it is theoretically feasible to increase the distance to 10,000 feet or more.

Nonetheless, the main span of the Golden Gate after 50 years is still the third longest in the world. It was surpassed marginally in 1964, by only 60 feet, by the 4,260-foot Verrazano in New York, which may have been stretched to set a record. Not until 1981 did the Humber Crossing in Britain achieve 4,626 feet, inaugurating a new phase of bridge building with huge towers of reinforced concrete rather than steel.

Yet these powerful 510-foot uprights are not so lofty as the Golden Gate's, which at 746 feet above water level remain the tallest bridge towers ever built. That's because the Humber estuary does not accommodate big ships, and the bridge's clearance is 98 feet, whereas the deck structure of the Golden Gate, clearing the channel by more than the official figure of 220 feet (it's actually closer to 235 feet), admits aircraft carriers and other very large vessels. But statistics mean less than the incalculable beauty of the bridge. And this turns out to be much more than sound engineering.

Much of its glamour seems due to the sweeping natural splendor of its emplacement. Yet Ansel Adams—no friend of technology in opposition to nature—said that the bridge improved the Golden Gate. The entrance to the Bay offered a "rather dull vista," he told me, before the tensed form of the bridge turned it into a spectacular portal; and his photographs prove the point.

The grand symmetry of the bridge seems almost perfectly wedded to the irregular site. This is all the more remarkable because the placement of the towers and the massive cable anchorages, especially on the southern side, was mainly dictated by geological considerations.

A stringent budget also affected aesthetics. The bridge's most serious flaw is the cumbersome triple-trussed arch framing Fort Point beneath its curve. The arched form is decent enough—far more handsome, say, than the cantilever section of the Bay Bridge—but it introduces a contradictory structural system where it is least wanted, interrupting what should have been a single smooth leap toward Marin. The arch was a thrifty expedient, to keep the main and side spans from growing even longer. If the bridge were built today, it could be easily lengthened, and the arch and its bulky piers omitted, or replaced by slender, widely spaced supports.

But at a distance the arch becomes almost a trifle in the majestic trajectory across the Gate. The main cables, 36 inches in diameter, are astonishingly fine for the enormous job they must perform. They lift in absolute confidence to the tops of the stepped-back towers, whose four rectangular openings diminish in size as they ascend, increasing the sense of height.

Then the cables swoop downward in a tremendous catenary, with a gathering impression of speed, almost touching the deck at mid-span, just short of the railing, before flying upward toward the opposite shore. There is no sign of strain or hesitation, only an unswerving statement of strength and decisiveness—the mark of a thrilling bridge.

This is perhaps the most exhilarating architectural experience ordinary people will ever enjoy; and it seems a pity to inform them that experts in such matters find the "sag" of the cables too deep and the roadway too low, although its height was unprecedented in a structure of this size.

Good engineers in the 1980s would almost routinely hang the main cables higher above the deck at mid-span, improving the proportions and emphasizing the extreme slenderness of the hanger ropes and the beautiful detailing of the clamps and connectors.

Another feature that can be criticized is the thick stiffening truss of the deck, 30 feet deep, which today could be replaced by a far less obtrusive aerodynamic structure tapering to thin edges.

In the 1930s, however, the heavy truss-work was not only prudent but indispensable. Wind stresses were not fully understood. At the end of the decade the disaster of the daring 2,800-foot Tacoma Narrows Bridge—"Galloping Gertie," which shook itself to death in a moderate wind—justified the conservatism of the Golden Gate's designers.

If anything, they underestimated the bridge's flexibility. Torsional problems appeared very early. In 1951 the span was briefly closed after it was slightly damaged in a storm. To dampen excessive movement, the truss was further stiffened by cross-bracing between its lower edges, changing the cross-section from an inverted "U" into a rectangular form that engineer Charles Seim likens to a shoebox. It is difficult to twist such a box, although the lid could be torn off if it were not fastened as securely as the deck, which has recently been lightened by a new asphalt-surfaced steel roadway.

All this, and much more, underlies the structural drama of the bridge, everywhere intensified—glorified—by its romantic "International Orange" color, the inspired contribution of bridge architect Irving F. Morrow.

Having built hardly anything on his own before this, although he had worked for leading architectural firms, the sensitive and rather shy designer was recommended by artist friends to the overpowering chief engineer Joseph B. Strauss. Morrow may have been hired because he would work for low fees and looked like a man whom Strauss could master.

Instead, Morrow's magnificent charcoal renderings had a major effect on the finished design. The stepped-back forms of the towers had already been roughly determined, possibly by Strauss himself with the help of an earlier architectural consultant. They had nothing like the opulence of Morrow's decorative details, including the Art Deco brackets of the tower portals, which disguise structure but do amazing things with light and subtly enhance the scale of the entire span and its approaches.

The ribbed surfaces of the seemingly solid tower crossbars, for instance, conceal X-bracing beneath, which handles the structural loads. But the ornamental furrows create a soaring effect. Morrow continued this theme on the great concrete piers and the underpinning of the towers, subtly softening ponderous forms. The open railings permit generous views of the Bay, in contrast to the crude barriers of the Bay Bridge. The lighting standards were models for their time. The tall, curving toll booths, now being replaced, were beauties.

Yet the bridge's color is Morrow's noblest legacy. Variously described as a kind of vermilion, it is largely a mixture of orange and lamp black, which produces the burnt reddish-orange that responds so eloquently to changing light, in sunshine or mist, from soft dawn to violet twilight.

The success of Morrow's sculptural and painterly architecture almost precludes the question of whether the bridge might not have appeared still stronger, purer, more "honest," if rationally engineered forms of the basic structure had been allowed to speak powerfully for themselves, without Morrow's operatic orchestration.

But there's no denying that the unjustly half-forgotten architect merged function and decoration in an extraordinary way. Precisely how he worked can be glimpsed in a rare show of his drawings, as well as correspondence and documents concerning the bridge, at the San Francisco chapter of the American Institute of Architects, 790 Market Street, until June 8[, 1987].

By sorting out the roles of Strauss, Morrow, the superb engineering staff, intrepid work crews, and a host of other talented people who designed and built the bridge, we are slowly arriving at an accurate historic record of the whole vast undertaking.

There was never any doubt that the masterly design was largely, if not entirely, the work of other hands than the chief engineer's. The question since the 1930s has been, whose?

The 50th anniversary has been an occasion for much squabbling over who did what, most recently in a kindly meant but misleading book, *The Gate* by John van der Zee (Simon & Schuster), which must be read with the utmost care.

Van der Zee has a double purpose. He not only is bent on denigrating the feisty, unlovable Joseph Strauss, an indomitable promoter who tried to hog credit for everything, but also has tried to elevate a rather obscure figure, Strauss' subordinate design engineer, Charles Alton Ellis, to the empyrean of structural art as the principal creator of the bridge, even though he never did anything else of nearly the same distinction.

The exhumation of Ellis is praiseworthy, since he was clearly an excellent engineer, but van der Zee's claim is made at the expense of the able Clifford E. Paine, chief assistant to Strauss, who before his death in 1983 told Harold Gilliam that he actually designed the bridge.

There must be truth in both of these versions, but it cannot be the full truth. As van der Zee concedes, an infinitely greater "genius" first proposed a 4,000-foot bridge for the Gate in 1925: Leon Solomon Moisseiff, one of the searching engineers of his generation, who later became the foremost member of the bridge advisory board and saw the design process through to the end, under separate contract to the Strauss engineering firm.

A concept of such grandeur seems utterly beyond the capacities of men like Strauss, Paine and Ellis. Yet each in his own way helped to help make the idea a reality; and when the story is put in final perspective, by someone without an ax to grind, Strauss especially may fare better than his detractors suspect.

This difficult man, far more than anyone else, got the bridge built against daunting odds. His role was analogous to that of the "building bishops" of the Middle Ages, like Maurice de Sully at Notre Dame, who were not designers but who made the crucial decisions, and took tremendous risks, to create the cathedrals. Even if the Golden Gate Bridge does not last 1,000 years, much less "forever," as Strauss vowed it would, he should always be thanked for that.

BRENDAN GILL

Brendan Gill was born in Hartford, Connecticut, in 1914. Joining the staff of *The New Yorker* in 1936, he reviewed theater, film, books, and architecture, in addition to writing fiction, poetry, biography, and history. Gill was the author of fifteen books, among them *Late Bloomers, Here at The New Yorker,* and *Many Masks,* a biography of Frank Lloyd Wright. Gill also wrote *The New Yorker's* "Skyline" column on architecture for ten years. Beyond his literary pursuits, Gill played an active role in architectural preservation. He died in New York City in 1997.

• •

In this excerpt from *The Dream Come True,* Gill gracefully distinguishes between the architecture of the California bungalow and that of the California ranch house. In so doing, he celebrates the vigorous fantasy life of Los Angeles as embodied in the ranch house architecture of Cliff May.

from **THE DREAM COME TRUE: GREAT HOUSES OF LOS ANGELES**

AN INNOVATION SUFFICIENTLY prolonged becomes a fashion and a fashion sufficiently prolonged becomes a style. California has long prided itself on initiating fashions, whether in swimsuits, tax-cuts, or religious sects, and it is certainly the case that at least twice in this century a distinctively Californian style of architecture has spread from coast to coast: the California bungalow style, which flourished before and just after the First World War and was characterized by low, broad gables and porch roofs supported on stubby columns of brick or wood; and the California ranch-house style, which has been gaining in popularity continuously since the end of the Second World War. (Specimens of a third style, a California version of Spanish Colonial, can often be found in large cities, in real-estate developments laid out prior to 1929 and the subsequent depression; they are rare in cities with populations of fewer than twenty-five thousand people and in certain areas, such as New England, they are almost non-existent.) As one approaches the East coast, where open land is hard to come by and therefore expensive and where the rigor of winter requires substantial central heating, the California ranch-house tends to draw in upon itself, making up in height what it lacks in breadth. From this huddled posture springs the curious neologism "splanch," which one encounters daily in the real-estate sections of Eastern newspapers and which stands for "split-level ranch." "Splanch" usually means that a couple of bedrooms and a bathroom have been fitted into a second story above a partly subterranean garage; it may also mean that a "family" room has been added to the usual living room, though the difference between what goes on in a family room and in a living room remains undefined—one suspects that the living room becomes the formal preserve of visitors. There are ranch-houses and splanch-houses all the way out to the furthermost rocky tip of Long Island, cleaving the Atlantic, and they seem not uncomfortable there (especially as the sun and the sea air gradually weather them), but one is tempted to assert that their natural setting is the Pacific coast; it is a Pacific climate and a Pacific culture that have brought them into being.

That dictum uttered, a formidable exception immediately springs to mind. By far the most skillful practitioner of the California ranch-house style is Cliff May, who in the course of a career that began in 1932 has designed ranch-houses in uncounted hundreds of different localities, most of them in California but some of them as far afield as Australia, Venezuela, Switzerland, Ireland, Italy, and several islands in the Caribbean. Ranch-houses by May, modified to accommodate to climate and topography, are to be found in forty-five of our fifty states; during a brief period in the early nineteen-fifties, he licensed on a fee basis to builders plans for a low-cost ranch-house, of which no fewer than eighteen thousand were built and sold. Of his individually designed ranch-houses, May estimates that they run into well over a thousand. Given the total number of May houses designed and built to date, it could be argued that May is probably the most popular architect who has ever lived. In books of architectural history, the tiny Eames house will no doubt take pride of place over the grandest of May's ranch-houses, but no matter. The quantity of work he has presided over is hard to take in; the quality of much of it is, under the circumstances, astonishingly high.

A true ranch-house of the nineteenth century was the main structure in a cluster of buildings that were flung up any which way over a period of years. May has perfected an apparent randomness of plan that convincingly resembles that cluster and evokes the simplicities of an earlier, more hospitable, and (we may pretend) more affectionate time. Rooms flow into one another and out onto terraces and enclosed patios; it is always an agreeable sensation to lose one's way not once but several times in getting from the front door of a May house to a distant bedroom. The bigger the ranch-house, the greater the opportunity: May's own house, at the head of a long canyon within the city limits but seeming to lie in some remote valley of the High Sierra (one hears from a nearby pasture the whinnying of horses, the baying of hounds), might be mistaken at first glance for a village. The scale is big but unintimidating. The living-room, for example, is fifty-five feet long, thirty-five feet wide, and fifteen feet high at the skylighted crest of its "cathedral" ceiling. It contains two grand pianos, thousands of ancient vellum-bound books, folk sculpture from half a dozen cultures, and innumerable oversized couches, tables, and chairs. Hard as it may be to believe, the room is cozily domestic, inviting one to rough it ranch-house style on a very high level of luxury. If one sits in the patio under the stars and the night air grows cold, underfoot the paving is warm; whether indoors or out, May takes care to provide heat when nature doesn't. Away in the dark, one hears the hissing of water in the thick ground-cover of a distant hillside. That, too, is May's handiwork; a miniature rain-forest flourishes where for months no rain is likely to fall. Closer to hand, the splash of a fountain, the glint of firelight on a grilled Spanish casement. Sparks fly up out of a crumbling pyramid of logs; the logs are real and so is the concealed jet of gas that keeps them flaring.

At the foot of the canyon road stretches a city of many millions, ablaze with lights, throbbing with activity. The quiet house and its accompaniment of shadowy fields and woods is a stage-set, but the wise student of Los Angeles perceives—and is content to perceive—that a stage-set is no more true or false than the dream it embodies. All those hundreds upon hundreds of May ranch-houses, big and small, like all the hundreds of thousands of anonymous dwellings that make up the loosely woven fabric of the city, are embodiments of dreams that, against high odds, have managed to come true. Wracked by floods, droughts, and earthquakes, in terms of safety Los Angeles might just as well be perched on the simmering upper slopes of Vesuvius, but it doesn't matter: nothing is as outrageous and everlasting as a dream, and a city founded on dreams and scorning prudence is likely to endure forever.

NEIL LEVINE

Neil Levine is the Emmet Blakeney Gleason Professor of History of Art and Architecture at Harvard University. *The Architecture of Frank Lloyd Wright* is one of his many books on architectural subjects.

• •

In "Hollyhock House," Levine shows how Frank Lloyd Wright connected one home with the theatrical spirit of 1920s Hollywood by infusing the structure with a stark monumentality.

from **"HOLLYHOCK HOUSE"**
in *The Architecture of Frank Lloyd Wright*

FEW MODERN HOUSES in the twentieth century have been designed with such monumental purpose as Hollyhock House. Fewer still have been invested with the degree of symbolic expression normally reserved for buildings of a more public nature. Soon after Wright had begun working on a project for a small theater for the wealthy oil heiress Aline Barnsdall, sometime in 1955 or early 1916, she urged him to stretch his imagination to the limit. "You will put your freest dreams into it, won't you!" she wrote. "For I believe so firmly in your genius that I want to make it the keynote of my work." Wright saw a major opportunity when it eventually came to designing an entire cultural center around a house for his enthusiastic client. "Why not make the architecture stand up and show itself...as Romance?" he asked. "The architect's plans joyfully traveled the upward road of poetic form and delighted Miss Barnsdall. I could scarcely have keyed the 'romanza' too high for her...had I made it a symphony." He later realized, however, that there were those who would feel "that the architect had indulged himself...regardless of the task with the machine he had set himself."

Hollyhock House was built in the Hollywood section of Los Angeles at the first peak of excitement over that city's role in the fast-growing motion picture industry. The house, which was to be the nucleus of a cultural center devoted mainly to the dramatic arts, is located on Olive Hill at the edge of the Los Angeles basin, just before the Hollywood foothills begin to rise.

With the city below to the southeast, the San Gabriel Mountains in the background to the north, the San Bernardino Mountains in the far distance to the east, and the Pacific Ocean sweeping across the horizon from west to south, the house is perched on the acropolis of Olive Hill like an ancient palace or citadel, isolated from the real world by a surrounding moat of boulevards and streets. Wright called it Aline Barnsdall's "little queendom" and said it was conceived as "a holiday adventure in Romanza."

"You'll want when you see it to call it Egyptian," wrote a reporter just after the house was completed, until "you realize that in the Nile country, in all the stretches of the north African plains, there is no building that could truly be called Parent of this one." Then, "the 'Aztec!' you exclaim; and you are closer to the truth, when your eyes equate it with the charm of the courts and the patios and the bowers, and the gardens and the siesta spots and the flat roof lines. But you are still wrong." Rather, he concluded, you should "think of a good size pueblo on one of New Mexico's mesas or low clean bluffs seen in some parts of the foothills of the Sierras. Refine the outline[s] somewhat, without losing their strength, tint it as near as an approach as possible to the silver green slopes of these same foothills and bower it with verdure and you will approach the conception of the exterior of Miss Barnsdall's home."

Hollywood had already become the land of make-believe in that "desert of shallow effects" Wright called Los Angeles. Soon after Colonel William Selig sent some of his staff there in 1907 to shoot *The Count of Monte Cristo*, the movie industry began establishing permanent studios to take advantage of the perpetual sunshine and extraordinary natural scenery. Movie lots began springing up all over Los Angeles, but especially in Hollywood, with sets resembling the rock-cut temples of Abu Simbel for Cecil B. DeMille's *Ten Commandments* (1923) or a Middle Eastern bazaar for Douglas Fairbanks's *Thief of Baghdad* (1925). The first and greatest of these spectacular outdoor dream worlds was D. W. Griffith's Babylonian palace for *Intolerance*, built in 1916 on Sunset Boulevard, just a block or so to the east of Olive Hill, and left standing for a number of years afterward as a kind of memorial to that epic. As the palaces in which the movies were shown, along with those in which the stars lived, were becoming as exotic as the sets themselves, a context was established that Wright could hardly ignore, especially when Nebuchadnezzar was the next-door neighbor.

Located just below the crown of Olive Hill and enclosing a central courtyard, Hollyhock House steps down to the south in a series of platforms and terraces that terminate in a low semicircular bastion, making the southern flank of the building seem impregnable from Sunset Boulevard. The private entrance on the north, from Hollywood Boulevard, is protected by a deep forecourt that reaches out to the driveway and is bordered by animal pens on one side and a forty-foot-long porte-cochere on the other. For most of its length, this covered passage has openings at eye level, recalling to the newspaper reporter "apertures in great moat walls," and providing intermittent glimpses of the Pacific Ocean that establish from the outset the thematic link between mountain and sea." Near the end, the passage narrows into a corbelled tunnel that finally pushes through a pair of swinging, solid concrete doors, like a ceremonial causeway opening into the shaft of a manmade mountain."

Inside, the verdant, sun-drenched courtyard offers a sanctuary of peace and serenity. Like a crater open to the sky, it is surrounded by shaded loggias and pergolas that were cooled by a stream of water fed by a fountain and pool. Outside, the monolithic appearance of the smooth, lightly tinted walls, roofs, and parapets—layered and canted as they rise, and almost completely unpunctured by windows or doors—makes the house seem to be part of the hill, at once reinforcing the temple-like character of the precinct and calling to mind the ancient monuments of Mesoamerica and the Middle East. But finally, the luxuriousness of the setting, the sleek beauty of the forms, and the sense of enchantment within provide a visual experience that, more than any other serious work of architecture, speaks of the world of romance represented by Hollywood in the late teens and twenties.[…]

Originally part of the Los Feliz Rancho, Olive Hill comprised a thirty-six-acre block bordered by Sunset Boulevard on the south, Hollywood Boulevard on the north, Vermont Avenue on the east, and Edgemont Street on the west. The hill took its name from the olive trees planted on its slopes in the 1890s. The hollyhocks growing wild there provided the decorative theme for the house and gave Barnsdall the idea of naming her house after "her favorite flower."

Rising to a height of nearly 490 feet above sea level and at least 100 feet above the surrounding streets, the site was a prominent landmark. Located at the northeastern corner of Hollywood, where the tracks of the Pacific Electric streetcars coming from downtown Los Angeles turned west from Vermont Avenue into Hollywood Boulevard, Olive Hill, along with Mount Hollywood to the north, formed a kind of natural gateway to Hollywood." For many years Angelenos had come to the "Mount of Olives" to celebrate Easter sunrise services, a purpose Barnsdall recognized in declaring to the press, upon announcing her plans for building, that she would "keep [the] gardens always open to the public...who wish to come here to view sunsets, dawn on the mountains, and other spectacles of nature visible in few other places in the heart of the city."

As Wright began to develop the plans for what Barnsdall ultimately intended to be a complete art center, including theaters for both drama and movies, residences for artists and production staff, income-producing shops, a rooftop restaurant above the theater, and public gardens—all surrounding her own hilltop residence—the nature of the hill site and its setting in the surrounding landscape seemed to demand a monumental solution. He turned the site into an outdoor sanctuary for the arts. Like a temple—or "a miniature palace of some ancient civilization," as Bel Geddes described an early version of the design—the house was to command the hill, with the buildings for cultural activities set around its base.[...]

Hollyhock House was one of the very few opportunities Wright had in domestic design to develop a program of such scope. Earlier there had been the Coonley estate and the McCormick project. The other major undertaking of a similar nature was, of course, Taliesin. After Hollyhock came Fallingwater and Wright's desert compound of Taliesin West. But Hollyhock House is different from all of these. It has the formality of the early Prairie Style, but none of its domesticity. It is more explicitly regional and more specifically oriented to the natural forms of the landscape, yet is nowhere nearly as naturalistic and integral to its site as the two Taliesins or Fallingwater. Like the Imperial Hotel, Hollyhock House is a "transitional" building; but unlike its immediate predecessor, it represents a single point of view and is prophetic in that regard. Its subject matter is nature—or, more precisely, the forces of nature—and the relation between building and landscape is expressed in a symbolic language that predicts the major themes of Wright's later work.

Southern California was a totally new experience for Wright. Its natural beauty made it seem to him "a land of romance." But he also felt, just as profoundly, that its natural beauty had not yet been recognized in any "type" of building "characteristic" of the region, and that most of its architecture was a misguided effort to escape from the realities of the landscape and to deny its potentially devastating effects. With the Barnsdall commission, Wright was, for the first time in his life, forced to confront the issue of American regionalism as an outsider. In the Imperial Hotel, he had deliberately chosen to make a compromise with his Prairie Style to avoid anything that might look too "Oriental." The architecture's relation to nature was ultimately an abstraction, for the downtown urban setting of the building had no immediate connection with the actual landscape.

In the case of Hollyhock House, Wright was presented first and foremost with a landscape situation. Early on in the process, Barnsdall had told him that the hill would be "the *real* inspiration," and throughout their later discussions both of them described the project as "working out this hill." Wright instinctively associated the situation with Taliesin, as can be seen in a notation on a series of sketches for the overall treatment of the site. But the scrubby hills and powerful mountain ranges of Southern California presented an austere environment quite alien to the lush, rolling countryside of south-central Wisconsin, which, Wright noted, "picks you up in its arms and so gently, almost lovingly, cradles you." Never before had Wright faced a landscape of such elemental power and dramatic presence. "Hollyhock House was to be a natural house in the changed circumstances," he later wrote. It was to be "native to the region of California" and thus embody and dramatize the characteristic features of the region for "a client who loved them and the theater."

Wright was hardly alone in this search for regional expression. Across America, the adoption of explicitly regional styles was already beginning to alter the course of modern architecture. Nowhere was this more apparent than in California, where the progressive work of Greene and Greene, Irving Gill, and Bernard Maybeck had come almost completely to a halt by 1916. Instead, the Spanish Colonial style of the early missions had been accepted as the most logical expression of local conditions, especially after the 1915 Panama-California Exposition in San Diego. While Wright despised such "sentimental bosh," he agreed that the style of the mission buildings "just happened to be more in keeping with California." To searching for an "imaginative California 'Form,'" something "romantic" and "beautiful in California in the way that California herself is beautiful," he felt inspiration could be found in "cool *patios*" enclosed by "plain, white-plastered walls," creating a "refreshing foil for exotic foliage" in "oases kept green by great mountain reservoirs." But Wright also believed his program called for something more monumental and "not so domestic as the popular neo-Spanish of the region." By reference to the native forms of Precolumbian Mexico and the American Southwest, he sought to achieve a more "elemental" expression of the powerful forces of nature that define the landscape of Southern California.

For the plan of Hollyhock House, Wright returned to the "zoned plan" he had developed for the main house of the Coonley estate and later used in modified form at Taliesin. As adapted to the Olive Hill site, it became the most classically balanced and self-contained composition he ever produced for a house. In the Coonley House, the major functions (living, dining, kitchen and servants' quarters, bedrooms, guest rooms) were placed in separate wings. These were raised above the driveway to form a *piano nobile* and were linked in a broad, open U to take advantage of the view to the Des Plaines River. At Taliesin the different wings were set along the contours of the hill, just below the crown, and were only loosely connected to one another. By contrast, the four main wings of Hollyhock House enclose a patio court in the local Spanish Colonial tradition. The axiality and symmetry of the design give it a specifically classical formality relating it to Midway Gardens and the Imperial Hotel; yet the plan of Hollyhock House is more domestic in type." In its complex play of longitudinal and transverse axes terminating in divergent circular shapes, it recalls certain eighteenth-century French *hôtel* plans, exemplified by the

Hôtel de Salm in Paris. (An exact replica of this was built in San Francisco in 1915 as the French pavilion for the Panama-Pacific Exposition and then rebuilt in 1919-24, on a site in Lincoln Park overlooking the Pacific Ocean, as the permanent home of the California Palace of the Legion of Honor.)

Hollyhock House is organized around two major axes: the central one runs east-west through the patio, or garden court; the other extends north-south through the entrance, or motor court. Each terminates in a semicircle, as in the Hôtel de Salm. A central opening into the patio on the east forms a monumental "courtyard entrance" along what would have been an almost ritually formal path through the woods from the theater below. But the main entrance to the house, from the motor court, is shifted off axis. It slides into the northwest corner, thus producing one of the many distortions that give the plan the pinwheeling effect characteristic of Wright's work in general. The long sides of the patio are bounded by the dining/kitchen/servants' wing on the north and the guest-bedroom wing on the south. The former closes the house off from the motor court, and the latter opens onto a walled garden, which in turn is ringed by the semicircular retaining wall.

The central east-west axis parallels the mountains to the north and connects the reflecting pools at each end of the house. To the east, the axis passes under the family bedroom wing, which forms a bridge over a circular pool marking the upper end of the patio. A stand of pine trees, backed by a taller one of eucalyptus, was to have formed a silvery green screen between the pale stucco walls of the house and the distant, sandy-colored mountain slopes. To the west, the axis passes through the loggia and then the living room, which faces the Pacific Ocean. A square reflecting pool in front of the living room balances the circular one to the east.

Unlike almost all Wright's earlier houses, Hollyhock House is a closed composition turning inward on itself. Despite its elevated site, the views are limited and highly controlled. All the spaces, however, open generously into the central patio, making the house seem "half house and half garden"—which is, Wright told Barnsdall, what "a California house should be." The patio was originally designed to be part formal and manicured, part informal and wild, again reminiscent of such eighteenth-century proto-types as the romantic *jardin anglais* set within the classical framework of

Ledoux's Hôtel de Thélusson. At Hollyhock House, a stream meandering through lush foliage and connecting the reflecting pools was originally separated from the rest of the garden by a stone path.

The secluded oasis thus became an idealized landscape suggesting, in its forms, an open-air theater. Although it is not known whether dramatic productions were ever intended to be staged there, the bedroom bridge could have functioned as a proscenium arch, separating the raised stage beyond the circular pool from the orchestra occupying the manicured garden, while the flat roofs of the surrounding wings could become balconies for overflow crowds. More in keeping with the antique source of Wright's design for the actual theater, however, the whole arrangement could be seen in reverse. Then the stepped semicircular *cavea* around the pool would define the perimeter of the auditorium. The action would take place, as in a Greek theater of the Hellenistic period, on top of the flat roof of the loggia, functioning as a true proscenium, in front of the episcenium formed by the canted roof of the living room.

However this central arena was used, its design was clearly more than a literal response to the program. The stylized, freestanding hollyhocks sprouting from the corner stairway are inset with mask-like faces. Recalling Mexican Gulf Coast agricultural deities guarding a sacred precinct, they recur in pairs to define a processional way up to the multilevel roof garden. The entire sequence takes on an extraordinarily ceremonial air. The roof terraces, like temple platforms, are linked to one another by stairways and bridges and seem to have been designed for some symbolic purpose beyond the viewing of contemporary drama and dance.

The movement follows a spiraling, counterclockwise path, fully encircling the open court and making one realize that this is not just a roof garden. Rather, it is a "roof observatory," as a contemporary newspaper report aptly called it, "to view sunsets, dawn on the mountains, and other spectacles of nature." As at an ancient Amerindian observatory, such as the Caracol at Chichén Itzá, or the Palace complex at Palenque, one mounts from one platform to the next, to yet a higher one, until the panorama of Los Angeles unfolds below and one has the impression of being suspended between the mountains and the sea under "the serene canopy of California blue."

The exterior of Hollyhock House reflects the surrounding mountain shapes, which Wright described as "curious tan-gold foothills ris[ing] from tattooed sand-stretches." Hollyhock House is the one building Wright placed *on* the hill (or nearly so) and for which he made the profile of the roof the most conspicuous feature of the design. After first trying a conventional hip and then a tall, tepee-like shape, he chose a truncated talus, which is banded by a ridge, or frieze, of conventionalized hollyhocks to "adorn the hill crown." Instead of relating house to ground through the extended horizontal line of the eaves, the truncated shape floating above the line of hollyhocks relates the building to the sky and allows for the effects of aerial perspective in a landscape where, as Wright noted, "foreground spreads to distances so vast" that "human scale is utterly lost as all features recede, turn blue, recede and become bluer still to merge their blue mountain shapes, snow capped, with the azure of the skies." It was "in the *silhouette* of the Olive Hill house" that Wright meant to express "a sense of the breadth and romance of the region."

As observers pointed out from the moment Hollyhock House was finished, its imagery derives from the two historical models Wright felt were most appropriate to the region. The stepped and layered horizontal masses recall the "mesa silhouette," as Wright's son Lloyd put it, "characterized and developed by Pueblo Indians" in their terraced adobe constructions. More significant and more obvious, perhaps, are the shapes of Precolumbian Mexican architecture. The profile of the high canted attic, and the squat proportions resulting from the mid-height placement of the continuous decorative frieze, immediately bring to mind the temples of Palenque, Uxmal, and Chichén Itzá, just as the banded, enframing moldings of the theater project recall the more compressed and earth-bound forms of Mitla and Monte Albán.[...]

Hollyhock House gave form to Wright's vision of the landscape and history of Southern California. A sham construction in itself, it is fittingly all about image—and image-making. Through its theatrical adaptation of historical forms, it represents an idealization of the powerful forces of nature in an elemental expression of Southern California. To appreciate its uniqueness and significance in this regard, one has only to contrast it with the casual Japanese-inspired bungalows of the Greene brothers, the simplicity of Irving Gill's stripped-down Mission Style, and the more explicit revivalism of Goodhue's Spanish Colonial. Those earlier attempts to fit in with the region were, Wright believed, either "sentimental," "antiseptic," or just "fashionable," designed to appeal to the Californian "née Iowan, Wisconsoniano, Ohioan." His vision of Los Angeles, the "poetic thing this land was before this homely mid-west invasion," derived from a cataclysmic interpretation of a landscape described by Southern California's poet laureate John Steven McGroarty in 1921 as "a city where it seemed that neither God nor man intended a city should be." It was a "place in the sun," as Frank Fenton later wrote, that "rested on a crust of earth at the edge of a sea that ended a world." [...]

Barnsdall probably never really thought of Hollyhock House as her "home." Wright made it quite clear, both in what he designed and in what he wrote, that his intention was never simply to provide a functional solution to a domestic problem. Monumentality was uppermost in both their minds. It is therefore not surprising that Barnsdall hardly ever lived in Hollyhock House and that she offered it to the City of Los Angeles, within two years of its completion, as the nucleus of a municipal art center. Following much debate, and after the California Art Club agreed to act as an intermediary, the city accepted the gift in early 1927, at which time the land and its buildings became known as Thomas Barnsdall Park, in memory of her father.

Many reasons have been put forth to explain this peremptory disposal: high taxes, exorbitant maintenance costs, problematic living conditions, lack of need for a permanent residence of such size, philanthropy, the demise of the theater component, even real estate profiteering. Interestingly, Wright stressed the social question. A friend of Emma Goldman, Barnsdall was well known as a promoter of left-wing causes. Wright acknowledged the enormous disparity between Barnsdall's ideological position and the house she had been given to live in: "They said in Hollywood, Aline Barnsdall was a Bolshevik....They rather sneered...at one whose ideas were 'proletariat' and hard, while living soft herself like a princess in aristocratic seclusion." But such an apparent mismatch cannot fully explain Barnsdall's action, for she commissioned Wright to design another house (in Beverly Hills) at about the same time she offered Hollyhock House to the city. Which leads one to suspect, as most observers have, that her fundamental reason for giving away Hollyhock House was the very one for which she initially commissioned Wright to design it: that it should become a public arena in which Los Angeles might find forms of artistic expression appropriate to its new "place in the sun."

For many years, however—indeed, until quite recently—Hollyhock House seemed hardly to fulfill its idealistic social mission. Abandoned and unused during the years of high modernism, it fell into a premature state of ruin. Whether or not it qualifies as the first modern ruin, this condition of dysfunction made its expression of the "spirit of place" even more poignant. One is forcefully reminded of Louis Kahn's conception of how meaning in architecture emerges out of the transcendence of mere building or function:

> When a building is being built, there is an impatience to bring it into being. Not a blade of grass can grow near this activity. Look at the building after it is built. Each part that was built with so much anxiety and joy and willingness to proceed tries to say when you're using the building, "Let me tell you about how I was made." Nobody is listening because the building is now satisfying need. The desire in its making is not evident. As time passes, when it is a ruin, the spirit of its making comes back. It welcomes the foliage that entwines and conceals. Everyone who passes can hear the story it wants to tell about its making. It is no longer in servitude; the spirit is back.

Hollyhock House will always be like a stage set for a play that could never be acted out, nor ever had to be, in reality. For the building itself was conceived as a work of pure representation, its fictional story line being understood in its mute, historic forms.

KEVIN STARR

Kevin Starr was born in 1940 in San Francisco. After graduating with a Ph.D. in American literature from Harvard University, Starr worked as an aide to the mayor of San Francisco and as a columnist for the *San Francisco Examiner*. During his career he has also served as the city librarian of San Francisco and as the state librarian of California. He is currently University Professor and Professor of History at the University of Southern California. Starr is the author of the acclaimed Americans and the California Dream series, a multifaceted examination of the state's history from the gold rush through the mid-twentieth century. The latest volume in the series is *Golden Dreams: California in an Age of Abundance: 1950–1963*. Among the many awards and honors Starr has received are a National Medal for the Humanities, the Centennial Medal of the Graduate School of Arts and Sciences of Harvard University, the Gold Medal of the Commonwealth Club of California, and a Guggenheim Fellowship.

• •

In this selection from *Material Dreams*, one of the volumes in the Americans and the California Dream series, Starr explains the connections between Hollywood stage sets and Wallace Neff's architecture of the Southland between the two world wars.

from *MATERIAL DREAMS: SOUTHERN CALIFORNIA THROUGH THE 1920S*

AMONG THESE GRAND eclectics, Wallace Neff distinguished himself as the most imaginative and playful: not as correct perhaps as the others but displaying an inventiveness, a storybook theatricality that in some ways made his work seem the most appropriately Southern Californian. Neff, first of all, was a native son born in 1895 in La Mirada, a subdivision near Altadena (itself near Pasadena), which Neff's grandfather, the multimillionaire Chicago map and gazeteer publisher Andrew McNally (as in Rand McNally), was developing as a community of country estates. McNally's chief assistant in the La Mirada scheme was his son-in-law Edwin Dorland Neff, a Chicago stockbroker of Swiss-Dutch descent. Moving permanently to La Mirada from Chicago, Neff proceeded to pursue a life of sports-related leisure—riding, hunting, some ranching—as described in the brochure *The Country Gentleman in California* (1897) which he wrote to sell the La Mirada estates. When the Neff children reached school age, the family moved to a home in Altadena which Andrew McNally had presented to the couple at the time of their marriage.

A scion of the same Southern Californianized Midwestern wealth which constituted the most appreciative clientele for architecture, Wallace Neff grew up with a strong sense of personal caste and regional identity. Southern California was for Neff not a locale adopted in later life for reasons of health or economic opportunity, but the internalized landscape of his earliest and most fundamental self. He understood the place instinctively—its climate, landforms, fauna, and flora, its capacity to speak directly to dreams. Wallace Neff's father, after all, empowered by wealth, had come to Southern California to lead a storybook life as a country squire, which he proceeded to do. In later life, Wallace Neff would show an instinctive understanding of the life-style and subliminal aspirations of his clients: why, that is, they had come to Southern California in the first place; and this rapport accounted in some measure for the storybook aspects, the mood of dreams come true, that characterized so much of his work.

Between 1909 and 1914 the Neffs lived in Europe, based initially in Switzerland where they had gone to seek medical treatment for Wallace's sister Marie, who had been born with a congenital heart condition. The Neffs later moved to Bavaria, where Wallace was sent to the German-American School in Munich. Marie Neff, unfortunately, succumbed to her heart condition in late 1912, and the entire Neff family relocated to Munich until the outbreak of war drove them back to the United States. For five impressionable years, from age 14 to 19, Wallace Neff experienced Europe—Switzerland, South Germany, France, and Italy—as a student and an ardent traveler. Instructed in drawing at Munich by the landscape painter Peter Paul Muller, Neff filled his sketchbooks with depictions of picturesque rural architecture (a castle rising from rock formations, a country church emerging from a copse of trees) that could already pass as illustrations for a book of fairy tales set in the Bavarian forest.

At MIT, where Neff studied architecture from 1915 to 1917, Dean Ralph Adams Cram encouraged his propensity towards a strong narrative line based on historical precedents. Himself the master of Gothic Revival (St. John the Divine in New York, the monastery of the Cowley Fathers in Cambridge, the Graduate School and Chapel at Princeton, the United States Military Academy at West Point), Cram rejected the Beaux Arts tradition of drawing and redrawing from classical models in favor of a more experimental approach based on travel, observation, and sketching in the field. Neff's drawings from Europe had encouraged Cram to overlook the young Southern Californian's spotty preparation (Neff had already been rejected by Throop College in Pasadena) and admit him to the program. Aside from honing his technical skills, the MIT of Ralph Adams Cram encouraged Wallace Neff to continue in that course of narrational eclecticism based on observed precedents upon which he had already embarked as a student and unpaid architectural apprentice in Munich. As an architect Wallace Neff possessed a highly developed ability to set scenes and tell stories through domestic design (throughout his long career, he would rarely do other than homes) in a manner appropriate to an emerging region desirous of identity through historical metaphors: of dreams materialized as architectural fairytales.

Entering the profession in the take-off year 1919, Neff immediately displayed his eclecticism with an exquisite Craftsman cottage for his mother in Santa Barbara (1919), a courtyard stable for Edward Drummond Libbey at Ojai based on French precedents (1923), and a country club at Ojai, again for Libbey, inspired by the low-lying horizontal haciendas of Spanish California (1923–1924). Neff thus began his career with a salute to the Craftsman era just ending, a perfect performance in the Spanish Revival era just beginning (the Ojai Country Club won an Honor Award from the Southern California chapter of the AIA), and a gesture via the Libbey stable to the rural French vernaculars Neff would begin adapting in the early 1930s for the film colony. The commission from Libbey, moreover, a multimillionaire Ohioan who wintered at Ojai, underscored another emergent pattern, Neff's ability to design for Southern Californianizing wealth—King Gillette of safety razor fame, cereal mogul Carol Post, brewer extraordinaire Adolphus Busch, Mary Pickford and Douglas Fairbanks—in such a way as to corroborate for them their newly elected identity as Southern Californians through homes that bore a signature, a trademark, almost as strong as the brand names Gillette, Post, and Busch. Through such homes, Wallace Neff told his clients the story of their new lives in Southern California.

Neff's homes were widely copied by other architects and were, many of them, passed off by realtors as authentic Neff houses thirty or forty years later when they reappeared on the market. Designers of tract homes were especially wont to borrow from Neff, and he himself was not above designing for tract developers such as Frank Meline—so that the Neff imprint on domestic design, like the Myron Hunt imprint on public and commercial structures, emerged as a visual norm throughout the Southland.

When clients wanted Italian, Wallace Neff gave them Italian: the poised Tuscan perfection of the Wilbur Collins House in Pasadena (1928), for example; or the splendiferous theatricality of the Bel-Air hilltop villa Neff designed for film mogul Sol Wurtzel in 1931, modeled on the Villa Giulia designed by Giacomo da Vignola for Pope Julius III. (A Hollywood producer and a Renaissance pope, after all, have much in common.) In the bulk of his 1920s designs, however, Neff adhered to Spanish Revival, which he chose for his own home in Altadena (1923). Throughout the 1920s, in Pasadena, San Marino, Beverly Hills, Bel-Air, Santa Barbara, and Los Angeles itself, Wallace Neff designed a series of notable Spanish Revival homes which today, sixty and more years later, preserve and epitomize—the Singer House (1925) and the Bourne House (1927) in San Marino being most conspicuous in this regard—the mood of poetic taste wedded to a regional identity itself fabricated through metaphors of Italy, Spain, Algiers, or Tripoli, which constituted such an important design for living in the Southern California of the 1920s.

When it came time in 1928 for Harry Culver, who had himself housed hundreds of thousands of Southern Californians, to house his own family on a four-acre lot across from the California Country Club in Cheviot Hills, Culver chose Wallace Neff to be his architect. Neff dissuaded Culver from his original preference for American Colonial in favor of a Spanish Revival creation with some Italian, even Secessionist (the chimney) overtones in the façade and Fenestration. Within, Neff provided the Culvers with a soaring two-story living room with a carved and gilded beamed ceiling and a gallery to one side fenced off in wrought iron, served by a circular stairway surmounted by a dome. Ensconced in a setting worthy of the Escorial or a Cecil B. De Mille movie set in Spain, Harry Culver might easily persuade himself that he had indeed come a long way from Omaha.

While most of Neff's prominent clients went along with the Spanish Revival preferences of the 1920s, Douglas Fairbanks and Mary Pickford chose an English Regency motif for the redesign and adaptation of Pickfair, the Buckingham Palace of Hollywood. Neff tried in vain to persuade the first couple of Hollywood to tear down their already existing Beverly Hills home and build anew. Had they done so, Neff would no doubt have led them to a Spanish Revival or Italian Revival solution; but Fairbanks and Pickford were well aware that they were acting out in their marriage and in Pickfair a drama of national significance. By keeping their design for living English, they kept Pickfair assimilable to most regions of the United States, not to mention Canada (Mary Pickford's birthplace), the United Kingdom, and the dominions of the British Empire. Built in Spanish Revival, Pickfair would have bespoken the highly localized identity of Southern California. Remodeled by Neff in English Regency, Pickfair flatteringly corroborated the general taste of the film-going public for whom the home had become a shrine of English-speaking taste. As if to authenticate the choice by Fairbanks and Pickford of English Regency, Lord and Lady Louis Mountbatten honeymooned at Pickfair in October 1922.

Already a connection between Hollywood and architecture had asserted itself. Initially, filmmakers used the existing architecture of Southern California, the Mediterranean mansions especially, as readily available locations. But then in 1915 D. W. Griffith, inspired by the Tower of Jewels at the Panama Pacific International Exposition in San Francisco, hired English stage designer Walter Hall to recreate Babylon at the corner of Sunset and Hollywood boulevards for the spectacle *Intolerance*. Surviving until 1919 before it was dismantled, the *Intolerance* set not only provided Hollywood and Los Angeles with one of its most important metaphors, the Babylonian ziggurat atop Los Angeles City Hall, it also introduced an element of theatricality into Los Angeles/Hollywood architecture itself. When the Goldwyn Studios constructed a cathedral

240 feet long and 90 feet wide dominated by an equally impressive crucifix for its 1920 production of *Earthbound,* Hollywood balanced off the
Babylon of *Intolerance* with an expressive Christian metaphor.

The more sets Hollywood created, including numerous back lots built
as towns, cities, or fantasies of every description (the domed minarets of
Baghdad, for instance, constructed for the 1924 Douglas Fairbanks epic), the
more expressively scenic became the popular architecture of the Southland.
If Hollywood, working through set designers and architects, could build
a perfect replica of a thatched Scottish cottage, a Montenegran villa, or
Dublin townhouse from the Grattan Ascendency for use as locations, then
it is not surprising that citizens of the nearby area, influenced by both the
movies and the sets themselves, should also be increasingly desirous of
stage-set values in their domestic architecture. In 1923, for instance, two
brothers, Adolph and Eugene Bernheimer, built a full-scale, historically
accurate sixteenth-century Japanese estate, Yama Shiro (the Castle on the
Hill), on the crest of the highest foothill in the Santa Monica Mountains
overlooking Hollywood. Fronted by a pagoda, a lake, and extensive gardens,
Yama Shiro featured a fully accurate interior as well, with any Western-
style furnishings specially adapted to the Asian decor. Once completed, the
Bernheimer estate became available as a location for films set in the Far
East, thus rechanneling the stage-set values of private architecture back
into the films that had inspired such eclecticism in the first place.

In the hands of a master such as Wallace Neff, who became by the late
1920s and early 1930s the architect of choice for Hollywood, such narrational eclecticism, properly employed, could and did result in much fine
architecture. The homes Neff designed for Hollywood clients such as Joan
Bennett, King Vidor, Darryl Zanuck, and Charles Chaplin and Paulette
Goddard during their brief marriage each bore the Neff imprint of skilled
siting, proportioning, and storytelling through historical motifs.

A case could be made for the urban folk art inspired by Hollywood
as well, the first hat-shaped Brown Derby Restaurant (1926) on Wilshire
Boulevard across from the Ambassador Hotel being the most famous
example. Why, after all, should not orange juice stands be shaped like
giant oranges or hot dog stands like dachshund pups? Highbrow critics
might cavil, but such folk creations became instantly accepted as signature

features of the Los Angeles/Hollywood cityscape, their good-humored fantasy universally enjoyed as sly fun by mid-America.

What disturbed eastern observers such as Edmund Wilson, however, was the fact that Hollywood eclecticism seemed by the early 1930s to have run amok across vast stretches of greater Los Angeles, resulting in a phantasmagoria of unassimilated, unintegrated, spurious styles which an eastern-seaboard highbrow such as Wilson might see as final evidence for his preconception that Southern California lacked depth and was merely eccentric. "The residential people of Los Angeles," Wilson observed caustically in 1932, "are cultivated enervated people, lovers of mixturesque beauty—and they like to express their emotivation in homes that symphonize their favorite historical films, their best-beloved movie actresses, their luckiest numerological combinations or their previous incarnations in old Greece, romantic Egypt, quaint Sussex or among the priestesses of love of old India. Here you will see a Pekinese pagoda made of fresh and crackly peanut brittle—there a snow-white marshmallow igloo—there a toothsome pink nougat in the Florentine manner, rich and delicious with embedded nuts. Yonder rears a clean pocket-size replica of heraldic Warwick Castle—yonder drowses a nausey old nance. A wee wonderful Swiss shilly-shally snuggles up beneath a bountiful bougainvillea which is by no means artificially colored. And there a hot little hacienda, a regular *enchilada con queso* with a roof made of rich red tomato sauce, barely lifts her long-lashed lavender shades on the soul of old Spanish days."

So much for historical eclecticism! Even the revered and contemporarily appreciated Spanish Revival falls before the Atlantic gale of Wilson's eastern-seaboard scorn. As in the case of most of his California observations, Wilson is at once correct and wrong-headed. No tradition, even that of New York, deserves to be defined exclusively by its excesses or abuses. Wilson's sense that Los Angeles had emerged as an idiosyncratic cityscape challenging to eastern eyes, however, drove directly to the point. In the last analysis, it would be by Los Angeles that the civilization of Southern California, architecturally and otherwise, would be defined and judged.

LYNNE OLSON

After graduating from the University of Arizona, Lynne Olson joined the staff of the Associated Press as a reporter and writer. From 1974 to 1976, she worked as the AP's Moscow correspondent, writing both human-interest items and pieces covering major news events. In 1976 she covered Jimmy Carter's successful campaign for the presidency and then moved to the *Baltimore Sun*, becoming a White House correspondent. She became a freelance writer in 1981 and has written for *Smithsonian, American Heritage*, the *Washington Post, Baltimore* magazine, and the *Los Angeles Times Magazine*, among other publications. Her 2007 book *Troublesome Young Men: The Rebels Who Brought Churchill to Power and Helped Save England* was a finalist for the *Los Angeles Times* Book Prize in history. Lynne Olson lives in Washington, D.C.

• •

"A Tycoon's Home Was His Petite Architect's Castle" underscores the intelligence, stamina, and strength of will of the pioneering architect Julia Morgan. Here Lynne Olson vividly recounts Morgan's indispensable role in the creation of William Randolph Hearst's *cuesta encantada* in San Simeon, on California's central coast.

A TYCOON'S HOME WAS HIS PETITE ARCHITECT'S CASTLE

THE TOURISTS FILE into the red-and-gilt movie theater, dazed and footsore. For 90 minutes they have tramped around the Hearst Castle at San Simeon on the central California coast, overwhelmed by its rococo splendors. Now it's time for a rest in what was once William Randolph Hearst's private theater—and a look back at San Simeon when it was a magnet for the famous, rich and powerful of the world. A film flickers on the screen: there's Marie Dressler clowning, Clark Cable mugging and Charlie Chaplin cavorting on the tennis court. And there's Hearst himself, standing with a wisp of a woman who reacts to the camera by covering her bespectacled face with a handful of papers. The narrator identifies her as Hearst's secretary.

Hardly. She is Julia Morgan, the architect and master builder of San Simeon, who, under Hearst's watchful eye, transformed a barren hill overlooking the Pacific into the site of what may be the 20th century's most lavish and ostentatious residence. For nearly 20 years this teetotaling spinster, her hair tucked in a schoolmarmish bun, supervised virtually every detail of erecting and furnishing Hearst's 144-room pleasure park. Since 1958, when San Simeon was opened to the public, more than 17 million visitors have seen the flamboyant fruit of Morgan's labors.

For Julia Morgan, however, San Simeon was a startling incongruity in a brilliant 46-year career. The first woman to graduate in architecture from the Ecole des Beaux-Arts in Paris, she was one of San Francisco's most renowned and prolific architects. Starting in 1902, she designed close to 800 buildings throughout California and the West, most of them as understated and beautifully proportioned as San Simeon is extravagant and jumbled. Several, like the Berkeley City Club and the YWCA of Oahu, have landmark status; two—San Simeon and the Asilomar Conference Center on the Monterey Peninsula—are California state monuments.

This drab, soft-spoken woman—who "looked like a nobody," according to a former employee—is regarded by some as America's most successful woman architect. "Who else has surpassed her?" asks architectural historian Sally Woodbridge. "No other woman has produced the volume of buildings that she did."

Why, then, have so few people ever heard of her? Because Morgan loathed personal publicity and did everything in her power to avoid celebrity. She shunned the press and refused to allow her name to be posted at construction sites. When she retired, she ordered all of her papers burned, believing that an architect should be like the usually anonymous medieval master builders who created Europe's vast monasteries, cathedrals and castles. In Morgan's view, a building should speak for itself.

SHE BELONGS WITH CASSATT AND WHARTON

When *Life* ran a story on San Simeon in 1957, it never mentioned Morgan's name. An irate art historian complained in a letter to the editor: "In American architecture she deserves at least as high a place as does Mary Cassatt in American painting, or Edith Wharton in American letters."

But Morgan is finally losing her aura of mystery, thanks to the dogged efforts of architectural historians like Sara Holmes Boutelle.[…] On one point, at least, there is no mystery: Julia Morgan's success stemmed from talent and an obsession with her profession that virtually precluded any private life. Often working 14 hours a day, six days a week, she kept tight control of all aspects of her commissions—interviewing clients, sketching preliminary drawings, monitoring preparation of final working drawings and supervising construction.

Born on January 26, 1872, Julia enjoyed a comfortable childhood, thanks to her maternal grandfather, a millionaire cotton speculator. A small, frail child, iron-willed Julia rebelled against Victorian ideas of proper girlish behavior, preferring to cavort on her brothers' gymnastic equipment and swing from the rafters in the family stable.

IN CIVIL ENGINEERING, A MINORITY OF ONE

By 1890, she knew that she wanted to have a career. Escorted to and from classes by her elder brother, she entered the University of California at Berkeley—one of only about two dozen women students. She chose architecture as her field of study. Because there was no school of architecture there, Julia enrolled in the civil engineering course—its only female student—where she learned about the mechanics of building but little about design. Providentially, she met Bernard Maybeck during her senior year. One of the most creative architects San Francisco has produced, he was then a 32-year-old instructor in the university's drawing department. An eccentric who sported a waist-length beard and trousers that reached almost to his armpits, he was already working on the style of domestic architecture for which he became famous: houses of native redwood which would "climb the hill" on a "goat lot" and blend into the landscape.

Maybeck was so impressed by Julia that he became her mentor, inviting her to informal classes on architectural design that he conducted at his home. After receiving her engineering degree in 1894, she went to work for Maybeck, who encouraged her to further her training at his alma mater, the prestigious Ecole des Beaux-Arts in Paris. There was one hitch. The Ecole discouraged women from enrolling and had never admitted a foreign female. Arriving in Paris in 1896, Julia was told that the faculty *"ne voudrant pas encourager les jeunes filles"*—did not wish to encourage young ladies. She wrote that she intended to stay "just to show '*les jeunes filles'* are not discouraged." Supporting herself by working as a draftsman for a French architect, she passed the rigorous entrance examinations and was finally admitted to the school.

Despite harassment from fellow students who poured water on her head and pushed her off the ends of benches, she excelled. Writing to her cousin, she noted that one teacher "always seems astonished if I do anything showing the least intelligence, '*Ah, mais, c'est intelligent*,' as though that was the last thing expected." In 1902, Julia Morgan was awarded a *Certificat d'étude* in architecture, the first given to a woman.

At the age of 30, she returned to San Francisco to work for John Galen Howard, a brilliant New York architect who had been imported to direct an ambitious building program for the University of California. She helped design the elegantly classical Hearst Memorial Mining Building, donated by Phoebe Hearst in memory of her late husband, George, a roughhewn miner who had struck it rich. The Hearsts' son, William Randolph, was a budding newspaper magnate; he financed an 8,000-seat Greek theater on the campus, which Morgan designed to resemble the theater at Epidaurus.

Mrs. Hearst, a philanthropist devoted to women's causes, was impressed by the independent Julia Morgan. The two had first met in Paris, where she had offered to finance Julia's education at the Ecole—an offer that was declined. In San Francisco, Mrs. Hearst took Julia under her wing and later commissioned her to remodel a family hunting lodge. Meanwhile, John Galen Howard was boasting to his colleagues about his achievement in capturing Julia, "the best and most talented designer, whom I have to pay almost nothing, as it is a woman." She left Howard in 1904 to open her own office in San Francisco.

Julia Morgan shunned the label "woman architect," but from the beginning was architect of choice for prominent women such as Phoebe Hearst and for the women's organizations to which they belonged. Her first major commission came from Mills College, a women's college in Oakland, which asked her to design a campanile. She created a gem of a bell tower in Mission Revival style. She later designed Mills' library, gymnasium and social hall.

The campanile, constructed of reinforced concrete, withstood San Francisco's devastating earthquake in 1906—a fact that may have helped her win the task of rebuilding the Fairmont Hotel, which the earthquake had reduced to a shell. Jane Armstrong, a local reporter, decided to check out the amazing news that a woman had been put in charge of the Fairmont renovation. Standing with Julia in the hotel's beautifully restored ivory, gold, gray and scarlet dining room, the newswoman assumed that the architect had done the interior decoration and gushed, "How you must have reveled in this chance to squeeze dry the loveliest tubes in the whole world of color." Smiling, Julia replied: "I don't think you understand just what my work here has been. The decorative part was all done by a New York firm....My work has all been structural."

It was the first—and last—interview that Julia Morgan is known to have given.

Her work on the Fairmont established her reputation, and from then on she had all of the commissions that she could handle. In the first dozen years of her practice, she and her staff, which numbered 16 architects at the height of her career, designed more than 300 homes, schools, churches, women's clubs and other small institutional buildings, most in the San Francisco Bay area.

Known as an architect who sublimated her own artistic ego to accommodate the needs and desires of her clients (she never rejected them because they had little money to spend), Morgan was neither interested in innovation for its own sake nor in developing a style readily identifiable as her own. Instead, she designed buildings "from the inside out"—concentrating on interiors that were practical, convenient and elegantly simple. The exteriors were understated, sober and carefully balanced. In the case of her residential commissions, which made up the bulk of her practice, "the object was first of all to build a home," said the late Walter Steilberg, her longtime structural engineer and a respected architect himself.

Eclectic in her choice of styles, willing to borrow from Gothic, Byzantine, Romanesque or any other period requested by a client, she usually added her own modifications. Often using the classicism of her Beaux-Arts training, she helped formulate a new form of architecture associated with Northern California's increasingly casual lifestyle: wood for both interiors and exteriors, a look of informality and a blending of the building with the landscape. Her houses generally had a light and airy outdoorsy feeling, with an abundance of windows, courtyards and open porches. The pleasure of occupying a Romanesque Morgan house for 30 years is described by former owner Constance Braver as "like living inside a work of art—the proportions are so classically comfortable."

Morgan was interested in structure—and in the use of structural materials as part of the design. In the Berkeley City Club, the soaring vaulted ceilings on the first floor are of unadorned concrete. The ornate club-hotel, Gothic and Romanesque in style, features cloister-style arcades that surround two interior courts. She paid extraordinary attention to detail and had a passion for quality. When the Oakland YWCA was under construction, she personally inspected each of the thousands of tiny tiles which were to cover the building's exterior columns, discarding those with even the tiniest flaws. She demanded perfection from contractors and laborers alike, expecting top-quality materials and workmanship. Some contractors who hadn't worked with her before took one look at the demure lady, barely more than five feet tall, and dismissed her complaints about what they'd done and how they'd done it. They did that only once: she could rip out faulty work with her bare hands. Said an employee: "Big men used to quail in her presence."

Always immaculately dressed in a dark tailored suit, white blouse and ample hat, Morgan would climb 100-foot ladders and clamber out on scaffolding 13 stories above the ground to inspect construction. Occasionally she'd be so busy inspecting that she wouldn't watch where she was going and would fall to the floor below. One day a strong wind blew her three or four stories down off a scaffolding into a river. But the bruises and scars never deterred her from climbing up again. When flying was not yet commonplace, she hired a stunt pilot to take her up "to see what it was like," and later chartered a Lockheed Vega to fly her to her farflung construction sites.

She liked young people, and her office became known to fledgling architects as a wonderful, if difficult, training ground. Walter Steilberg recalled that after he graduated from architectural school, a prominent San Francisco architect told him to go see Julia Morgan for a job. "I hadn't even heard of Miss Morgan," Steilberg said. "I looked a little startled and he said, 'Don't fool yourself, young man. She's one of the best architects in this city.'"

"She was a perfectionist, and each job was a maximum effort," said Dorothy Wormser Coblentz, one of several women who worked as draftsmen for Morgan. "Nothing was left incomplete…nothing was left to chance.…The pressure was terrible." She would present a draftsman with an eight-inch sketch of a proposed building, just "a little scratch of something, and then you'd have to work from that.…You'd come to a place where you couldn't go further, but you couldn't try any other line of reasoning until she came back and gave you permission."

Morgan thought of her staff as her children and herself as the stern but loving matriarch. Satisfied with only a few hours of sleep a night and sometimes only a candy bar for dinner, she felt that her employees should be as consumed with work as she was and seemed unable to understand why they might want a private life. Never interested in money, she divided the profits among the staff, keeping only enough to pay for her limited personal expenses and office overhead. "Her total earnings were seldom over 10,000 a year, and I don't think any year she made as much as $15,000," said her late nephew, Morgan North.

Julia's true affection for children probably helped during her 30-year collaboration with William Randolph Hearst—a man whose willful behavior often tested her patience. When Hearst began work on San Simeon, he was the notorious lord of a publishing empire encompassing six magazines and 13 newspapers. The hallmarks of his newspapers were scandal, crime, sensation, exaggeration and downright fabrication. He was anathema to many (the *North American Review* called him "a blazing disgrace to the craft"), but increasingly rich and powerful. Hearst had gone into journalism at 22, after expulsion from Harvard for presenting chamber pots—engraved with their names—to his instructors. After making his first newspaper, the failing San Francisco *Examiner*, a success, he performed the same feat with the New York *Journal*.

MORGAN AT BEAUX-ARTS, HEARST AT WAR

As a tactic in his fierce circulation war with Joseph Pulitzer's New York *World*, Hearst in the 1890s called for war with Spain over its occupation of Cuba. In a famous exchange of telegrams, artist Frederic Remington, whom Hearst had sent to Cuba, wired: "Everything is quiet. There is no trouble here. There will be no war. I wish to return." Hearst wired back: "Please remain. You furnish the pictures and I'll furnish the war." Goaded by the *Journal's* inflammatory coverage of the sinking of the U.S. battleship *Maine* in Havana harbor, Congress declared war against Spain in 1898—the year that Julia Morgan entered the Beaux-Arts.

Exulting in his journalistic influence, Hearst decided that he wanted political power as well, but except for two terms as Congressman from New York, he was doomed to disappointment. Foiled in his 1904 bid for the Democratic Presidential nomination (the year Morgan opened her office), he turned to his other passions—architecture, art collecting and Marion Davies. Hearst met Davies, a 1917 Ziegfeld Follies showgirl, promptly fell in love with her and decided to make her a movie star. His wife refused to divorce him, but he lived with Marion Davies, the true mistress of San Simeon, until his death in 1951.

In 1919 Hearst, by then a publishing tycoon, told Julia Morgan that he wanted her to build a few bungalows on his 275,000-acre ranch at San Simeon, where he and his family camped every summer. He had come across a style he rather liked, a "Jappo-Swisso bungalow." They both laughed at the absurd name, little dreaming of the mammoth undertaking and monumental headaches that lay ahead.

Hearst insisted that he wanted simple, rustic structures with plaster walls and wooden ceilings. Morgan drew up set after set of plans; Hearst constantly altered them as he moved toward the florid, unrestrained style that would be San Simeon's hallmark. What emerged were drawings for a twin-tower castle which dominated the crest of the hill, and three guesthouses which cascaded down the hillside, all surrounded by terraced gardens and groves of trees. The cost of construction, from 1919 to 1942, totaled $4.7 million.

An obsessive international art collector over the years, Hearst had amassed an amazing array of paintings, tapestries, carpets, beds, tables, secretaries, church statuary, mantels, columns, carved doors, choir stalls, window grilles, sarcophagi, wellheads—even stairways and ceilings. "Every time Willie feels badly, he goes out and buys something," his mother once observed. Morgan soon realized that Hearst wanted San Simeon to be not only a personal retreat, but a museum for his hoard of treasures, which by then had overrun several warehouses. Hers was the task of integrating these disparate elements into a unified whole.

Even with Hearst's original idea of simple bungalows, construction would have been arduous. The serpentine road climbing 1,600 feet from the foot of a chaparral-covered hill to San Simeon, a road that makes tourists uneasy even today, was only a dirt path in 1919 and was frequently flooded by rainstorms. At first, building materials were carried up the hill by horse and wagon, later by early-model Mack trucks that groaned their way to the summit at one mile an hour. Docks at the nearby Pacific shore were rebuilt for steamers that brought supplies from San Francisco: a camp was constructed at the base of the hill for workers. From the beginning, Julia Morgan was in charge of every aspect of construction.

San Simeon's guesthouses, each a mansion in its own right, were built first. They were relatively simple: red tile roofs and white walls, with intricate grillwork and handpainted tiles. But Casa Grande, atop the summit, was a cathedral-like edifice made of reinforced concrete to withstand the strongest earthquakes, a wild mix of styles jammed with art treasures from many periods. Nor was the castle planned functionally; it grew to satisfy Hearst's changing fancies and "didn't give Miss Morgan and me a real chance to use her real talent as a planner," complained Steilberg. "She was like a man playing the piano backwards."

From the beginning, Julia was bombarded with detailed instructions, suggestions and admonitions from Hearst, who was eager to move in as soon as possible. Yet he repeatedly changed his mind about what he wanted, often after work based on the original designs had been completed. Once, according to Steilberg, Hearst was inspecting one of the guesthouses and decided, on a whim, to have a fireplace moved to another spot in the room. Six months later, he decided the move had been a mistake. He ordered the fireplace rebuilt in its original location. The workers, many of them top craftsmen in their fields, were infuriated, Steilberg said. "Some of them told me, 'I can't stand that, doing the best I can on something, and then having someone just come and tear it down because he hasn't given it thought.'"

Even as he made his changes, Hearst—astonishingly—complained to Julia about slow construction and high costs. She would sometimes lose patience and let him know, in her mild way, that building his dream house was far from an easy task. "The shortage of every kind of material and of workmen out here is incredible, from draughtsmen to window glass inclusive," she wrote him in April 1920. "I had to take one of the modelers up to San Simeon this week and convince him that it was a 'lovely place' and then have him telephone…that I was veracious, before the cast-cement crew would agree to go up." Workmen imported from San Francisco often took one look at the isolated construction site and left, occasionally without unpacking, because "they didn't like feeling so far away from things," she added. They also didn't like the lack of a paycheck. Hearst was notoriously slow in paying his bills and, said Morgan North, Aunt Julia "suffered the tortures of the damned" in staving off workmen and contractors who hadn't been paid.

Morgan maintained her thriving San Francisco practice while supervising construction at San Simeon. Several times a month, she traveled down on the night train and spent a day or two at the castle. During her visits, Hearst paid little attention to anyone or anything else. In a little wooden shack in Casa Grande's courtyard, which served as her office, the pair conferred for hours. And at dinner in the splendid 67-foot-long Refectory, Hearst would ignore the world-famous celebrities around him and speak only to Julia, sometimes sketching designs on his paper napkin.

AN EGREGIOUS ERROR ENDS IN ORCHIDS

In 1928, Morgan underwent an operation for a chronically infected ear, which ended with the complete removal of her inner ear and permanent impairment of her equilibrium. Even worse, the surgeon accidentally severed a facial nerve, giving Julia's face the paralyzed look of a stroke victim. She felt as sorry for the doctor as he felt sorry about his mistake, and every year sent his wife orchids to ease his guilt. Sometimes she delivered the flowers herself.

Morgan didn't let her physical problems slow her down. Besides her work for other clients, she designed several more structures for Hearst, including the *Examiner* building in Los Angeles and three Bavarian-style cottages at Wyntoon, Hearst's 67,000-acre estate in Northern California. (He and Marion Davies took refuge in Wyntoon's forest wilderness from

1942 through 1944 as an economy measure, but also to escape the possibility of being shelled at San Simeon by Japanese submarines off the Pacific coast.)

Julia still clambered over scaffolding, though often on her hands and knees because of her faulty balance. She jokingly spoke of the problems of walking down the street and trying to pass a drunk who was having balance troubles, too. But she *was* sensitive about her facial paralysis, refusing to go to dinner at San Simeon on the grounds that "an architect should never appear asymmetrical."

During World War II, Julia, then in her 70s, began to phase out her practice. She later replaced architecture with travel and roamed Europe. But her mind was starting to fail: she got lost on foreign jaunts and searches had to be organized (a major problem was that she wouldn't ask for help in finding her way). She died in 1957 at the age of 85, just six years after Hearst. She wanted no funeral and had told her nephew, "Please give me a quick tuck-in with my own." At her death she was penniless. Her legacy: the buildings she had designed.

CHARLES W. MOORE

Born in Michigan in 1925, Charles Willard Moore was an influential post-modern architect, professor, and author of many books and articles on architecture. He taught at the University of California, Berkeley; Yale University; and the University of Texas at Austin. He gained widespread acclaim in the 1960s for his design of Sea Ranch, a planned community on the coast of Northern California. Having designed dozens of noteworthy buildings across California and the United States over several decades, Moore received the Gold Medal of the American Institute of Architects in 1991. He died in 1993 in Austin, Texas.

• •

In his essay "You Have to Pay for the Public Life" (originally published in *Perspecta*, Yale's architecture journal, in 1965), Moore explores the public significance of monuments and urban spaces, from the Santa Barbara County Courthouse and the Stanford University campus to the Nut Tree restaurant and Disneyland.

"YOU HAVE TO PAY FOR THE PUBLIC LIFE"

THIS ISSUE OF *PERSPECTA* considers monumental architecture as part of the urban scene. I was asked to ferret out some on the West Coast, especially in California. *Perspecta*'s editors suspected, I presume, that I would discover that in California there is no contemporary monumental architecture, or that there is no urban scene (except in a sector of San Francisco), or more probably, that both monumental architecture and the urban scene are missing. Their suspicions were well founded; any discussion from California in 1964 about monumental urban architecture (as it is coming to exist, for instance, in New Haven) is bound to be less about what we have than about what we have instead.

Any discussion of monumental architecture in its urban setting should proceed from a definition of (or, if you prefer, an airing of prejudice about) what constitutes "monumental," and what "urban" means to us. The two adjectives are closely related: both of them involve the individual's giving up something, space or money or prominence or concern, to the public realm.

Monumentality, I take it, has to do with monuments. And a monument is an object whose function is to mark a place, either at that place's boundary or at its heart. There are, of course, private monuments, over such places as the graves of the obscure, but to merit our attention here, and to be of any interest to most of the people who view it, a monument must mark a place of more than private importance or interest. The act of marking is then a public act, and the act of recognition an expectable public act among the members of the society that possesses the place. Monumentality, considered this way, is not a product of compositional techniques (such as symmetry about several axes), of flamboyance of form, or even of conspicuous consumption of space, time, or money. It is, rather, a function of the society's taking possession of or agreeing upon extraordinarily important places on the earth's surface, and of the society's celebrating their preeminence.

A version of this agreement and this celebration was developed by José Ortega y Gasset, in *The Revolt of the Masses*, into a definition of urbanity itself. "The *urbs* or *polis*," he says, "starts by being an empty space, the *forum*, the *agora*, and all the rest is just a means of fixing that empty space, of limiting its outlines....The square, thanks to the walls which enclose it, is a portion of the countryside which turns its back on the rest, eliminates the rest, and sets up in opposition to it."

Ortega y Gasset's product is the city, the urban unit based upon the Mediterranean open square, a politically as well as physically comprehensible unit that people used to be willing to die for. The process of achieving an urban focus is the same as that of achieving monumentality: it starts with the selection, by some inhabitants, of a place which is to be of particular importance, and continues when they invest that place with attributes of importance, such as edges or some kind of marker. This process, the establishing of cities and the marking of important places, constitutes most of the physical part of establishing civilization. Charles Eames has made the point that the crux of this civilizing process is the giving up by individuals of something in order that the public realm may be enhanced. In the city, say, urban and monumental places, indeed urbanity and monumentality themselves, can occur when something is given over by people to the public.

Planners have a way of starting every speech by articulating their (private) discovery that the public body's chief concern is *people*. The speech then says unrelatedly that it's too bad the sprawl of metropolis is so formless. It might well be that if the shibboleth about people were turned inside out, if planning efforts went toward enlarging people's concerns—and sacrifices—for the *public* realm, then the urban scene would more closely approach the planners' vision, and the pleasures of the people would be better served.

The most evident thing about Los Angeles, especially, and the other new cities of the West is that, in the terms of any of the traditions we have inherited, hardly anybody gives anything to the public realm. Instead, it is not at all clear what the public realm consists of, or even, for the time being, who needs it. What is clear is that civic amenities of the sort architects think of as "monumental," which were highly regarded earlier in the century, are of much less concern today. A frivolous but pointed example is the small city of Atascadero, which lies in a particularly handsome coastal valley between Los Angeles and San Francisco. It was first developed in the 1920s as a real estate venture with heavy cultural overtones and extensive architectural amplification. Extraordinarily ambitious "monumental" architecture popped up all over the town site. Buildings of a vague Italian Romanesque persuasion with a classic revival touch, symmetrical about several axes, faced onto wide malls punctuated or terminated by Canovaesque sculptural groups. The effect was undeniably grand, if a bit surreal, exploiting wide grassy vistas among the dense California oaks. But there wasn't much of a town until the 1940s. Then, on the major mall, an elaborately sunken panel of irrigated green, there cropped up a peninsula of fill surmounted by a gas station. Later there came another, and more recently an elevated freeway has continued the destruction of the grand design. All this has happened during the very period in which Philadelphians, with staggering energy and expense, have been achieving in their Center City long malls north from Independence Hall and west from a point just off their City Hall, grand vistas at every scale, an architectural expression overwhelmingly serene, all urban desiderata which the Atascaderans did not especially want or need and have been blithely liquidating. Doesn't this liquidation constitute some sort of crime against the public? Before we start proceedings, we should consider what the public realm is, or rather, what it might be in California now and during the decades ahead, so that the "monumentality" and the "urbanity" that we seek may be appropriate as functions of our own society and not of some other one.

In California cities, as in new cities all over the country (and in California just about all cities are new cities), the pattern of buildings on the land is as standard as it is explosive. Everywhere near population centers, new little houses surrounded by incipient lawns appear. They could be said to be at the edge of the city, except that there is no real edge, thanks to the speed of growth, the leapfrogging of rural areas, and the long commercial fingers that follow the highways out farther than the houses have yet reached. Meanwhile, in areas not much older, houses are pulled down as soon as zoning regulations allow, to be replaced with apartments whose only amenity is a location handily near a garage in the basement.

The new houses are separate and private, it has been pointed out: islands, alongside which are moored the automobiles that take the inhabitants off to other places. It might be more useful and more accurate to note that the houses and the automobiles are very much alike, and that each is very like the mobile homes which share both their characteristics. All are fairly new, and their future is short; all are quite standard, but have allowed their buyers the agonies of choice, demonstrating enough differences so that they can readily be identified during the period of ownership, and so that the sense of privacy is complete, in the car as well as in the house. This is privacy with at least psychic mobility. The houses are not tied down to any *place* much more than the trailer homes are, or the automobiles. They are adrift in the suburban sea, not so mobile as the cars, but just as unattached. They are less islands alongside which the cars are moored than little yachts, dwarfed by the great chrome-trimmed dinghys that seek their lee.

This is, after all, a floating world in which a floating population can island-hop with impunity; one need almost never go ashore. There are the drive-in banks, the drive-in movies, the drive-in shoe repair. There is even, in Marin County, Frank Lloyd Wright's drive-in Civic Center, a structure of major biographical and perhaps historical importance, about whose forms a great deal of surprisingly respectful comment has already appeared in the press. Here, for a county filling up with adjacent and increasingly indistinguishable suburban communities, quite without a major center, was going to be *the* center for civic activities, this public realm, one would have supposed, for which a number of public-spirited leaders in the community had fought long and hard. It might have been, to continue our figure, a sort of dock to which our floating populace might come, monumental in that it marked a special place which was some-where and which, for its importance, was civic if not urban. But instead of a dock for floating suburbanites, it is just another ship, much larger than most, to be sure, and presently beached (wedged, in fact) between two hills. It demands little of the people who float by, and gives them little back. It allows them to penetrate its interior from a point on its underside next to the delivery entrance, but further relations are discouraged, and lingering is most often the result of inability to find the exit.

A monster of equivalent rootlessness hoves into view from the free-way entrance to California's one established, anchored city, San Francisco. The immense new Federal Building just being completed by John Carl Warnecke and a host of associated architects stands aloof from the city's skyline, out of scale with it, unrelated to anything in the topography, no part even of the grandiose civic center nearby. Slick details, giant foun-tains, and all, it draws back from the street and just stands there. It is one of the West's largest filing cabinets, and it is unfair, of course, to expect from it any attributes of the public realm. Indeed, if San Francisco, one gathers, had not grudgingly stepped aside for it, some distant bureaucrats would spitefully have removed it to Oakland. So much for the Federal Heart of the city.

Even in the few years of Yankee California's existence, this kind of placelessness has not always been characteristic. During the twenties and into the thirties, with what was doubtless an enormous assist from the Hollywood vision in the days of its greatest splendor, an architectural image of California developed that was exotic but specific, derivative but exhilaratingly free. It had something to do with Helen Hunt Jackson's *Ramona*, with the benign climate, with the splendor of the sites and their floral luxuriance, with the general availability of wood and stucco, and with the assurance supplied by Hollywood that appearances *did* matter, along with the assumption (for which Hollywood was not necessary but to which it gave a boost) that we, the inheritors of a hundred traditions, had our pick. What came of this was an architecture that owed something to Spain, very little to the people who were introducing the International Style, and a great deal to the movie camera's moving eye. It seemed perfectly appropriate to the energetic citizens of Santa Barbara, for instance, that after their city had been devastated by an earthquake, it should rise again Spanish. The railroad roundhouse appeared to become a bullring, the movie house a castle. Everywhere in the town, the act of recalling another quite imaginary civilization created a new and powerful public realm.

Out of this public act came one of the most extraordinary buildings in the United States, probably the most richly complex and extensively rewarding stew of spatial and sculptural excitements west of Le Corbusier's Carpenter Center for the Visual Arts: the Santa Barbara County Courthouse. It was completed in 1929. William Mooser was the architect, and the inspiration, say the guidebooks, was Spanish. But nothing in Spain was ever like this. Instead of setting itself off against the landscape, in Mediterranean fashion, this assemblage of huge white forms opens itself up to it. The landscape is a big and dramatic one in Santa Barbara, where the coastal plain is narrow, the ocean close at hand, and the mountains behind unusually high and startlingly near. The Courthouse takes it all in: it piles around one end of a large open park, whose major forms are sunk into the ground, thus allowing the giant arch, the main feature among the dozens of features visible from the street side, to lead not into the building but through it and immediately out the other side, so that the building minimizes its enclosure function and asserts itself as backdrop—a stage set, if you will—with the power to transform the giant landscape. It is almost too easy to make a comparison with Le Corbusier's new Harvard building, similarly pierced (in Cambridge, in 1963, by a make-believe freeway ramp) and similarly composed of an immensely rich but strongly ordered concatenation of sculptural forms. At Harvard they are twisted enough and powerful enough to dislocate all the polite Georgian buildings around, to wrench them loose and set them whirling. Fewer structures are set whirling by the Courthouse, but a full complement of phantoms is raised up out of the lush landscape.

The Santa Barbara County Courthouse did so much about sweeping the whole landscape up and in that one might expect the really large-scale projects of the sixties to catch even more of the grandeur of the place. Whole new college campuses, for instance, which are springing magically out of fields across the state, surely present unparalleled chances to order a public realm, to invest a place of public importance with the physical attributes of that importance. Yet, by any standards, the clearest and strongest campus to be found in the state is still the old campus at Stanford, designed in Boston by Shepley, Rutan and Coolidge and built in the years just after 1887. The buildings in the old campus are H. H. Richardson warmed over (and cooled off again in the long passage from the architects' Boston kitchens); the gaudy mosaic facade of the chapel, the centerpiece of the composition, is an affront to the soft yellow stone surfaces around. But the play of the fabled local sunshine with the long arcades, the endlessly surprising development of interior spaces from big to small to big again, the excitement of a sensible framework that is strong and supple enough to include the most disparate of academic activities—all combine to make this a complete and memorable place. Even though the surrounding countryside is not swept into the picture, as at Santa Barbara, at least there is an orchestration of spaces varied and complete enough to evoke a complex public use. It is a place, however, that dates from the previous century, and this is a survey of our own times, times that have multiplied opportunities for spatial and functional orchestrations like the ones at Stanford and Santa Barbara. What, then, do we have?

Foothill College in Los Altos, by Ernest J. Kump and Masten and Hurd, comes first to mind, because it has won every prize in sight, and because it is a beguiling place. It sits strong on a pleasant rolling site, on which prodigies of bulldozing have created earthworks worthy of a Vauban, though a bit dulled by a foreground of parking lot. Its nicely detailed buildings share the charm of the best Bay Region domestic architecture, topped by memorable shingle roofs, which have added the glories of old Newport and older Japan to the idiom of the Bay, without ever losing control. Yet I am bound to report that their sensitive and disciplined complex is simply not in the same league as the older campus or the Courthouse. There is no heightening of importance, no beginnings, even, of the establishment of a *place* singled out for special public importance and illuminated by that recognition—a place, for instance, important enough for an academic procession to occur. The old Stanford campus may not culminate in anything of special beauty or worth, but it works at culminating. Foothill, rather, with great charm, dissipates itself and loses its powers. Sasaki and Walker's landscaping senses well this urge to dissipate, and devotes itself to filling with impenetrable bosques the places where the spaces might have been. Equalitarian it is: every tree and every building is as important as the next.

And so the public realm is made scarcely distinguishable from the private; the college's fortress base of earth does not anchor it, and it floats, as free as the houses in the suburban seas around.

The same firm's newer campus, for Cabrillo College near Santa Cruz, is far less beguiling and floats even more free. The buildings, carefully and sophisticatedly detailed, stick close to the idiom established when California was young and places were Places, but the idiom does not stretch to cover the requirements, and the act of multiplying varying sites of hipped-roof buildings surrounded by porches only serves to confirm the rigidity of a whole campus made of a single verandaed form. A window is a simple thing, and not new. In the cool climate of coastal northern California, the sunshine it can admit is pleasant if there is not a wide veranda in front to reduce north, east, south, and west to shady equality. The citizens of old Monterey built porches like these in the cool fog, lived behind them, and died like flies from tuberculosis; presumably medical science and the mechanical engineer will save us this time.

Meanwhile, the attempt to stuff the functions of a whole college into this rigid domestic idiom puts Cabrillo in strong contrast with the old Stanford campus, where the spaces evoke a wide variety of uses; here everything is not only equalitarian but equal. Impeccable details and all, it makes nothing special, it adds nothing to the public realm.

During the years of California's growth, as its cities have appeared, the extravagances of the settlers upon it have suggested to many that straight opulence might create centers of the public realm. Three city halls, especially, clamor for our attention. The San Francisco City Hall probably heads the list for sheer expensive grandeur. The expensiveness was, one gathers, as much a political as a physical phenomenon, but the grandeur is a manifestation of the highly developed Beaux-Arts compositional skills of architects Bakewell and Brown. These great skills, though, have been curiously ineffectual in commending themselves to public concern. It is a curious experience, for instance, to stand in the towering space under the aggressively magnificent dome and to notice that hardly anyone looks up. And the development of the extensive and very formal civic center outside has had remarkably little effect on the growth of the downtown area, which has remained resolutely separate from all this architectural assertion. Surely a part of the failure to achieve an important public place rests with the entirely abstract nature of the Beaux-Arts' earlier International Style. It takes a major master, like Sir Edwin Lutyens at New Delhi, to lift this idiom out of the abstract to give some point to its being somewhere. San Francisco City Hall demonstrates skill but no such mastery, so the city is not specifically enriched by this building's being here; it could be anywhere.

Or almost anywhere. It could not easily be in Gilroy. A small garlic-farming community of the Salinas region, Gilroy relied on a similar, if more relaxed, show of opulence in the building of its own City Hall in 1905. An elaborateness of vaguely Flemish antecedent served the town's desires; a truly remarkable array of whirls and volutes was concentrated here to signal the center of the public realm. But, alas, this concentration has not kept its hold on the public mind much more effectively than San Francisco's City Hall has, and now this fancy pile is leading a precarious life as temporary headquarters for the town's Chamber of Commerce and police station.

The citizens of Los Angeles adopted a slightly different route to achieve importance for their City Hall. In their wide horizontal sprawl of city, they went *up* as far as seemed practical, and organized their statutes so no other buildings could go higher. But economic pressure has mounted, and now commercial structures bulk larger on the skyline than the City Hall. The Angelenos' vertical gesture should get some credit, in any case, for being a gesture, an attempt to make a center for a city which otherwise had none. As a formal gesture, it has even had some little hold on the public mind, although its popular image now involves a familiar tower rising in the smoggy background, while a freeway interchange fills the sharp foreground. Investing it with life, and relating the life behind its windows to the life of the city, may never have been possible; such investment, of course, has never happened.

It is interesting, if not useful, to consider where one would go in Los Angeles to have an effective revolution of the Latin American sort: presumably, that place would be the heart of the city. If one took over some public square, some urban open space in Los Angeles, who would know? A march on City Hall would be equally inconclusive. The heart of the city would have to be sought elsewhere. The only hope would seem to be to take over the freeways, or to emplane for New York to organize sedition on Madison Avenue; word would quickly enough get back.

Thus the opulence and the effort involved in the San Francisco, Gilroy, and Los Angeles city halls seem to come to very little in the public mind, lacking as these buildings all do any activity that elicits public participation or is somewhat related to public participation. Whatever the nature of the welfare state, these public buildings seem to offer far less to the passerby than such typical—and remarkable—California institutions as the Nut Tree, a roadside restaurant on the highway from Sacramento to San Francisco, which offers in the middle of a bucolic area such comforts as a miniature railroad, an airport, an extensive toy shop, highly sophisticated gifts and notions, a small bar serving imported beers and cheeses, a heartily elegant—and expensive—restaurant, exhibitions of paintings and crafts, and even an aviary—all of them surrounded and presented with graphic design of consummate sophistication and great flair. This is entirely a commercial venture, but judging from the crowds, it offers the traveler a gift of great importance. It is an offering of urbanity, of sophistication and chic, a kind of foretaste, for those bound west, of the urban joys of San Francisco.

In the days before television, moving picture theaters afforded one of the clearest and easiest ways for people to participate in the National Dream. In California, especially southern California, where movies came from and where the climate allowed forecourts for theaters to be largely out of doors, some of the most image-filled places for the public to congregate, some of the most important parts of what at least seemed to be the public realm, were these theaters. The Fox in Santa Barbara invites our inspection on many of the same grounds as the Santa Barbara County Courthouse. The idiom is a movieland Spanish (again, like nothing in Spain), the architectural opportunity a double one: First, to make of the immense auditorium, set a block back from the theater's entrance on the main street, one of the city's noblest bastions, with high white walls sprouting turrets and balconies and follies. Only the grandest of the princes of the other hemisphere could have afforded walls this size to stick their balconies onto. Second, and more importantly for the city, to make partly roofed and partly open the block-long passageway from the box office to the ticket taker, thus providing the opportunity to extend the sidewalks of the city, still outdoors, past gardens and along a tiled esplanade, where soft lights play at night, and where by day the sun filters down among the leaves. Santa Barbara's sidewalks are ordinary enough, but in the mind's eye they merge with the passage to the Fox Theater and other commercial arcades and patios off State Street to form a public realm filled with architectural nuance and, even more importantly, filled with the public.

Another such public monument, which should not soon be forgotten, although it has been left isolated by Los Angeles's swiftly changing patterns, is Grauman's Chinese Theater, on Hollywood Boulevard, which seems more astonishingly grand today than it did in the days when millions in their neighborhood theaters watched movie stars immortalizing bits of its wet concrete with their hands and feet.

More recent years have their monuments as well. Indeed, by almost any conceivable method of evaluation that does not exclude the public, Disneyland must be regarded as the most important single piece of construction in the West in the past several decades. The assumption inevitably made by people who have not yet been there—that it is some sort of physical extension of Mickey Mouse—is wildly inaccurate. Instead, singlehanded, it is engaged in replacing many of those elements of the public realm which have vanished in the featureless private floating world of southern California, whose only edge is the ocean and whose center is otherwise undiscoverable (unless by our revolution test it turns out to be on Manhattan Island). Curiously, for a public place, Disneyland is not free. You buy tickets at the gate. But then, Versailles cost someone a great deal of money, too. Now, as then, you have to pay for the public life.

Disneyland, it appears, is enormously important and successful just because it recreates all the chances to respond to a public environment, which Los Angeles particularly no longer has. It allows play-acting, both to be watched and to be participated in, in a public sphere. In as unlikely a place as could be conceived, just off the Santa Ana Freeway, a little over an hour from the Los Angeles City Hall, in an unchartable sea of suburbia, Disney has created a place, indeed a whole public world, full of sequential occurrences, of big and little drama, full of hierarchies of importance and excitement, with opportunities to respond at the speed of rocketing bobsleds (or rocketing rockets, for all that) or of horse-drawn streetcars. An American Main Street of about 1910 is the principal theme, against which play fairy-tale fantasies, frontier adventure situations, jungles, and the world of tomorrow. And all this diversity, with unerring sensitivity, is keyed to the kind of participation without embarrassment which apparently at this point in our history we crave. (This is not the point, nor am I the appropriate critic, to analyze our society's notions of entertainment, but certainly a civilization whose clearest recent image of feminine desirability involves scantily dressed and extravagantly formed young ladies— occasionally with fur ears—who disport themselves with wild abandon in gaudily make-believe bordellos, while they perforce maintain the deportment of vestal virgins—certainly a civilization which seeks this sort of image is in need of pretty special entertainment.) No raw edges spoil the picture at Disneyland; everything is as immaculate as in the musical comedy villages that Hollywood has provided for our viewing pleasure for the last three generations. Nice-looking, handsomely costumed young people sweep away the gum wrappers almost before they fall to the spotless pavement. Everything works, the way it doesn't seem to any more in the world outside. As I write this, Berkeley, which was the proud recipient not long ago of a set of fountains in the middle of its main street, where interurbans once had run and cars since had parked, has announced that the fountains are soon being turned off for good, since the chief public use developed for them so far has been to put detergent in them, and the city cannot afford constantly to clean the pipes. Life is not like that in Disneyland; it is much more real: fountains play, waterfalls splash, tiny bulbs light the trees at night, and everything is clean.

The skill demonstrated here in recalling with thrilling accuracy all sorts of other times and places is of course one which has been developing in Hollywood through this century. Disney's experts are breathtakingly precise when they recall the gingerbread of a turn-of-the-century Main Street or a side-wheeler Mississippi River steamboat, even while they remove the grime and mess, and reduce the scale to the tricky zone between delicacy and make-believe. Curiously, the Mickey Mouse–Snow White sort of thing, which is most memorably Disney's and which figures heavily in an area called Fantasyland, is not nearly so successful as the rest, since it perforce drops all the way over into the world of make-believe. Other occurrences stretch credulity, but somehow avoid snapping it. The single most exciting experience in the place, surely, is that which involves taking a cable car (as above a ski slope) in Fantasyland, soaring above its make-believe castles, then ducking through a large papier-maché mountain called the Matterhorn, which turns out to be hollow and full of bobsleds darting about in astonishingly vertical directions. Thence one swings out above Tomorrowland. Now nobody thinks that that mountain is the Matterhorn or even a mountain, or that those bobsleds are loose upon its slopes—slopes being on the outsides of mountains. Yet the experience of being in that space is a real one, and an immensely exciting one, like looking at a Piranesi prison or escalating in the London Underground.

Of course Disneyland, in spite of the skill and variety of its enchantments, does not offer the full range of public experience. The political experience, for instance, is not manifested here, and the place would not pass our revolution test. Yet there is a variety of forms and activities great enough to ensure an excellent chance that the individual visitor will find something to identify with. A strong contrast is the poverty or absurdity of single images offered up by architects, presumably as part of an elaborate (and expensive) in-group professional joke. The brown-derby-shaped Brown Derbies of an earlier generation, which at least were recognizable by the general public, have given way to such phenomena as the new Coachella Valley Savings and Loan in Palm Springs which rises out of vacant lots to repeat Niemeyer's Palace of the Dawn in Brasília. Across the street from this, a similar institution pays similar in-group tribute to Ronchamp. The most conspicuous entry in this category of searches after monumentality, though, is architect Edward Durrell Stone's revisitation of Mussolini's Third Rome in Beverly Hills. This one has plants growing out of each aerial arch. Apparently there was a plethora of these arches, for they crop up, again along Wilshire Boulevard, as far away as Westwood Village, without, however, contributing much continuity to that thoroughfare.

Methods of seeking "character" for buildings in northern California are mostly much less theatrical, and adhere most strictly to a single pattern, an outgrowth of the redwood Bay Region Style in the direction of the standard universal American motel, employing stucco walls, aluminum windows, wooden shakes, and casual, if not cavalier, attitudes toward form. A case in point is a recent competition conducted by Los Gatos, a small and pleasant residential city near San Jose, for its city hall and civic center, to be located on a block near the center of the town, which backs onto a wooded hill and boasts some magnificent trees. Most of the entries were less concerned with responding to the site than with attempting to create a local character from long blocks roofed with widely overhung gables, and roofs covered with thick wood shakes, usually verandaed, and smothered in shrubbery—where there were no parking lots. It really isn't fair to describe this newer shagginess by invoking the Bay Region Style, an appellation devised to describe wooden houses of chaste simplicity, clarity, and economy of means. It is better, perhaps, to cast the blame across the seas and christen the idiom, as an Arizonan of my acquaintance has, "Califuji." The winner of the Los Gatos competition, I hasten to point out, was not at all of this persuasion. The scheme, by Stickney and Hall, is a completely simple and smoothly functioning set of flat-roofed blocks placed around a central space built on the top of the council chamber. The group of buildings fronts on the main street—the buildings relating to each other and to parking—and opens up, thanks to the plaza above the council chamber, to the wooded hill behind.

New monumental buildings in northern California, which sometimes bear firm recollection of the residential Bay Region Style, have achieved varying degrees of architectural and critical success. John Carl Warnecke's post office and bookstore adjoining the old campus at Stanford University uses its materials, masonry walls, and Mediterranean red tile roofs as a point of departure to make, with two large, steep overhanging roofs, a form almost strong enough to take its place beside the old campus. A finely detailed colonnade roofed with hyperbolic paraboloids (presumably the approved late twentieth-century successor to the arcuated colonnade) tucks rather redundantly under the great tile overhang, and fails to measure up to the rest. The care taken in framing its concrete members is, however, heartening assurance that the arts of construction have not yet died out.

At the University of California Student Union, in Berkeley, Vernon De Mars has sought to induce an active public response by devising (in a manner that closely parallels Disney's) astonishing juxtapositions of fragments which, individually, are often exquisitely designed but are left to fend for themselves in a hubbub meant to recall, within a planned environment, the chaos of the city. The forms, like Disney's, sometimes unabashedly recall another time or place: a steel trellis surmounting the major block of the building is said to owe allegiance to Bernard Maybeck's wooden ones of an earlier generation, which generally bore vines; the spaces around the building are by way of appreciation of the Piazza San Marco; and the carefully developed street furnishings recall Scandinavia. But the scope offered for this collection of occurrences is by no means Disney's, so that the chance to recreate the moods of the city is severely restricted, and the Student Union has just one mood: it is cheerful, unremittingly cheerful. Mostly this is fine, but on the occasions when a sober tone is wanted, something is missing: from the Student Union there is no aerial tramway direct to Tomorrowland, no Disneyland chance to create still another world.

Whatever is missing, however, this collector's approach to enlivening the public realm demonstrates certain advantages over the singlemindedness of, say, the San Francisco City Hall or some of the sober classroom blocks that stand about on the Berkeley campus. The simplicity and anonymity of these high blocks, mostly tile-roofed, set on knolls in groves of oaks and giant eucalypti, are in the spirit of the Bay Area, are praiseworthy, and have often been praised. But success eludes most of them, probably because they are set out to recall the area's last two lively idioms, but seldom with enough conviction to rise above the perfunctory. The two local idioms they seek to recall were lively ones, and look lively still.

The first, a high-spirited explosion of classical or other borrowed forms, which break apart to leave voids in astonishing places, so as to create lofty spaces and dark shadows, has left a major monument on the campus, the Hearst Mining Building of 1907. John Galen Howard was its architect, but in it the magnificent mad hand of Bernard Maybeck, the local cultural hero, is evident. The second local idiom, in whose development William W. Wurster has been the central figure, usually comes out best at small scale, since the carefully understated, spare, and almost anonymous efficiency of a well-understood carpenters' constructional system is clearly in evidence here. "No matter how much it costs," Mrs. Wurster points out about her husband's work—and the best of the rest of the vernacular—"it will never show." The new language of buildings on the Berkeley campus of the University of California, where they succeed, succeed because they share either in the exuberance of the first local idiom or in the naturalness of the second. When they fail, they fail from dispiritedly attempting continuity with the first local idiom (their great tile roofs lifted up and out of sight) or from seeking to cash in on the apparent casualness of the second local idiom, without noting that that is a casualness born of an intimate understanding of a constructional system and a way of life.

Not only the university but all of California and the West now face an architectural crisis different in many ways from the problems of the rest of the country. The Boston architects of the nineteenth-century railroad tycoon Leland Stanford had their own clear notions, social and architectural, of the nature of hierarchy, and they manifested them with great success in the old Stanford campus. But twentieth-century California has been equalitarian. As its population grows phenomenally, the people who comprise it, rich and poor, come from all sorts of places and owe no allegiance to any establishment of the sort that exercises at least some control of money and taste in areas less burgeoning. While California was largely rural, this equalitarianism lent special delights to living here. In southern California, from a combination of white-walled story-book Spanish and white-walled International Style, there developed, through

Gill and Schindler and Neutra and *Arts and Architecture* magazine, and thanks to the climate and the landscape, a way of building large numbers of private houses of a charm and comfort never before possible anywhere on such a scale. This development was surpassed only in northern California, where, if the climate was a bit moodier, the views of bays and forests were better, and there were architects, first of the generation of Bernard Maybeck, then of the generation of William Wurster, Gardner Dailey, and Hervey Parke Clark, who were willing and eminently able to make the most of the opportunities, to develop a domestic architecture not only esteemed by architects but almost universally accepted and enjoyed by the people for whom it was made. This is the domestic architecture we can call (though the architects who made it don't much like the appellation) the Bay Region Style.

When California was rural, a golden never-never land with plenty of room, with open fields for the public realm, with magnificent scenery for a sharable image, and with Hollywood's grandiose offerings for a publicly sharable experience, nothing could have been more natural than this emphasis on provision for domestic life, nothing more understandable than the gradual atrophying of concern for a public realm that people go to and use. The public weal was being extensively considered in projects built hundreds of miles from Los Angeles and San Francisco to provide those cities with water and electric power; but the kind of monumentality that occurs when the Establishment requires buildings more important than other buildings, in places of special importance, when skilled architects give physical form to this requirement, and when human use and the public imagination confirm this importance, never occurred. It never occurred because the Establishment didn't exist, and because there was no need for it. California during the first four decades of the twentieth century was being developed mostly at a domestic scale, and very well, too; it seemed quite proper that man's impact on the land should be of this cozy, equalitarian, and very pleasant sort.

The process, however, is continuing in 1964, and by now it brings worry. The domestic arrangements of the earlier decades are being reproduced endlessly, no longer in the places that laid some claim to public attention—places like Bel Air, Berkeley, and Sausalito for the view; San

Francisco and San Diego for the bay; Hollywood for a very special activity; and Santa Barbara for high mountains coming close to the sea—but in the no-places in between, such as Hayward, Daly City, Inglewood, Manchester, and other municipal fictions even less memorable. The character and the sense of special place that came to the first communities for free, from the oak trees around them and the yellow hills and the mountains and the sea, do not similarly serve the later comers or anyone: the oak trees go and the yellow hills vanish, the smaller mountains are flattened and even portions of the sea are filled in, all to be covered in a most equalitarian way with endless houses. Even the movie studios are being covered up.

It occurs to some, as the gray domestic waves of suburban sea fill in the valleys and the bays, and lap at and erode the hills, that something should be done, and that the something should be urban and monumental. The Bay Region Style, for all its domestic triumphs, offers no architectural framework for making a special celebration; the characteristic Wurster reticence, which has served so well in helping to create the continuous domestic fabric of the Bay cities, is too deeply ingrained to allow that. In southern California a latter-day straightforwardness born mostly of a habit of commercial expediency militates against architectural celebration of a particular place. But even more basic than the absence of a viable architectural idiom for making public centers is the absence of any Establishment ready to shoulder the responsibility for, to take a proprietary interest in, the public realm. So what, as we started out by asking, might we have instead, for an architectural framework and for an opportunity?

The hope exists that the first best chance for differentiation in these floating gray suburbs will come from our developing an interest in and techniques for a much more accurate definition than we seek presently of what the problems really are. If all places and problems are similar (as we might suspect from our endlessly repetitive new cities), then the whole act of marking something special is spurious and futile. If, on the other hand, there is a valid basis for differentiating one place from another and one building from another, and if the differentiation is not now made because techniques for defining a problem are too crude, then the use by architects of other tools already available, among them the tools of mathematics and of operations research, might offer help. We should be able to expect that our developing industrial plant, controlled by electronic devices of incredible sensitivity and complexity, should be able to give us a much wider, rather than a more restricted, range of products. Just so we might expect, as architects, that by using the techniques available to us, from computer and operations research methods to our own underused analytical capacities, in order to discover more accurately and completely than we do now the particularities, even the peculiarities, of the problems we are assigned, we might achieve a much wider, fuller, more differentiated and specific range of solutions than we do now. We should, then, at least have a method. Given the chance, we might rescue the dreary suburban sea from the sameness forced upon it as much by the blindness of our analytical tools and our tendency as architects to generalize on an insufficient base, as by the social and economic restrictions thrust upon us.

A few houses (since it is California, inevitably they are houses) by a few architects, mostly under the immediate influence of Joseph Esherick, are especially concerned with the specific analysis of and response to problems of site, its outlooks and climate, the client and his needs. This is not a revolution, really, away from the attitudes of the second Bay Region idiom; it embodies many of the same methods of direct response to the problem; but it seeks to clarify and extend these methods to cope with the aggravated situation.

Esherick's Cary House in Marin County, for instance, given a wooded view, does not rely on a wall of glass pointed generally in that direction, but has instead a wall with glass openings, each carefully placed to perform a specific function of admitting light, lighting a surface, or exposing a carefully selected portion of the view. The Rubin House in Albany, by George Homsey, though on a less dramatic site, reacts even more specifically to such local delights as the dappled light coming between eucalyptus leaves, and the usually hazy sun of the bay shore sliding through skylights and along white walls. The exterior of the Graham House, by Richard Peters and Peter Dodge, on a steep Berkeley hillside, also demonstrates forms that grow not from a generalized formal impulse but from a specific search for light, air, space, and outlooks. All this extends the simpler idiom of the earlier unformal Bay Region work, toward what promises to be a much fuller vocabulary, generated like its precursor not by restrictive formal systems but by specific response to specific problems. So far these are restricted domestic problems; but there is no reason visible yet why the elusive problems of the public realm should not respond, in an area with hardly a public realm, to sophisticated extensions of the same efforts.

For the opportunity, the actual commission to create a public realm, we must look to other sources than the Establishment of other times or other places, to people or institutions interested at once in public activity and in place. We depend, in part, on more Disneys, on men willing to submerge their own Mickey Mouse visions in a broader vision of greater public interest, and who are nonetheless willing and able to focus their attention on a particular problem and a particular place. Disneyland, however arbitrary its location, is unique, even as Los Angeles is, and much of its power over the imagination comes from the fact.

A chain of Disneylands would have a disquieting effect not unlike that of the new transcontinental chains of identical motels that weigh the tired traveler with the hopelessness of driving all day to arrive at a place just like the one he started from. One can hope, too, for the day when the gradual loss of differentiated place, the gradual emerging of the gray no-places and the inundation of the places of special significance, will cause the slumbering citizenry to awaken, to demand to spend its money to have a public life. But it seems unwise to wait for that.

Right now the largest single patron available to be pressed into the service of the public realm is the State Highway Department. Freeways until now have been one of the most serious generalizers of place in the state, ruthlessly and thoughtlessly severing some communities, congesting others, and obliterating still others, marring, gouging, and wiping out whole landscapes. Yet, for all that, they loom large in the public eye as one of the strongest, most exciting, and most characteristic elements of the new California. If one had to name the center of southern California, it would surely be the place not far from the Los Angeles City Hall where the area's major freeways wrap together in a graceful, strong, and much photographed three-level interchange (in the photographs, the tower of City Hall rises through the distant smog). Much of the public excitement about San Francisco's small dramatic skyline is a function of the capacity to see it, a capacity which is greatly enhanced by the bridges (themselves major California monuments), by the freeways that lead to them, and now by the freeway that comes up from the south and breaks through the hills in the nick of time for a magnificent view of San Francisco. Indeed, in San Francisco as in few places, the view which gives a sense of the whole city is one of the most valuable parts of the public realm, one of the parts that is most frequently attacked and must be most zealously defended. One of the public views' most effective defenders could be the freeway builders, though admittedly they have more often acted as saboteurs, as when they tried and partly succeeded, in San Francisco, in building a freeway wall between the city and the bay.

I am writing this in Guanajuato, a middle-sized town in the middle of Mexico, crammed into a narrow canyon, with just two narrow streets (one up and one down) in the bottom of the canyon, and with a maze of stepped pedestrian ways climbing up the canyon's slopes through the most remorselessly picturesque townscape this side of Greece. Under this runs a river, which used to inundate the city from time to time. Ten years ago a suburban portion of the river was still further depressed, and its former bed was lined with a handsome pink stone to serve as a canyon for cars, moving downhill above the river. Now, in a bold project happily called "the urbanization of the river," this development is being continued through the center of the town to let the river run with cars as well as water, sometimes behind buildings, sometimes under the ancient vaults over which the buildings of the town center spanned the river bed. None of the picturesque eighteenth-century delights is being threatened; a whole new twentieth-century layer of visual delights, at the scale of the automobile, is being added instead. The urbanity that results from this enlargement of the public realm is even more striking than the visual charm. The pedestrian spaces remain undefiled, even unattacked, while cars grind below, as in a miniature of a Hugh Ferriss City of the Future that loses, miraculously, none of the delights of the past.

Guanajuato should offer us some lessons. The cities of California are much bigger, broader, and grayer, but then their budgets are larger, too (especially the items for freeway construction). They urgently need attention, before the characteristics that distinguish them at all are obliterated. There is no need and no time to wait for a not-yet-existent Establishment to build us the traditional kind of monuments or for a disaster gripping enough to wake the public conscience to the vanishing Places of the public realm we got for free. Most effectively, we might, as architects, first seek to develop a vocabulary of forms responsive to the marvelously complex and varied functions of our society, instead of continuing to impose the vague generalizations with which we presently add to the grayness of the sub-urban sea. Then, we might start sorting out for our special attention those things for which the public has to pay, from which we might derive the public life. These things would not be the city halls and equestrian statues of another place and time, but had better be something far bigger and better, and of far more public use. They might, for instance, be freeways: freeways are not for individual people, as living rooms are and as confused planners would have you believe the whole city ought to be; they are for the public use, a part of the public realm; and if the fidgety structures beside them and the deserts for parking—or for nothing—under them don't yet make sense, it is surely because there has so far been too little provision for and contribution to and understanding of the public realm, not too much. The freeways could be the real monuments of the future, the places set aside for special celebration by people able to experience space and light and motion and relationships to other people and things at a speed that so far only this century has allowed. Here are structures big enough and strong enough, once they are regarded as a part of the city, to re-excite the public imagination about the city. This is no shame to be covered by suburban bushes or quarantined behind cyclone fences. It is the marker for a place set in motion, transforming itself to another place. The exciting prospects, not surprisingly, show up best at Disneyland. There, from the aerial tramway over the bobsled run on the inside of the plastic mountain, is a vision of a place marked out for the public life, of a kind of rocketing monumentality, more dynamic, bigger, and, who knows? even more useful to people and the public than any the world has seen yet.

ROBERT DUNCAN

Robert Duncan was born in 1919 in Oakland. A poet and essayist and the editor of the *Experimental Review,* he was a colleague of writers ranging from Henry Miller and Anaïs Nin to Kenneth Rexroth and Jack Spicer. In the 1950s, Duncan taught at Black Mountain College, in North Carolina, where he developed much of his poetic sensibility in collaboration with Charles Olson. Duncan was also a lifelong follower of theosophy and open about his homosexuality, both of which were continuing influences in his work. He gained wide recognition in the 1960s for his poetry collections, *The Opening of the Field, Roots and Branches,* and *Bending the Bow.* Duncan was the recipient of a Guggenheim Fellowship, three fellowships in writing from the National Endowment for the Arts, and the National Poetry Award. He died in San Francisco in 1988.

• •

In "Nel mezzo del cammin di nostra vita," Duncan celebrates Simon Rodia's Watts Towers in Los Angeles as a creation of grace out of materials that many would consider trash.

NEL MEZZO DEL CAMMIN DI NOSTRA VITA,

at 42, Simon Rodilla, tile-setter,
    "to do something big for America" began
the Watts towers
(this year, 1959, the officials of which city
  having initiated condemnation hearings
  against which masterpiece)

          three spires
    rising 104 feet, bejewelld with glass,
shells, fragments of tile, scavenged
    from the city dump, from sea-wrack,
taller than the Holy Roman Catholic church
    steeples, and, moreover,
inspired; built up from bits of beauty
    sorted out—thirty-three years of it—
the great mitred structure rising

out of squalid suburbs where the
mind is beaten back to the traffic, ground
    down to the drugstore, the mean regular houses
straggling out of downtown sections
    of imagination defeated. "They're
taller than the Church," he told us
    proudly.

                Art, dedicated to itself!

The cathedral at Palma too
    soard above church doctrine,
with art-nouveau windows and baldachine by Gaudí
    gatherd its children
under one roof of the imagination.

                The poem…

"The poet,"
Charles Olson writes,
"cannot afford to traffic in any other *sign* than his one"
"his self," he says, "the man
  or woman he is" Who? Rodia
    at 81 is through work.
Whatever man or woman he is,
    he is a tower, three towers,
a trinity upraised by himself.
    "Otherwise God does rush in."

Finisht.   "There are only his own
    composed forms, and each one
the issue of the time of the moment of its creation,
not any ultimate except what he in his heat
and that instant in its solidity yield";

like the Tower of Jewels at the San Francisco
    Panama-Pacific Exposition in 1915, this
"phantom kingdom to symbolize man's
    highest aims", glittering, but

an original, accretion of disregarded
    splendors
resurrected against the rules,
having in this its personal joke; its genius
    misfitting
the expected mediocre; an ecstasy
    of broken bottles
and colord dishes thrown up against whatever
    piety, city ordinance, plans,
risking height;

              a fairy citadel,
a fabulous construction out of
    Christianity where Morgan le Fay
carries the King to her enchanted Isle
    —all glass beads of many colors
and ricketty towers, concrete gardens,
    that imitate magnificence.

"Art," Burckhardt writes:
"the most arrogant traitor of all
  putting eyes and ears…in place of
    profounder worship"
"substituting figures for feelings."

    The rounds contain crowns.
    The increases climb by bridges.

    The whole
planned to occupy life and allow
    for death:

              a skeletal remain
as glory, a raised image, sceptre,
    spectral island, most arrogant,
"to do something big for America"

    Rodia.

JOHN FANTE

Born in 1909 in Denver, John Fante moved to Los Angeles in 1930. While working a series of menial jobs, he published his first short story, "Altar Boy," in H. L. Mencken's *American Mercury* in 1932. Later in the 1930s, Fante began a career as a screenwriter and a novelist. He explored the implications of his Italian American ethnicity and working-class background in a series of novels featuring the protagonist Arturo Bandini. Among these are *The Road to Los Angeles; Wait Until Spring, Bandini; Ask the Dust;* and *Dreams from Bunker Hill*. In the late 1970s and early 1980s, Fante gained renewed admiration for his work, especially with the republication in 1979 of *Ask the Dust* with a preface by Charles Bukowski.

• •

In this excerpt from *Ask the Dust*, Bandini recalls the trauma of an earthquake and frenetically considers the merits of different construction methods in earthquake-prone Los Angeles.

from *ASK THE DUST*

GOT BACK TO Los Angeles the next day. The city was the same, but I was afraid. The streets lurked with danger. The tall buildings forming black canyons were traps to kill you when the earth shook. The pavement might open. The street cars might topple. Something had happened to Arturo Bandini. He walked the streets of one-story buildings. He clung to the curbstone, away from the overhanging neon signs. It was inside me, deeply. I could not shake it. I saw men walking through deep, dark alleys. I marveled at their madness. I crossed Hill Street and breathed easier when I entered Pershing Square. No tall buildings in the Square. The earth could shake, but no debris could crush you.

I sat in the Square, smoked cigarets and felt sweat oozing from my palms. The Columbia Buffet was five blocks away. I knew I would not go down there. Somewhere within me was a change. I was a coward. I said it aloud to myself: you are a coward. I didn't care. It was better to be a live coward than a dead madman. These people walking in and out of huge concrete buildings—someone should warn them. It would come again; it had to come again, another earthquake to level the city and destroy it forever. It would happen any minute. It would kill a lot of people, but not me. Because I was going to keep out of these streets, and away from falling debris.

I walked up Bunker Hill to my hotel. I considered every building. The frame buildings could stand a quake. They merely shook and writhed, but they did not come down. But look out for the brick places. Here and there were evidences of the quake; a tumbled brick wall, a fallen chimney. Los Angeles was doomed. It was a city with a curse upon it. This particular earthquake had not destroyed it, but any day now another would raze it to the ground. They wouldn't get me, they'd never catch me inside a brick building. I was a coward, but that was my business. Sure I'm a coward, talking to myself, sure I'm a coward, but you be brave, you lunatic, go ahead and be brave and walk around under those big buildings. They'll kill you. Today, tomorrow, next week, next year, but they'll kill you and they won't kill me.

And now listen to the man who was in the earthquake. I sat on the porch of the Alta Loma Hotel and told them about it. I saw it happen. I saw the dead carried out. I saw the blood and the wounded. I was in a six-story building, fast asleep when it happened. I ran down the corridor to the elevator. It was jammed. A woman rushed out of one of the offices and was struck on the head by a steel girder. I fought my way back through the ruins and got to her. I slung her over my shoulders, it was six floors to the ground, but I made it. All night I was with the rescuers, knee deep in blood and misery. I pulled an old woman out whose hand stuck through the debris like a piece of statue. I flung myself through a smoking doorway to rescue a girl unconscious in her bathtub. I dressed the wounded, led battalions of rescuers into the ruins, hacked and fought my way to the dead and dying. Sure I was scared, but it had to be done. It was a crisis, calling for action and not words. I saw the earth open like a huge mouth, then close again over the paved street. An old man was trapped by the foot. I ran to him, told him to be brave while I hacked the pavement with a fireman's axe. But I was too late. The vise tightened, bit his leg off at the knee. I carried him away. His knee is still there, a bloody souvenir sticking out of the earth. I saw it happen, and it was awful. Maybe they believed me, maybe they didn't. It was all the same to me.

I went down to my room and looked for cracks in the wall. I inspected Hellfrick's room. He was stooped over his stove, frying a pan of hamburger. I saw it happen, Hellfrick. I was atop the highest point of the Roller Coaster when the quake hit. The Coaster jammed in its tracks. We had to climb down. A girl and myself. A hundred and fifty feet to the ground, with a girl on my back and the structure shaking like St. Vitus Dance. I made it though. I saw a little girl buried feet first in debris. I saw an old woman pinned under her car, dead and crushed, but holding her hand out to signal for a right hand turn. I saw three men dead at a poker table. Hellfrick whistled: is that so? Is that so? Too bad, too bad. And would I lend him fifty cents? I gave it to him and inspected his walls for cracks. I went down the halls, into the garage and laundry room. There were evidences of the shock, not serious, but indicative of the calamity that would inevitably destroy Los Angeles. I didn't sleep in my room that night. Not with the earth still trembling. Not me, Hellfrick. And Hellfrick looked out the window to where I lay on the hillside, wrapped in blankets. I was crazy, Hellfrick said. But Hellfrick remembered that I had been lending him money, so maybe I wasn't crazy. Maybe you're right, Hellfrick said. He turned out his light and I heard his thin body settle upon the bed.

HERB CAEN

Born in Sacramento in 1916, Herb Caen became a sports reporter for
the *Sacramento Union* while still a teenager. In 1936 he began writing for the
San Francisco Chronicle as a columnist, first covering radio, later writing about
the city's nightlife in "It's News to Me." Not counting an eight-year stint at the
San Francisco Examiner, Caen wrote continuously about San Francisco for the
Chronicle, six days each week, from 1938 to 1991. The author of eleven
books, notably *Baghdad-by-the-Bay* and *One Man's San Francisco,* Caen won
a special Pulitzer Prize in 1996 for his journalistic contributions to San Francisco. Herb Caen died in San Francisco in 1997.

• •

In "Edifice Wrecks" Caen laments the destruction of several historic San
Francisco buildings, including the Montgomery Block and the old Hall of
Justice building, and extols the still-extant Flood Building and Garden Court
restaurant at the Palace Hotel, inveighing against their possible demise.

"EDIFICE WRECKS"
from *One Man's San Francisco*

"I CAN'T THINK OF a building I've put up that's one tenth as beautiful as
the one I had to tear down to make room for it."

Speaking was one of San Francisco's most successful builders, a veri-
table Maharajah of Eyesore. He spoke mournfully, and you half expected
him to add, as in an old movie melodrama, "Stop me before I kill again!"
But kill again he will, and so will all his confreres in the "building" business.

I thought about his words as I stood on Nob Hill, gazing at the gaping
hole where the old Sproule mansion had stood. It wasn't a particularly
old house, and architecturally it was closer to zircon than diamond, but
still it had more charm than the ice-trays-in-the-sky that will rise there
someday. In denying pleas that the house be saved, a city official said,
"What's so special about it? Did Washington or Lincoln ever sleep here?"

Funny in a tough way, but not particularly cogent, since Washington
or Lincoln is not known to have slept anywhere in San Francisco, although

Lincoln, had he come West, *might* have slept at the Montgomery Block—and now that's long gone. The Monkey Block (that's what everybody called it, Junior) was built in 1853 by Henry Halleck, who went on to become a general in the Union Army.

Every time the Chinese celebrate "Double Ten" Day, to commemorate the revolution against the Manchu Dynasty by Sun Yat-sen on October 10, 1911, I think about the Monkey Block, for it was there, at one point, that Sun Yat-sen lived while plotting his coup. It used to be enjoyable for a San Franciscan to look at the Monkey Block and think about the venerable Oriental and the other venerables who lived and worked there: Frank Norris, Kathleen and Charles G. Norris, Maynard Dixon, Charles Caldwell Dobie, George Sterling…

The Monkey Block was torn down a few years ago for a parking lot, a flat piece of real estate that sings no songs but tells quite eloquently about our scale of values. Now the Transamerica pyramid occupies the site. Words fail.

I thought about the Maharajah of Eyesore's words again as I watched the wreckers go to work on the old Hall of Justice on Kearny. Here again we have a building that was not particularly old—slightly more than fifty years—but even in its death throes, it has a somber Florentine magnificence impossible to duplicate. To San Franciscans of my generation, it is/was a storybook building, alive with tales of violence, echoing with the arguments of lawyers dead and dying, redolent (especially on a wet-foggy night) of sirens and screams. Another sterile stack of ice trays has risen in its place, a Holiday Inn, and someday, perhaps, this building, too, will tell strange and moving stories of life in Baghdad-by-the-Bay. It doesn't seem like an especially good bet.

The most dangerous men in town may well be our Maharajahs of Eyesore, killing The City That Was—and what a city that was, think you not to the contrary. Day by day, the concrete evidence is being ground to rubble, even when the evidence was as undistinguished as the derelicts that disappeared so that Fifth Street could eventually cross Market. But if anybody cares to know where Painless Parker got his start, the address is now gone forever. Don't laugh: Painless Parker was a historic figure too, and his patients slept there, even if Washington or Lincoln didn't.

Soon, as somebody once said, the only thing old in San Francisco will be the young men's faces, and if you prefer Plastic Inevitable to a fluted column of stone, you're well ahead of the game. If you feel otherwise, miss no opportunity to walk through the Flood Building lobby with its massive pillars and great lanterns, its marble floors and polished brass mailbox; it was built to last forever, but it won't. When you look at the gilded and crystal magnificence of the Palace's Garden Court, look twice, for you will never see its like again—not in this city, not in this lifetime. You may even start worrying about the Ferry Tower: its days are numbered. Faster and faster the city changes, and the people in it; those who never heard of the Monkey Block or the Slot can't tell you where Goat Island is, either. Soon, all will be new, bright, shiny and soulless—and then the legends will be gone forever, ground to dust by the relentless jackhammers.

MALVINA REYNOLDS

Born in San Francisco in 1900, Malvina Reynolds earned a Ph.D. in English from the University of California, Berkeley, in 1939. Unable to find a teaching position during the Depression, she became a social worker and wrote for the *People's World*. During the late 1940s, Reynolds and her husband operated a tailor shop in Long Beach, where she met Pete Seeger, Earl Robinson, and other folksingers. At this time she began to write songs of her own. She later returned to Berkeley, writing and performing songs for both adults and children, often on behalf of social and political causes. By the 1960s, Reynolds's songs were being recorded by many well-known performers, including Joan Baez, Judy Collins, Harry Belafonte, Pete Seeger, and Marianne Faithful. Reynolds released six albums for adults and three for children. She died in 1978.

• •

In the song "Little Boxes," Reynolds skewers the conformity and architectural sameness that dominate many a contemporary neighborhood.

LITTLE BOXES

Little boxes on the hillside,
Little boxes made of ticky tacky,
Little boxes on the hillside,
Little boxes all the same.
There's a green one and a pink one
And a blue one and a yellow one,
And they're all made out of ticky tacky
And they all look just the same.

And the people in the houses
All went to the university,
Where they were put in boxes
And they came out all the same,
And there's doctors and lawyers,
And business executives,
And they're all made out of ticky tacky
And they all look just the same.

And they all play on the golf course
And drink their martinis dry,
And they all have pretty children
And the children go to school,
And the children go to summer camp
And then to the university,
Where they are put in boxes
And they come out all the same.

And the boys go into business
And marry and raise a family
In boxes made of ticky tacky
And they all look just the same.
There's a green one and a pink one
And a blue one and a yellow one,
And they're all made out of ticky tacky
And they all look just the same.

ALLEN G. SIPLE

Allen G. Siple was born in Otsego, Michigan, in 1900. After studies at the School of Architecture at the University of Southern California, Siple served for six years as editor of the bulletin of the Los Angeles–Long Beach chapter of the American Institute of Architects. He also wrote a column for the *Los Angeles Times* called "We Like This Plan Because," in which he commented on a variety of plans for houses. Siple designed an enclave of middle-class housing in Westdale, a suburb of Los Angeles, in the late 1940s. Among his other designs were the headquarters for the Beverly Hills Police Department, several homes within the Trousdale Estates in Beverly Hills, and sections of the Webb School in Claremont. He was a Fellow of the American Institute of Architects. Allen Siple died in 1972.

• •

In "Suburbia Revisited," Siple distinguishes clearly between the various factors at play in the construction and reconstruction of suburban houses. With witty and literate prose, he beautifully profiles change and adaptation in domestic architecture.

SUBURBIA REVISITED

FROM WHERE I SIT, in a somewhat dilapidated ivory tower in the City of Beverly Hills, there appear to be two equally popular ways of looking at "housing tracts," or *dormitory suburbia* for those who prefer the Latin: 1 Through the rose-colored spectacles of the merchant builder, the real estate agent, the lending institution and the eager young couples who sign up for "Non-Vets–No-Down"; 2 Through the smoked goggles usually worn by land philosophers and urban sophisticates, comforting to the jaundiced eye and giving the currently preferred dim view of the suburbs.

A third optical approach seems at the moment not in vogue—to look at Urban Sprawl as it now is *after the fact* and without "corrective lenses," to give it the hard look, to try to observe realistically its plus and minus values, to note its appeal by contrast with decaying urbs, the damage already wrought both to the city and the countryside, to see the problem in its entirety, the problem of exploding numbers, more roofs for more people, more houses on less land, and to try to learn what our past mistakes have been, taking full advantage of "twenty-twenty hindsight," a faculty with which we are all so generously endowed.

Thinking about these weighty matters the other noon on the fourth cup of coffee, I recalled a housing development that I had a bit to do with a few years ago, and I felt attracted, as they say in police reports, to revisit the scene of the crime.

Accordingly, toward evening I left my tower and drove to that suburb known as Westdale now deep in the ever-sprawling outskirts of the Pueblo of the Queen of the Angels. Fifteen years had passed since I last made this eight-mile journey and it seemed timely to investigate how things were doing in that early post-war subdivision, both with my little ziggurats and with the inhabitants now at mid-point on the thirty-year mortgage plan.

In the year FHA 12 and AD 1946, I had accepted an offer to join a tract building team as "design consultant"—a title sufficiently innocuous to relieve me of total responsibility but adequate to justify the monthly stipend of $1500 on a two-year run with all drafting to be performed in and paid for by the tract developers' office.

I may be subjected to disciplinary action but I have always considered the Boiling of the Pot a normal and necessary sideline of the architectural career. I was thus afforded a living while pursuing in off-hours my own elevated professional practice and an undisturbed contemplation of the irregular Greek verbs. I also enjoyed the camaraderie of the company's drafting room—the whistling virtuoso head-draftsman, Ray Abos, doing *La Tosca*—as the boys apparently enjoyed my early morning recitations of the first chapter of Genesis. Morale was high, in spite of the job at hand and in spite of the beguiling pink horizon of the "brave new world." Bear in mind, if you will and can, that in 1946 the word "modern" had not yet disturbed the calm puddle of FHA policy—in fact, "modern stuff" was then frowned upon and sniffed at, with official skepticism—at arm's length.

"DREAM" HOUSES

We were engaged upon a mildly entertaining enterprise—designing 782 houses—"each to be different with sales appeal," said the office memo from on high! We went ahead on three basic common-sense plans, rather pedestrian in view of later developments but locating the principal rooms generally on the "rear" or garden side. For variation, we had a bedroom wing that could jut or not jut, a sliding trombone garage that could be turned sideways to give the much-to-be-desired half-moon driveway. We had a breakfast alcove that could jut and become a "formal" dining room separated by a door from the kitchen. There were at least 782 different entrance variations easily inventable. Color schemes suggested infinity. So the show was on the road.

The sales wing clobbered for the "homey" touch. It and the advertising man, known to us as "the enemy," believed that dormer windows were much desired and low eaves gave a bedroom that early girlish nostalgia, a feeling of rain on the roof, and all that sort of thing! Shutters enhanced the hole-in-the-wall window. *Treillage* and winding stepping-stones enhanced the front entrance, recalling moonlit nights, high school romance, or something. Our living room fireplaces usually had mantels with a plug for an electric clock and ample width for the household gods and Christmas cards. Our "convertible den" could somehow accommodate a studio couch and a large leather chair for Daddy and the evening paper.

Our garages—not carports!—had *doors* and were intended for automobiles of modest size, not 300 HP spaceships with fins, and were planned for normal accumulation of junk, without which everyday life was then and still is improbable, even with latter-day storage walls.

As I drove along toward Westdale, I reviewed these plan considerations of times gone by and wondered how far-sighted they really were. And how about the New Look, now so successfully entrenched? I thought of "the enemy"—the sales wing, and for old time's sake, whistled a strain from La Tosca. I thought of the "population explosion" and what it might have done to the little houses…"and God said unto them, be fruitful, and multiply, and replenish the earth, and subdue it." Surely in fifteen years I could expect or hope for extensive remodellings.

NO CHANGE AT ALL?

My first impression on turning into the main street of Westdale was crushing! The little houses looked at first sight about the same as I remembered them! Trees had grown and shingled roofs had weathered; but the whole place seemed wrapt in self-sufficient slumber.

True, there were a few applied stone facings, brick plant-boxes, plastic fences, chinoiseries, and other gestures toward contemporary design in *treillage, brise-soleils,* louvers, perforated cement-block grilles, etc. But not more than a half-dozen out of 782 had gone all out for remodelling on the street-facing side. All of them, however, looked well-kept and freshly painted, the color schemes departing occasionally from the original, featured by touches of black trim intended perhaps as an evidence of advanced taste to point up the status symbol. In fact, the black *motif* has swept the whole subdivision—a kind of neighborhood *comme il faut!* If you still have green shutters, you probably still play Canasta.

All of the front yards, imposed by the legal setback restriction, showed signs of hard work and loving care. Many, indeed, were like submissions in a garden club show with groupings of birches, banana palms and bamboo, or an off-center dwarf pine on a mound of oriental grass complete with stone lantern. A few front yard fences had been timidly introduced—little white pickets or rustic rails overgrown with rioting roses, all held down to the restricted height of 3´-6˝ as required by the building ordinance.

The parkway trees were a positive value after fifteen years of growth since I remembered them with trunks the girth of my thumb. Some had died or for other reasons were no more, and I found the gaps pleasing, especially when other trees in the front yards had achieved enough size to carry the continuity of the leafy tops in and out of the monotonous parkway pattern.

In general, the whole street scene looked inhibited and self-conscious,— contrived to conform to legal restrictions and neighborhood respectability. Pride of ownership and possible "re-sale value" appeared as equally motivating factors.

But a real surprise was waiting back of those pretty and cosmetic façades!

Pushing a few door-bells with due misgivings and in the embarrassing role of a pollster, I found that great things had been happening. Partitions had been torn out, doors walled in, and walls pushed out into the rear patios to gain more elbow room within. One house had doubled its original 1400 square feet! Bedrooms and baths had been tacked on to the full limit of legal land coverage. Garages had been taken over as "family" or "hobby" rooms, carports then being added only to be remodelled again into something else with another carport added in tandem. So-called "service porches" had become "breakfast alcoves" or "offices," the laundry then moving on into the attached garage with a maid's room and bath displacing the second car.

When patios were gobbled up by the new "lanai" or added bedrooms to the full limit of the rear-yard ordinance restriction, new patios were built farther back, in many cases with swimming pools. Clothes driers had relieved the demand for service yards. *Sic transit gloria Monday*, with multi-colored undies whipping in the breeze!

But to offset this decorative loss, most householders had bestrewn their own kingdoms (back of the front yards!) with all the normal and healthy clutter accessory to well-adjusted taxpaying life. All the little juniors had left their wagons and battle-ships just where they had left them, as a perfect booby-trap for father sauntering forth through the newly installed sliding glass doors in the dead of night. Older juniors had taken over the new pebbled-cement patio for the dissection of a vintage Model-A. Still older "juniors" had left a striped bath-towel, a high-ball glass with lemon rind, and a floating funny-paper to decorate the pool. Most garage gable-ends held basket-ball hoops and high over every sentimental roof-line a TV antenna etched its "contemporary" pattern in the sky.

PEOPLE ARE PEOPLE

I found the whole expression most heartening! People were behaving like people, in spite of pretty and conforming façades, in spite of "zoning" restrictions. Urban Sprawl was beginning to consolidate, to tighten and occupy its sprawl!

I talked at some length with Doris Palmer, an early purchaser now at mid-way on the thirty-year payment plan. With a balance yet to go of $6500 against a current market value of $45,000, the financial status seems fairly secure. After remodelling her own house to bring it to that handsome value, she went on to do others in the tract as designer-decorator and has worked up an expanding clientele, having special knowledge of the Westdale houses, their problems and possibilities. "About 70% of the houses have had interior remodellings at least once!" she said. "They were pretty well built to start with, and can take it!"

There is the paper-cup, throw-away school of built-in obsolescence in housing philosophy. As my English secretary said: "How frightfully unsporting!" Give those who are to follow houses worth owning, paying for and keeping, and they will correct our "mistakes," each in his own way!

There is the wise-guy school who wryly remark: "Those shacks won't be there thirty years from now. The new forty-year mortgage is nothing but a rental plan—with the government holding the bag." Then the crystal ball, esthetic gentry who look forward with gleeful enthusiasm to massive clearances of the "future slums," and a chance to say: "We told you so!"

All of these slants on housing theory are based on the notion of more or less temporary structures, nothing to be taken too seriously. But our little tract houses, even for the land philosopher, are disgustingly durable, thanks to the Uniform Code and FHA standard requirements.

Even the California product of tar paper, chicken wire and stucco nailed to a framework of "genuine Douglas Fir" is, from an engineering and common-sense view-point, a very worthy and long-lived box, more than adequate for withstanding the nonexistent inclemencies of the heavens and for challenging the unpredictable but always possible earthquake. The disturbing fact is that the less seriously a structure is built the better chance it has to survive that fatal hour.

Five hundred years would probably be fairly severe on our little houses built of two-by-fours, considering the termite, not a novelty to Ashurbanipal, King of Assyria in the seventh century, BC. But we now have chemistry to fight the ant, and (barring general catastrophe) a life expectancy of two hundred years with luck should be quite probable.

New roofs and water-heaters would be as predictable as death and taxes. More coats of paint with periodic sand-blasting, new floors from time to time to replace the "life-long vinyl," new plumbing every fifty years, new gadgets every fifteen years—all this should be understood by any reasonable home owner.

But the little house will be standing there a century or two from now in spite of mutations and lean-tos, just as wooden houses still stand in

New England after two centuries of useful life. One in Old Lyme that I inspected, built in 1781, had a full course of oak timbers laid into the central stone chimney as a kind of "bond beam" to support the kitchen hearth. The termites had finally begun to chew with enough food on hand for another fifty years!

Well! There would seem to be enough time on hand in which to look at suburbia realistically and constructively, *as now built* for better or for worse. As architects, we can deplore the stupidity of land waste, the inflicted lot size and street pattern. We can deplore the continued spawning of Mother Goose cottages and the Squirrely Renaissance, and give prizes for designs which at least acknowledge the intelligence and dignity of man. We can plan houses with more thought toward remodelling and adapting to individual needs in a restless age. But as architects in the larger sense, we must hammer away on the basic issues of land use, both for projects now on the boards and with an eye for what must and will happen to suburbs already built.

Looking ahead a few years, maybe fifty, when deeded restrictions will have expired and "setback" ordinances are certain to have been overruled by a practical and vigorous population, multiplied by "x" according to our prophets, the street scene of Westdale may at last be altered. I find it no strain on clairvoyance to imagine the little houses built out to the front property line, beginning with high walls and screens for privacy, or to see whole streets dead-ended or turned into wooded greenways, the automobile by that time either under control or obsolete. Perhaps an ivory tower rumination—but munching on real grass fresh-cropped from the "grass roots" of Westdale.

KURT ANDERSEN

Kurt Andersen was born in 1954 in Omaha and has enjoyed a varied career as a journalist, architecture critic, editor, screenwriter, novelist, and film and television producer. He founded and edited *Spy* magazine with Graydon Carter, was a columnist for *Time*, *The New Yorker*, and *New York*, and has started several online publications. Andersen has contributed his writing to television specials and a number of musicals. At present, he serves as editor-at-large in charge of nonfiction for Random House as well as host of *Studio 360*, a Peabody Award–winning public radio program. He is Visionary in Residence at Art Center College of Design in Pasadena. Kurt Andersen lives in Brooklyn, New York.

• •

"Desert Cool," first published in *The New Yorker*, chronicles the 1990s return to popularity of Cold War modernist architecture, as exemplified in the buildings of Palm Springs.

DESERT COOL

THE FIRST TIME a no longer fashionable style came back into fashion was probably in the eighteenth century, when architects became obsessed with classical Greek and Roman forms. The cycle of aesthetic rejection, oblivion, and renaissance, which took a millennium to play out in that instance, had speeded up considerably by the middle of this century: Tiffany lamps and Victorian houses, for instance, were only sixty or seventy years old when, to a gay and proto-yuppie avant-garde, these fusty great-auntish grotesqueries suddenly came to seem charming and desirable. In our present hypertrophied consumer age, it takes even less time for the culture to move through a complete taste wave, from peak to valley to peak again—no more than thirty or forty years. The phenomenon has now become predictable enough to constitute a kind of postmodern socio-cultural law.

Take Palm Springs, California. From the beginning of the great freeway era until the time of the last New York World's Fair—or, put another

way, from Marilyn Monroe's motion-picture debut until her death—
Palm Springs oozed California smart-set swank. Palm Springs was to
the oversexed Hollywood of the fifties what East Hampton was to the
overmoneyed Manhattan of the eighties: the getaway place a couple of
hours east for all the swingingest people.

But after its first twenty years of chic, the place became decidedly,
deeply uncool, and it stayed that way for another twenty years. The new
golf-o-centric pseudo towns like Rancho Mirage and Palm Desert, which
grew up during the seventies and eighties east of the city, between Dinah
Shore Drive and P.G.A. Boulevard, reinforced the image of a character-
free, climate-controlled elephants' graveyard, the world according to
Gerald Ford. Harold Robbing and Zsa Zsa Gabor lived in Palm Springs;
Sonny Bono became mayor.

But then comes the third, rehabilitative phase, which is now under
way in Palm Springs. At first, the embrace is ironic, campy. In the nineteen-
seventies, for instance, pediments and columns began appearing in serious
new American architecture as tongue-in-cheek gestures, around the same
time that the southern end of Miami Beach began to seem fetchingly
zany. Soon tongues are removed from cheeks, and the aesthetically correct take goes from contempt to amusement and on to earnest adoration,
all within a decade.

The connoisseurship by baby boomers of mod, kitschy artifacts from
their youth (amoeboid tabletops, plastic chairs, lava lamps) acquired serious
momentum during the eighties. As this appreciation has extended outward
and downward into the young heterosexual masses, it has taken the form of
vicarious life-style nostalgia—nostalgia for the idealized young adulthood
of one's parents (giant cocktails, lounge music, cigars, Sinatra, poolside cha-
cha-cha). The 1996 film "Swingers" was a hit, and now Martin Scorsese is
planning a Dean Martin biopic. Given this ascendant retro vector, plus the
fact that the desert itself is a stylishly nineties kind of landscape—mini-
malist, unsentimental, extreme—the hipster rediscovery of Palm Springs
was probably inevitable. Even the infrastructure seems serendipitously
au courant: the four thousand sleek, giant white metal windmills west of
town, acres and desolate acres of them in the desert along the highway from

L.A., look like a collaboration between Philippe Starck, Richard Meier, and George Lucas.

Because Palm Springs itself did not prosper during the seventies and eighties, developers had no incentive to rip down the first-generation architecture. So the snazzy haute–Cold War houses survive—entire time-warped neighborhoods of them. And, unlike the rich neighborhoods of Los Angeles, where nineteen-thirties pseudo-Colonials are next to nineteen-eighties pseudo-Mediterraneans that are next to nineteen-fifties pseudo-Tudors and seventies suburboid mansions, Palm Springs posh sprang up in a single moment and shared a single architectural dream: desert modernism—low, glassy, horizontal, sleek. It remains perfect. Before the twenty-first century is finished, Palm Springs will seem as remarkable and precious as places like Georgetown or Brooklyn Heights do today, an American urban period piece preserved in situ.

There's a surprisingly high concentration of houses whose significance derives not from the fact that Elvis or Zsa Zsa once slept in them. The California modernist star John Lautner designed Bob Hope's house, and Richard Neutra designed a Palm Springs house in 1947 for the Edgar Kaufmanns—the Fallingwater Kaufmanns. Albert Frey, who emigrated from Zurich sixty-seven years ago and still lives in his own glass house up on a San Jacinto Mountain ledge, designed the city hall, a 1946 house for the industrial designer Raymond Loewy, and an early-sixties gas station that is currently the subject of a contentious preservationist battle. (The local establishment doesn't quite get it: Palm Springs' official city architecture guide lists twenty-six notable buildings, none built after the thirties and almost all of them cute Spanish stucco or Old West Vernacular.)

It's not just the buildings from the forties, fifties, and sixties that are remarkably well preserved and that seem to 1998 sensibilities unwittingly hip. Human vestiges of the Rat Pack resort milieu survive as well, which is definitely part of the ironic-cum-anthropological attraction of the place: imagine Williamsburg or Sturbridge Village if the actors in Colonial drag were real people from the eighteenth century. In Palm Springs, old guys and dolls of the Peter Lawford and Angie Dickinson generation, still well tanned and lubricious, drive their Cadillacs to supper at Melvyn's Restaurant and Lounge.

Do not rebuild it, and they will come. The people in black are now arriving and meeting with real-estate agents. The word "fabulous" is being uttered on Palm Canyon Drive. At John's Mid-Century Modern, a two-year-old resale store in a building designed by Frey, cosmopolite newcomers buy their plywood Eames chairs and George Nelson coffee tables (for a song, still). In 1992, an Ian Schrageresque hotelier refurbished the nineteen-twenties Korakia Pensione, which is now booked weeks in advance by movie people—cool movie people, like Laura Dern. During the last five years, hyperstylish men from New York and Los Angeles (the creative directors of GQ and Clinique, the director of the Isaac Mizrahi documentary *Unzipped*, and so on) have bought houses. Magazines are using Palm Springs for fashion shoots, which has the effect of making the space-age desert-swinger aesthetic seem more intensely voguish to more people, which will result in more fashion shoots and videos, and then the arrival of more emigrants from Manhattan and Los Angeles. There's still no Miamified Scene—no surplus tuna tartare, no V.I.P. rooms, no roving packs of supermodels. Give it a few years. "There's a feeling of Camelot," says Jim Moore, the GQ creative director, who bought his 1962 steel house in 1993 and has meticulously restored it. "I don't want it to change."

DAVID LITTLEJOHN

Born in San Francisco in 1937, David Littlejohn is a fourth-generation Californian. He taught writing at the University of California, Berkeley, for thirty-five years and served as the arts critic for KQED-TV in San Francisco for ten years. He has also been a Critic at Large for the PBS network. A contributor to the *Wall Street Journal* since 1990, Littlejohn has written for *The Times* (London) as well. He is the author of nearly six hundred literary and arts reviews and fourteen books, including *Architect: The Life and Work of Charles W. Moore.* An honorary member of the American Institute of Architects, David Littlejohn lives in Berkeley.

• •

In "The Sea Ranch," Littlejohn presents a memorable account of the innovative buildings designed by Charles Moore's architectural firm, MLTW, and their setting within the climate and landscape of coastal Northern California.

from **"THE SEA RANCH"**

THE MOST WRITTEN-ABOUT building erected in Northern California during the last 25 years is a perversely odd-looking, rustic-redwood, ten-unit condominium built smack against the unpacific Pacific Ocean's edge, on the Sonoma County coast. Called simply "Condominium I" (there were once plans for many more), it was designed in 1963 by a young firm of Berkeley architects to serve as a display piece for the developers of a new coastal tract called the Sea Ranch, 120 miles north of San Francisco. Completed in 1965, it has been described and illustrated in scores of magazines and books. It has been imitated far and wide by the designers of thousands of other buildings, often in locales where the unique design features of the building clashed against, rather than resonated with, the features of the landscape. Condominium I made celebrities of its four architects—Charles Moore (who was 38 in 1963), Donlyn Lyndon (then 27), William Turnbull Jr. (28) and Richard Whitaker (34). Their firm, which operated out of a disused little train station across from the Heinz factory in Berkeley, was called simply "MLTW."

The trip up to their most famous building, by whatever route one takes, involves at least a last 25-mile drive on the cliffside curves of Highway 1. In thick fog, when only the yellow center line of the road is visible, the narrow, uphill-downhill bends can be a nerve-straining ordeal. In clearer weather, the Pacific Ocean is almost always one's immediate companion, a vast spread of hammered gray or glittering blue that pulls one's eyes constantly from the road. Occasionally, the road itself is hooded with foliage. After the 1982 and 1983 "killer" storms, long stretches were buried in mud and chunks of the western roadway fell into the sea. North of Jenner and the mouth of the Russian River, a few farms, crossroads stores and resorts interrupt the landscape with buildings. Cows and sheep still graze in the long grasses of the meadows and rolling hills, which rise rapidly into forest to the east.

However much one expects it, the first glimpse of the now-famous silhouette comes as a surprise. The ten-unit MLTW condominium rises from its oceanfront cliff like a more shapely cliff itself, answering the land forms with the appearance of a cluster of deftly tumbled rocks half a mile across a cove of the sea. The shape, dominated by the sliced tower of Unit 10, the echoing angles of its eaveless prisms and one long downsloping roof, is at once commanding and discreet, ordinary and refined. There is much about it in common with neighboring barns. Its dark, weathered shapes seem to have grown naturally, like the outbuildings of a farm—when you need a shed, you add a shed. In the right light, the building looks as if it had grown there, like a tree, or had been built ages ago—until you realize how artfully, and with what conscious care, these lines, planes and volumes have been disposed.

Condominium I is the first building of the Sea Ranch seen by drivers from the south. (Larry and Anna Halprin's five-acre estate actually comes first, but it's invisible to passersby.) Along with the sign of a stylized ram's head, it announces one's entry to this compromised utopia. The private drive, winding down past the buildings of a small store and lodge, ends inside the palisaded shelter of a parking court, where the owners' cars are hidden from view. A further, ruggedly landscaped interior courtyard slopes steeply down to an opening onto the sea. Most of the individuated residences present their blank, Fort Laramie-like walls to this, their private spaces; their windows face the ocean.

Charles Moore, the M of MLTW, bought Unit 9 of the condominium as his own private place of escape; he has owned it for the past nineteen years. When he is in residence—usually four or five times a year—he loves to invite friends up to feast and party and (in winter) watch the whales swimming south. A blank redwood wall conceals his small entry court. When you open his front door, you discover astonishing space games that are repeated, with variations, in all ten units of the complex.

Twenty-four-foot-square boxes, framed in rough, massive ten-by-ten timbers—which occasionally cut diagonally through space—rise to whatever height the great oversloping roof allows. The high and low spaces this yields are then punched out for windows, projecting bays, window-seat alcoves and solaria, positioned to seize most felicitously the sun (when there is sun) and the rampaging sea. The vista of Pacific Ocean waves breaking over dark brown rock islands, directly below a corner window, can hold a viewer transfixed for hours.

Inside the high box of each unit are set two almost free-standing pieces of architectural furniture: a floating, unwalled bedroom loft raised on four wooden columns, which shelters a fireplace nook underneath; and a two-story "cabinet," into which Moore deftly fit a kitchen below and a bath and storage space above. A tight, steep stairway joins the two. (Higher still, up a ladder, is another sleeping loft.) Minute balconies and bridges link the upper levels of these two units. Depending on where they are set inside the box, these units (which are sometimes brightly painted, to assert their status as "furniture") carve out the interior space, direct the changing views and define one's movement and experiences inside.

Not everyone confronting the building for the first time feels pleased or at ease. I once took a class of Cal freshmen up to spend a weekend exploring this and other MLTW buildings at the Sea Ranch, then asked them to write up their responses. "As I roamed about the lower level and around the upper floors via narrow passageways and steep ladders," wrote one, "I felt the way a mouse must feel wandering through a maze. The Moore house is simply not livable."

"At times my eyes caught stage fright," wrote another. "The house vacillated between being playful and nightmarish, like a disorienting labyrinth, or a fun house at an amusement park. Once within the walls of weathered wood, under the heavy beams, I could no longer feel where I was in space. I felt a sense of entrapment in all this seeming spatial freedom."

But other students—like most visitors—grew to love it. "There were no doors (except to the bathroom) to separate the different living spaces," wrote a third. "At first I found this disturbing, even threatening. But when I started crawling into the cubbyholes and climbing up to the sleeping loft, I got the feeling that I was in a playhouse or a treehouse, and that this was another adventure. These spaces act as vehicles into a fantasy world: Moore's master bedroom, with its canvas drops and ropes, might be a ship sailing on the sea, or a mountain high above the world. Everything above the ground floor feels like islands in space instead of compartments."

"Have you ever seen the Swiss Family Robinson Tree House at Disneyland?" asked a fourth. "It has exactly the same kind of appeal—like living in a jungle gym. Fantasy, playfulness, freedom: Moore's houses are more free than anything I've ever lived in. They're uniquely liberated and liberating."

Unit 10 caught fire a few years ago. Dry rot and moles have invaded from below. One window in Unit 4 cracked in a storm. There have been some leaks. ("Don't all prize-winning buildings leak?" one owner asked me.) But most of the residents I talked to (four of the ten are original owners) professed an almost sacred dedication to the place and seemed to be ardent devotees of the original "Sea Ranch ideal."

Condominium I at the Sea Ranch was, in fact, designed as part of one of the most idealistic schemes in American regional planning. A territory of 5,200 acres along the north coast of California, fronted by ten miles of one of the most soul-stirring shorelines in the world, came on the market in 1962, when the Ohlson brothers decided that they had had enough of unprofitable sheep farming. Prompted by a pair of ecological visionaries, planner Alfred Boeke and landscape architect Lawrence Halprin, Oceanic Properties, the new owners and developers of the ranch, agreed to try to treat it with particular sensitivity. To design some model vacation homes on the site and demonstrate its possibilities, they hired Joseph Esherick, the most respected living practitioner of the Bay Region style, and the fledgling Berkeley firm of MLTW.

Since that time, the four MLTW architects have designed dozens of prize-winning buildings, separately and together. But in 1963, they had nothing but time. They were over-rich in ideas but poor in commissions; they wanted very much to make a mark. So they snapped at Halprin's offer to design a model set of clustered residences on one of California's most awe-inspiring bluffs.

Moore, Lyndon, Turnbull and (to a lesser degree) Whitaker—with Moore as the first among equals, and a lot of help from their friends— devoted several unbroken months of their combined and harmonious skills to this dream project, on a dream site, for a dream client. The result, both Lyndon and Turnbull now believe, was "the best thing any of us has ever done." They played with sugar cubes on cardboard contour maps, drew up lists of ideal objectives and juggled around all of the radical, anti- modernist ideas they and Moore had been toying with ever since their years together at Princeton in the '50s.

The result was at once astonishing and fitting. It achieved all of Boeke's and Halprin's utopian goals—and Oceanic Properties' worldly goals as well: The ten units in the cluster sold quickly. In the process, it created a new ethic and a new aesthetic for American architecture. Suddenly it was all right to do serious buildings that were cheap looking, shack-like, defiant of symmetry and right angles, because they worked, and could—if you looked at them long enough—come to seem beautiful.

Condominium I at the Sea Ranch won a Progressive Architecture citation in 1965 and an American Institute of Architects national honor award in 1967. But the popular and professional success of this build- ing was not simply the result of a spontaneous outpouring of respect and admiration. Partly, in order to earn a return on their $4.7 million, but partly also because it soon became clear that they had fortuitously underwritten something historic, Oceanic Properties hired a wizard San Francisco press agent to spread the word. Marian Conrad was able to persuade representatives of the national and international press to fly out to San Francisco, where she met them at the airport, drove them up the coast and sent them home searching out new metaphors for this instant classic structure: "perhaps," wrote Fortune, "the roughest hewn and most romantic building since Fort Laramie."

It was featured in design magazines in the United States, Japan, France, Britain, Spain, Germany and Italy; in *Time, Newsweek, Sports Illustrated, Look, Elle, Paris-Match,* the *Los Angeles Times* and the *New York Times.* Values in American architecture have never been quite the same since. It has been cited, and usually illustrated, in virtually every book written on the architecture of the last twenty years. A lavish Japanese photo album published in 1970 was devoted entirely to a sampling of MLTW work at the Sea Ranch: the condominium, two recreation centers and two houses designed by Bill Turnbull. Half the houses at the Sea Ranch now look like MLTW creations, and about 30 of them, including seventeen almost identical "barn"-houses, actually are.

Innumerable copies of Condominium I sprouted up all over the United States within a few years after it was built, praised and publicized—whether or not heavy timbers, rough wood siding, shed roofs, oddly punched windows and jutting bays were suited to the site and the owner's needs. You can see them in innumerable second home tracts and condominium clusters in California and elsewhere. "I'd drive up a rise on some dead straight Kansas highway," says Bill Turnbull, "and sure enough, there it would be: another Sea Ranch condo, out in the middle of the prairie where none of that stuff made sense." […]

To see Moore inhabit his habitat is to fully appreciate the genius of its design. I was fortunate enough to observe him in the midst of one traveling house party at Sea Ranch leading up to a New Year's Eve:

The editor of the *New York Times* Home Section is supervising a radical, but apparently ineffectual job of housecleaning and closet-clearing in Unit 9, trying to empty the place of all sorts of baskets, toys, puzzles and junk. The things she believes would fit better in Moore's current Los Angeles perch are carried by a visiting student out to the architect's beat-up Pinto. A former student, now an architect in New York, arrives with a load of metal light fixtures he has deigned, for everyone to admire. The owner of Moore's prize Los Angeles home (a colleague of his at UCLA) has commandeered one of the window seats overlooking the rocks and foam. Four of Moore's fantasy landscapes are being handed around—pennants on steep turrets, fairytale bridges to gem-like islands. One, already watercolored, will go to his sister and brother-in-law as this season's holiday gift, to join a series of dream landscapes on their living room wall.

The ostensible host stands in the middle of it all, looking a bit lost. He makes futile gestures of help with the housecleaning, joins in half a dozen conversations, makes and receives numerous calls over a phone on the kitchen counter with a very long cord.

More guests arrive, bearing food, wine, gifts. An old Princeton classmate arrives, with his new poet wife (who is later to sprain her ankle falling down the precipitous stairs to the upper reaches of the house). A professor of architecture from New Mexico and his wife arrive. A distinguished architect—slim, Southern, dressed in determinedly electric colors—arrives with his banker friend. The Berkeley architect nips into the tiny kitchen to make his special mayonnaise, which is a signal for the whole company to sit on the floor and begin cracking and then eating a mountain of fresh crab. They wolf down salad and French bread spread with Stilton butter, empty bottles of white wine, pile up crab shells on a cloth. The talk is personal and professional, wide-ranging and allusive, with little darts tossed now and then at the current East Coast architectural elite.

After this midday feast, most of the men in the crowd head up the road to MLTW's spectacular Northern Recreation Center, to play tennis, swim in the turquoise waters and sweat in the sauna. Inside the sauna, the talk is of a pink villa in Cuernavaca, lecture audiences in Barcelona, plans for an exhibition in Frankfurt. Arrangements are made to stow surplus guests at Dmitri Vedensky's house up the hill. Back at Unit 9 of the condo, the non-athletes have prepared a second feast: baked ham and potatoes au gratin for seventeen. Champagne is opened to celebrate the editor's birthday.

After dinner—the guests cook, the guests clean up—Moore is presented with a gift of an old geography class chart of land forms, rolled on a stick. It is instantly hung near the door. Later, sitting on chairs or the floor near the window seat corner, most of the company stay up till after 2 a.m., drinking more wine and singing old songs, the words to all of which Charles knows by heart. Some of the singers are drunk, some glowingly near. Moore and his friends work their way through the more obscure airs of *Kiss Me, Kate*, Noel Coward classics, the *Marseillaise*, two Shirley Temple hits (which Charles does in a Shirley Temple voice, with coy winks and gestures), college fight songs, Christmas carols, Irish ballads and propaganda hits from World War II. Charles Moore is sitting cross-legged like a Buddha, happy to be onstage among his friends. Finally, ever genial, ever deferential, the architect accompanies the uphill contingent to their quarters for the night, leaving his bed, on its crow's-nest perch, for other guests.

ALAN CARTNAL

Alan Cartnal, born in 1950, is a former fashion writer for the *Los Angeles Times* and has also written for *New West, Esquire*, and KABC-TV in Los Angeles. Cartnal was formerly the host of the Hollywood segment on ABC's *Good Morning America*. He is the author of *California Crazy* and *Warren Beatty*. Alan Cartnal lives in California.

• •

In the following selection from *California Crazy*, Cartnal delivers a comic take on feel-good religion as it is broadcast from the Crystal Cathedral in suburban Southern California.

from *CALIFORNIA CRAZY*

HONK YOUR HORN if you love Jesus. The "Let's Boogie" van pulled into the drive-in religious sanctuary for Sunday services that sun-kissed morning. The couple in the van were Orange County regulars. They resembled Dale Evans and Roy Rogers. She wore a bouffant hairdo and a lime and white, peppermint-striped pantsuit. He wore the latest in leisure suits, a denim job, which looked as if it had been borrowed from a used-car salesman down the sun-bleached boulevard.

There was a traffic jam for the car-culture pews. But nobody cared. This drive-in religion thing was big. Dr. Robert Schuller, its founder, had not only attracted the masses and celebrities like Frank Sinatra and Doris Day but had officiated at Hubert Humphrey's nationally televised funeral. Schuller had, praise be to God, built the $14-million Crystal Cathedral bigger than Notre Dame in Paris.

Well, Little Miss Orange County, about five-foot-four and cute as a button, and Mr. Macho Orange County, with a mustache, Mr. America pectorals, and totally into this Jesus thing to boot, had changed their lifestyle. Like some residents of the White House, they had gone the Born-Again route. Before conversion, they had been into recreational vehicles and dirt bikes in the desert. That was all over, those let's-do-it-in-the-dirt days. They had seen the glory from the windshields.

One day the van couple had been out cruising in Garden Grove, California, a bottom-of-the-pit, High Tack town of 80,000 or so in the vast frontierland of Southern California near Disneyland. There they had been struck by the most awesome sight of their life. It reminded them of a set from *The Empire Strikes Back*. Both of them were stoned out of their minds on home-grown Laguna Beach grass.

Suddenly, not far from a 7-11 fast-food store and a Pup 'n Taco Acapulco gold-colored hot-dog stand shaped like a plastic Swiss chalet, there appeared the Crystal Cathedral, a totally mirrored monstrosity, which looked like something they had seen in the pages of the *Whole Earth Catalog*—but bigger, much bigger—and it rose in the flatland spaces around the tract-home paradises like a space ship. "Jesus," Mr. Macho Orange County said to his cutie-pie, who was munching on a Hostess cupcake at the time, "it's *Close Encounters of the Third Kind*."

Hordes of tourists, other car-culture adventurers out for a day of fun in the sun, had also stopped to observe the architectural phenomenon. Japanese tour buses, filled with miniature businessmen dressed in white shirts, ties, and tailored wool-blend trousers, were lined up for blocks. Instamatics popped. Some of the more devout fell to their knees and began praying.

"What is it?" Mr. Macho Orange County asked one of the spectators, a woman dressed in the latest Orange County style—a powder pink princess dress with a fifties Elizabeth Taylor hairstyle and a cross as a comb.

"It's drive-in religion," she answered, her eyes reaching for the heaven above.

They steered the van, a citrus orange beauty, inside the huge compound. It felt so peaceful. But it was unlike any church they could remember. There were 2000 parking spaces, built in the exact style of California drive-in movie theaters.

The interior seemed more like a national park than a church. Someone, some ding-dong gardener, had filled the gardens with bird of paradise flowers and sculptured hedges.

The worshipers strolling inside the gardens, although straightforward folk who probably read the *Saturday Evening Post* and shopped for days at J. C. Penney's, had Born-Again smiles on their faces. There were several new California species which the young van couple had never encountered before. Everybody was friendly. Positive. Filled with polyester inspiration. Chimes tolled, filling the sanctified stillness with the sounds of "The Old Rugged Cross." In front of the van couple, next to the dazzling drive-in cathedral, stood a fourteen-story neon cross. Amazing.

It was the most important moment in the young couple's courtship. They had heard of the Jesus thing, but never experienced it before. They decided it might be a great club to join.

Sunday morning service was even more fantastic. The young couple parked the van on a stiff incline and set the emergency brake. You didn't want to have your car drift back and collide with the other worshipers singing hymns at the steering wheels in their cars.

A young usher whose golden hair was truly blinding passed them a church bulletin through a front window. As usual the young couple was responding in a positive way to the messages of inspiration within the bulletin. The woman turned the dial of the car radio to 540 KC, and they held hands while the church chorus on the drive-in loudspeaker sang upbeat, sunny hymns.

The scene before them was currently broadcast to 2 million worldwide TV-religious-hour fans in places like Sydney, Australia, and the Philippines and Puerto Rico, as well as inspiration seekers in the United States and California. The program, "The Hour of Power," had from the very beginning, back in 1968, been popular. How could electronic religion miss? The TV cameras aimed at the drive-in congregation, their multicolored cars basking in the gleam of the sun, and telecast scenes of nature from the gardens of the cathedral which rivaled the most cheery Hallmark cards.

But that was nothing compared to being there. Schuller, the most famous parking-lot padre in America, walked outside the Crystal Cathedral and glass walls parted like nothing since a Hollywood version of the Red Sea. Twelve fountains, one for each apostle, sprung skyward as Schuller beamed his message of eternal glow. "This is the day that God has made," exulted the fifty-five-year-old, silver-haired, drive-in preacher. "Let us be glad and rejoice in it."

Between Schuller's sermonettes, thanks to the presence of the TV cameras, things never got boring as they did in those other hell-and-damnation churches in Orange County. There were beach-boy rock-'n-roll bands—usually two sun-sensibility young men and one Olivia Newton-John look-alike—who rocked out for Jesus. For the older crowd—the senior citizens or keen-agers, as Schuller referred to them—who sat in their recreational vehicles sporting "We visited Yellowstone National Park" bumper stickers, there was also the Christian version of vaudeville. Norma Zimmer, the latest Lawrence Welk champagne girl, would use her powerful TV soprano to bring the crowds to tears.

The church organs were unbelievable. One of them had been purchased by the Reverend Schuller for $100,000 from Avery Fisher Hall in New York's Lincoln Center. The other was equally famous. You didn't merely attend church when you worshiped at Schuller's Garden Grove Community Church, you were watching a full-scale Broadway show at what was conversationally called the fastest-growing indoor/outdoor religious institution in the world.

By the time the ushers arrived at your vehicle for tithes and offerings, you had also heard from a Hollywood celebrity confessing how drive-in religion had released him from the Sodom and Gomorrah of fame and fortune. It literally poured from the confessionals at the pulpit. Doris Day. Rhonda Fleming. Glenn Ford. Even Ruth Carter Stapleton, the ex-President's sister, had come clean at Schuller's command. It was the best soap opera on Sunday morning TV religious hours.

Then Dr. Schuller bounded up to the pulpit and began pressing buttons for the dancing waters. You couldn't actually see the waters from your car, but there was a wonderful commotion on the loudspeakers. The spectators inside were going into ecstasy.

Schuller was dressed in crimson robes. But people didn't remember the robes. They remembered the smile. The sparkling, I've-seen-God-and-he-is-terrific eyes. Schuller never used a prepared sermon. He believed in spontaneous delivery and he was a born actor. They didn't give Emmy awards to TV preachers, or Most Promising Newcomer plaques to God's messengers, but Schuller's revival style of preaching was as explosive as a rock act. He thundered like Charlton Heston playing Moses. He raised his hands, the velvet sleeves of his preacher robes, and the drive-in sanctuary was calmed to silence.

Schuller was an Iowa farmboy who had decided to follow the ministry at four. He had been inspired by an uncle, one of Christ's missionaries to the heathens in China. When Schuller had chanced upon Orange County back in 1955, it seemed like the perfect place to plant seeds. So he personally rang 3500 doorbells of the modest, garden-blessed homes in the area and learned that the inhabitants loved two things—TV and cars.

Around Schuller's neck hung a gold medallion. Its slogan represented the main focus of his philosophy, a low-rent version of Dr. Norman Vincent Peale's *Power of Positive Thinking.* Schuller's version was dubbed Possibility Thinking. "A Possibility Thinker," according to the inscription on the medallion that was being worn in high places everywhere that year, "is a person who, when faced with a mountain, does not quit. He keeps on striving until he climbs over, finds a pass through, tunnels underneath, or simply stays and turns his mountain into a gold mine with God's help. A Possibility Thinker looks for all the possibilities in every situation instead of the impossibilities." It was very big in California that summer.

Not everyone could dream up a drive-in church. Or could induce the multitudes to bless him with $10 million per annum. One day the idea of religion via loudspeaker simply popped into his mind. Why not? The snack bar could be the pulpit. The refreshment stand the baptismal room. The middle-class, family-oriented burghers of Orange County relished new concepts. It was one of the fastest-growing areas in the United States and the home of such all-American attractions as Disneyland, the Movie Star Wax Museum, Knott's Berry Farm—an old boysenberry ranch which had been bulldozed to provide space for the log rides and the Debbie Reynolds concerts—and Lion Country Safari. It had become the test tube of the hinterlands. Not as well entrenched with the trend makers as the rich arena of Los Angeles to the north, but rising…rising.

Orange County needed a religious leader. Not some old country-boy slick-o like Billy Graham. Kathryn Kulman and Reverend Ike were much too R-rated for mass culture, traditional tastes. They wanted a religious Barry Goldwater. They got Dr. Schuller.

Reverend Schuller realized what Orange County wanted. To lead the country back to God and peach pie. To send off powerful vibrations that could raise the nation from its deep sleep, wash away the sins and cynicism of Watergate. The Orange County middle class would be attracted to the values of the 1950s dressed up in space-age, technological trimmings. Affluence. Spirituality. Sunny smiles. Wouldn't it be wonderful?

Dr. Schuller was like the American flag to them. Christian. Successful. Businesslike. Brooks Brothers. Positive. Healthy. Clean. *Up.*

The couples in the drive-in congregation were often moved to tears by Schuller's inspiring messages. Sometimes they even turned on the windshield wipers in their more devastated moments. They always got what they came to hear. That in the common folk of Orange County lived the saviors of American morality. That hundreds of years from now the whole world would have heard about the fantastic events in Garden Grove. That even if they came from a hick town, and shopped in mammoth prefab shopping centers, and did their hair all wrong, were faced at home with the kids on drugs, and alcoholism, and their jobs were filled with worry and boredom, their troubles would vanish if they believed in the possibilities offered by instant car-culture religion.

It kind of hit you where you lived. Especially if you were like the van couple, totally lost in the anonymity of suburban life and unaware until Schuller that they were actually the new nobility, magnificent enough to worship in the $14-million Crystal Cathedral. The grassroots hadn't heard about the beauty of the common man to this extent since Roosevelt lifted them out of the Depression.

Back on stage, Dr. Schuller worked the majestic cathedral, as the dancing waters rose and the evangelical choirs sang hosannas from on high. The services were simultaneously translated into five languages. Four thousand seated worshipers filled the hall with divine applause. They *loved* the church. It was theirs. It was modern, open, more talked about than any religious building since Westminster Abbey. The cathedral was not only solar powered, but ecologically air-conditioned by the sea breezes of the region.

For couples like the van sweethearts it presented the most astounding mural in their rearview mirrors. The couple, as well as the other members of the 10,000-strong church, *loved* the cathedral. The two of them had given Dr. Schuller $500 the previous summer in order to become members of the Pillar of Steel Club. They had received a beautiful certificate, to hang on a wall at home, that acknowledged their membership in the group of 16,500 other Possibility Thinkers who had raised the lacy steel framework of the cathedral.

Dr. Schuller had sent them a color rendition of the cathedral. The message enclosed reminded them that their children, as well as their children's children, would remember them as founding builders of the great center of drive-in religion. Five hundred dollars seemed a bargain price for immortality.

They were no longer nobodies, but somebodies. The compound was filled with reporters and sociologists studying their every moment. Stories about them and their church appeared in *Time, Newsweek, People,* the *Saturday Evening Post, Us, Now, Success Unlimited, New West,* and *Vogue.* The architect of Schuller's dream palace, Philip Johnson, was a cover boy on *Time* magazine. The members of the church consorted with the most talented, most honored architects. The "Today Show" had given viewers across America progress reports on the wonder of religious wonders. In 1955 Dr. Schuller had begun his ministry by climbing atop the rusty roof of a snack bar in an Orange County drive-in movie theater. There were eleven cars in attendance. Schuller had $200 to his name. Now he was being invited to the White House and performing for millions from his own version of Chartres.

There were five services that Sunday. The biggie being the 9:30 A.M. service, since that was when the crowds got to see themselves smiling and praying on television. Hardly anyone at Schuller's cathedral wanted to be baptized at any other hour. Because if they got baptized at the 9:30 service people all over the world would see the TV cameras zoom in on them as they knelt to meet their maker and smile the smile of self-esteem as Dr. Schuller, resplendent in his robes, anointed them with the Biblical waters.

That had been another major moment in the lives of the van couple. Coast-to-coast baptism. They had held a party for their friends the day their baptism was telecast. And were presented with a videotape of the proceedings by their best friends, also advocates of Schullerism.

Often the couple would arrive for the early 7:30 service and remain until sunset to hear the last service; it reminded them of Easter sunrise services or a religious holiday on the church campus, which Dr. Schuller referred to as a 250-acre shopping center for Christ.

There was fresh-perked coffee served by the lay ministry. Much to ponder. For each week Schuller devised another trinket for them to take home and fill their walls with joyful wisdom. That Sunday it was a miniature wooden boomerang which read, "Blessings Always Boomerang." For $7 they could attend classes at the drive-in educational facilities in such varied subjects as Growing Through Grief or a course called To Bind Up the Broken Hearted ("National coordinator of Suiciders Anonymous shares insights into depression—how to recognize it, accept it, and move on to positive Christianity").

There was usually some new game introduced at the church. Not pinball or any of your Las Vegas card tricks or slot machines—that would be sacrilegious—but what passed for services in the eighties breeding ground of electronic religion. If anything was troubling a member of the parish, there was a twenty-four-hour crisis line for which one would dial 714 and the words NEW HOPE. Vast Sunday school facilities were provided so that the children could play with miniature cars on the carpets while they watched Dr. Schuller on television. One could, if one wished, take tours of the TV production facilities, which were more sophisticated than many Hollywood sound stages. Or review a few of the 40,000 letters which poured in each week, addressed only to Dr. Robert Schuller, Garden Grove, California.

Mostly the van couple wanted to kick back in their car, crank up the volume dial on their car radio, and cassette tape-record all of Dr. Schuller's sermons. The speeches, which they played for inspiration while driving the freeways, frequently contained an uplifting theme. Schuller's brand of religion didn't focus much on Jesus or Scripture or any of the more traditional preaching methods. Instead, the good doctor prepared his flock for the anxiety and depression of daily life by lifting them above their worries to an imaginary level where all their dreams would come true. They could have anything they wanted, as long as they believed. One of the couple's favorite tapes was currently climbing on the Schuller hit parade. It was called "Turn Your Scars into Stars."

Everyone was treated royally at Schuller's religious drive-in resort. Reverend Schuller was not only a theology freak but a connoisseur of the latest developments in California's rich human potential movement. Esalen met TV religion at the Crystal Cathedral. Not only were the multitudes fed Sunday school stories, and incredible arrays of musical entertainment, but the latest psychobabble of the California transformation movement.

The congregation appeared so ordinary—so "Father Knows Best" TV situation comedy squeaky clean. Yet they were being fed the basic California soma drugs of total joy. Through the message of the soul administered by Schuller and his huge staff the van couple had moved from self-doubt to self-confidence. From self-condemnation to self-effectiveness, self-acceptance, and self-love. They would drive into the compound unconscious, but Schuller, who often screamed as if he had received the word from God that instant, woke them up and charged them with holding the banners for The American Way of Life.

The van couple always kept Windex inside their glove compartment when they attended Sunday services. Sometimes flies and bugs splattered the windshield and ruined the view of Schuller as he stepped out onto the cement patio and blessed the cars.

They no longer did drugs. After a sermon from Schuller they were amazingly high—and they would drive to lunch or breakfast at the nearby coffee shops with plastic white roosters atop the thatch roofs and share their good will with their lost neighbors.

Nobody knew the truth about Dr. Schuller. Some of the more liberated members of the laity had wondered just what was going on underneath those crimson velvet robes. There were rumors in religious circles that the good doctor got up every morning and hollered out his front door: "I feel happy, healthy, and terrific." The underground gossip network also reported that Schuller had "happy spells" all the time, and would stand on tiptoe, quivering with be-here-and-now joy. Of course he had been visited by God many times. But then, who hadn't?

Schuller never resorted to laying-on-of-hands tricks. Or rode into services atop a white horse, as some of his California religious brothers had done. Schuller didn't buy the old gimmicks of American revivalists. To Schuller Jesus was the greatest psychologist of all time. Growth, that was the ticket. Why was everyone leaving the church in droves? Schuller thought the flight was connected to hell-and-damnation fundamentalism. He was not interested in that. Schuller not only intended to be the Lawrence Welk of TV religion but also the Dear Abby of the silver chalice set.

That Sunday morning, while the congregation queued up waiting for the gates to open for church, Schuller rose early in his three-bedroom home in Orange, just a few freeway exits from the cathedral. He was greeted by his Ultra-Brite wife of thirty years, Arvella, who, according to articles in Christian monthlies, did all the ironing, washing, and cooking and still contributed forty hours a week for her "church duties." The Schullers shared the family home, their Laguna Beach apartment, and their Lake Arrowhead mountain cabin with their five children. There were no *down* moods, as Schuller described them, around the fireside at the Schuller home. When faced with an angry child given to tantrums, Schuller simply informed the child that his radio was receiving a bad station and asked him to dial to a more positive program. It was nothing like *The Exorcist*.

Schuller would jump—he never walked, but bounded, jogged, or flew—into his brown Cadillac Seville for the pleasant ride to the sanctuary. Pink Cadillacs were no longer in style for Southern California religious leaders that year. But neither were VW Rabbits. The plush, comfortable automobile—like many of Schuller's possessions—was a gift from one of his parish members, who told the *New York Times* that a Great Man like the father of drive-in religion shouldn't have to ride around in just any gas-eater.

Schuller tooled down the freeways, his face lit up like a searchlight, seemingly tranquil. Recently his reputation had reached a new apex, the network TV breakthrough—he had conducted Hubert Humphrey's nationally broadcast funeral. Billy Graham may still be at the top of the religious charts, but Schuller was number two with a bullet.

Schuller was the TV prophet of good times. There was enough vengeance on the six o'clock news. Maybe Marvin Hamlisch would write a musical about his life. Perhaps Julie Andrews could play his wife. Schuller told reporters he was holding out for John Denver to recreate him on the silver screen.

The good people of Orange County applauded him as he entered the huge religious compound. Some yearned to touch his robes. School children lined up around the entranceways to the church, telling their parents they hoped to see a good man once in their lives. They wanted to see what a good man *looked like*.

What a scene. Schuller in his Cadillac zooming up to his parking space near the Crystal Cathedral. Then, to the cheers of the congregation as for a football hero, the glass doors parted and he would rise high above the throngs to a tune that sounded like a Christian version of *Thus Spake Zarathustra*.

A little organ music, please. Some Max Factor pancake makeup to erase the slightest imperfection on the brow of the TV culture hero. Quick shots of California clouds and trees swaying in harmonious winds for the vast television audience. Schuller's market research had shown that unless you used quick cuts viewers would get bored and move on to other religious programs.

Zoom in on a little safe sex appeal. Schuller may not be Hugh Hefner, but he did have a healthy Madonna complex. There was a big TV market of men like Schuller who appreciated the simple, wholesome beauty of the supermarket, schoolteacher, homemaker sex symbols in the choir. Schuller's Angels, some called them.

Dr. Schuller on stage had managed to amplify religion. It was small-screen ecstasy held just at the brink of orgasm.

For an hour birds chirped, Schuller preached, celebrities (today, Mickey Rooney) confessed, and Schuller forgave every transgression, casting such a golden light of goodness on the throngs that his show was one of the highest-rated TV hours on Sunday morning.

The car-culture congregation in the Drive-In Sanctuary, as well as the peasants dialing in via satellite in Mexico, listened to Schuller's voice washing over them, caressing them. The good doctor looked into their eyes from his side of the TV cameras, and he had so much he wanted to tell them. So much.

MIKE DAVIS

Mike Davis was born in Fontana in 1946. An urban theorist, sociographer, and social commentator, Davis received a MacArthur Fellowship in 1998 and an award for nonfiction writing from the Lannan Literary Foundation in 2007. He teaches in the Department of Creative Writing at the University of California, Riverside. Davis's books include *City of Quartz, Ecology of Fear, Magical Urbanism, Planet of Slums*, and *In Praise of Barbarians*. He lives in San Diego.

• •

In this excerpt from *City of Quartz*, Davis shows how preoccupation with security has produced an architecture of social division in contemporary Los Angeles.

from *CITY OF QUARTZ:*
EXCAVATING THE FUTURE IN LOS ANGELES

THE CAREFULLY MANICURED lawns of Los Angeles's Westside sprout forests of ominous little signs warning: "Armed Response!" Even richer neighborhoods in the canyons and hillsides isolate themselves behind walls guarded by gun-toting private police and state-of-the-art electronic surveillance. Downtown, a publicly-subsidized "urban renaissance" has raised the nation's largest corporate citadel, segregated from the poor neighborhoods around it by a monumental architectural glacis. In Hollywood, celebrity architect Frank Gehry, renowned for his "humanism," apotheosizes the siege look in a library designed to resemble a foreign-legion fort. In the Westlake district and the San Fernando Valley the Los Angeles Police barricade streets and seal off poor neighborhoods as part of their "war on drugs." In Watts, developer Alexander Haagen demonstrates his strategy for recolonizing inner-city retail markets: a panoptican shopping mall surrounded by staked metal fences and a substation of the LAPD in a central surveillance tower. Finally on the horizon of the next millennium, an ex-chief of police crusades for an anti-crime "giant eye"—a geo-synchronous law enforcement satellite—while other cops discreetly tend versions of "Garden Plot," a hoary but still viable 1960s plan for a law-and-order armageddon.

Welcome to post-liberal Los Angeles, where the defense of luxury lifestyles is translated into a proliferation of new repressions in space and movement, undergirded by the ubiquitous "armed response." This obsession with physical security systems, and, collaterally, with the architectural policing of social boundaries, has become a zeitgeist of urban restructuring, a master narrative in the emerging built environment of the 1990s. Yet contemporary urban theory, whether debating the role of electronic technologies in precipitating "postmodern space," or discussing the dispersion of urban functions across poly-centered metropolitan "galaxies," has been strangely silent about the militarization of city life so grimly visible at the street level. Hollywood's pop apocalypses and pulp science fiction have been more realistic, and politically perceptive, in representing the programmed hardening of the urban surface in the wake of the social polarizations of the Reagan era. Images of carceral inner cities (*Escape from New York, Running Man*), high-tech police death squads (*Blade Runner*), sentient buildings (*Die Hard*), urban bantustans (*They Live!*), Vietnam-like street wars (*Colors*), and so on, only extrapolate from actually existing trends.

Such dystopian visions grasp the extent to which today's pharaonic scales of residential and commercial security supplant residual hopes for urban reform and social integration. The dire predictions of Richard Nixon's 1969 National Commission on the Causes and Prevention of Violence have been tragically fulfilled: we live in "fortress cities" brutally divided between "fortified cells" of affluent society and "places of terror" where the police battle the criminalized poor. The "Second Civil War" that began in the long hot summers of the 1960s has been institutionalized into the very structure of urban space. The old liberal paradigm of social control, attempting to balance repression with reform, has long been superseded by a rhetoric of social warfare that calculates the interests of the urban poor and the middle classes as a zero-sum game. In cities like Los Angeles, on the bad edge of postmodernity, one observes an unprecedented tendency to merge urban design, architecture and the police apparatus into a single, comprehensive security effort.

This epochal coalescence has far-reaching consequences for the social relations of the built environment. In the first place, the market provision of "security" generates its own paranoid demand. "Security" becomes a positional good defined by income access to private "protective services" and membership in some hardened residential enclave or restricted suburb. As a prestige symbol—and sometimes as the decisive borderline between the merely well-off and the "truly rich"—"security" has less to do with personal safety than with the degree of personal insulation, in residential, work, consumption and travel environments, from "unsavory" groups and individuals, even crowds in general.

Secondly, as William Whyte has observed of social intercourse in New York, "fear proves itself." The social perception of threat becomes a function of the security mobilization itself, not crime rates. Where there is an actual rising arc of street violence, as in Southcentral Los Angeles or Downtown Washington D.C., most of the carnage is self-contained within ethnic or class boundaries. Yet white middle-class imagination, absent from any firsthand knowledge of inner-city conditions, magnifies the perceived threat through a demonological lens. Surveys show that Milwaukee suburbanites are just as worried about violent crime as inner-city Washingtonians, despite a twenty-fold difference in relative levels of mayhem. The media, whose function in this arena is to bury and obscure the daily economic violence of the city, ceaselessly throw up spectres of criminal underclasses and psychotic stalkers. Sensationalized accounts of killer youth gangs high on crack and shrilly racist evocations of marauding Willie Hortons foment the moral panics that reinforce and justify urban apartheid.

Moreover, the neo-military syntax of contemporary architecture insinuates violence and conjures imaginary dangers. In many instances the semiotics of so-called "defensible space" are just about as subtle as a swaggering white cop. Today's upscale, pseudo-public spaces—sumptuary malls, office centers, culture acropolises, and so on—are full of invisible signs warning off the underclass "Other." Although architectural critics are usually oblivious to how the built environment contributes to segregation, pariah groups—whether poor Latino families, young Black men, or elderly homeless white females—read the meaning immediately.

HERBERT MUSCHAMP

Herbert Muschamp was born in Philadelphia in 1947. As a young man, he was part of The Factory, Andy Warhol's studio in New York City. Trained in architecture and architectural history at the Parsons School of Design in New York and at the Architecture Association in London, Muschamp was also an architecture critic, first for *The New Republic* and later for the *New York Times*. His criticism was also featured in *Vogue*, *Artforum*, and *House and Garden*. His books include *File under Architecture* and *Man about Town: Frank Lloyd Wright in New York City*. He died in 2007.

• •

In "Rude Awakening," Muschamp relates his experience of a 1994 earthquake in Southern California and demonstrates that the surface-level exuberance of Los Angeles architecture conceals the fragility of California's built environment.

RUDE AWAKENING; QUAKE JARS ASSUMPTIONS: A CRITIC'S VIEW

BUILDINGS AREN'T SUPPOSED to murder architecture critics. It's meant to be the other way around. And it is particularly wounding to be menaced by a building you love: the Shangri-La Hotel in Santa Monica, a hostelry beloved by architects and photographers for its sleek Art Deco design and its spectacular views of sea, sky and palm trees. But these features didn't amount to much when the earthquake struck last Monday.

After the bounce out of bed, the crawl across a heaving floor toward the supposed haven of a doorway, the prayers and curses, the amazement that any building could survive the jolts this one had just been put through, I pulled on clothes and went five flights down to the sidewalk.

The darkness, the cold, the starry sky, the impromptu dress and dazed demeanor of the guests, and even the marine look of the hotel itself inspired thoughts of the Titanic, particularly when the word went around that the 6.6 quake might be just the foreshock of a bigger one. The sea that ordinarily looked so idyllic could rise up and swallow us. The whiffs of gas that teased the nostrils could signal an imminent explosion.

For me, the gut issue of survival was suddenly superimposed on professional concerns. I was scheduled to visit two buildings that day, both designed by architects I admire. And for many architecture critics today, the entire city of Los Angeles is Shangri-La—home to some of the most gifted architects now practicing.

But the earthquake made brutally clear that, however remarkable their talents, these architects are operating on a very thin veneer. Indeed, their job is to create that veneer. They design the alluring visual surface that enables people to imagine that they can enjoy a stable life on top of quicksand. After the quake, there was much praise for the maintenance of civility in the face of chaos. Architects translate civility into steel, stone and glass. But the earthquake showed that architectural civility is not so benign. In a flash, it inverted the usual relationship of the city to its surroundings, revealing that nature is the order, civilization the chaos. At 7 A.M., an inspector came by and declared the Shangri-La unsafe.

Eric Owen Moss showed up two hours later, as planned. A luminary of Los Angeles architecture, Mr. Moss drove me to Culver City to look at one of his projects, a commercial building nearing completion. On the way, we took in the sights that those without power couldn't see on their televisions: the cracks in the walls of high-rises; the piles of shattered glass and tumbled-down brick; the ugly fissures in expanses of tile that only a day before had looked pristine. The most unusual sight of all was the people walking on streets where people never walk.

We were also scanning the windshield, on this insultingly sunny day, for some correlation between what we were seeing and the facts coming in over the radio, though the constant adjustment of the numbers gave even facts the unstable quality of the earth under pressure. The death toll that by week's end exceeded 50 people dashed the optimism of early announcements. Not until nightfall would it be estimated that 47,000 people had sought refuge at Red Cross shelters. Since this was a holiday, we saw no sign of the impact that the collapse of three freeway overpasses would make on the traffic circulation that is this city's lifeblood.

WHAT CAN'T BE MEASURED

Effects on the quality of people's lives are not easily quantifiable. The estimate of $7 billion in damages, repeated endlessly, began to sound more like superstition than fact: a tribute to an ideal of objectivity that the earthquake itself made mockery of. The news that the quake originated with a previously unknown fault rocked the security that flows from our investment in scientific expertise.

Attempts to explain why some structures are safer than others repeatedly collided against the information that there are different kinds of quakes, that they affect structures differently, and that the greatest hazard may lie in supposing that earthquake-proof design is an absolute proposition. The facts were geared to one dubious idea: that recovery, however expensive, however long it takes, is ultimately possible.

When we finally reached Mr. Moss's building, it turned out to be an anticlimax, even though the design appeared to have much in common with the fractured cityscape we'd just driven through. A large, tilted cube dramatically cantilevered on curved steel trusses, it is a poem of precariousness, a precisely controlled upheaval in space. When completed, the building will deliver a strong esthetic jolt. On Monday, with the construction scaffolding jiggling around it, the project barely set off a mild perceptual tremor. The building wasn't damaged, only upstaged.

My next stop was a building that expresses even more emphatically the artificiality of California's urban veneer. Designed by the San Francisco firm Holt Hinshaw Pfau Jones, U.C.L.A.'s nearly completed Chiller Plant is a tour de force of expressionistic technology. With a muscular superstructure of cooling towers, chimneys and ducts rising boldly from a red brick base, the plant houses the equipment that air-conditions buildings throughout U.C.L.A.'s vast Westwood campus. The building's job, in short, is to change the climate. To its credit, the building makes no effort to hide what it's about. On the contrary, Wes Jones, the project's chief designer, is strongly committed to the idea that architecture should reveal the forces that fuel the social engine. "Architecture is supposed to mediate between people and nature," he said. But he acknowledged that buildings can be a means of refusing to reckon with nature. The Chiller

Plant enables U.C.L.A.'s architects to design buildings without full regard for the natural climate. Although it's honest about its function, the function itself is dubious.

Mr. Moss's building puts the critic in a similar quandary. It, too, expresses something pertinent about the built environment. Instead of perpetuating an appearance of ordered normality, the design's skewed forms call attention to the profound lack of order that has led America's second-largest city to be built where perhaps there should be no city at all.

Both buildings deal knowingly with the condition of inhabiting an artificial veneer. But they also extend the veneer. The work of these architects is far superior to countless buildings that do not even acknowledge the veneer. But their excellence will do nothing to remove people from harm's way when the earth rumbles.

And neither will the rumbling. People went out of their way to say they wouldn't think of leaving. The pleasure of living in the warm, golden light; the proximity to ocean, mountains and desert; the glamour of the California lifestyle, not to mention the schools, museums, industries, agriculture and everything else that makes civilization worth talking about— these, they say, are worth the risk of earthquakes, fires and droughts.

Yet is it fair to expect the taxpayers to subsidize that risk? Californians bridle at the question. Elsewhere, Americans live at risk of hurricanes, floods, tornadoes. A fault line runs through Manhattan. Las Vegas is a mirage that thinks it's an oasis. The country is subsidized by cheap oil, cheap labor, the profligate consumption of natural resources. An earthquake should alert people to the folly of disregarding nature. But who wants to wake up from the American dream.

SIM VAN DER RYN

Born in the Netherlands, Sim Van der Ryn came to New York City with his family in 1939 at the age of five. A longtime advocate of sustainable design, Van der Ryn was a professor of ecological design at the University of California, Berkeley, for thirty-five years and has also held the position of California State Architect. He has won numerous awards and honors over several decades, including a Guggenheim Fellowship, a Lindisfarne Fellowship, and a Nathaniel A. Owings Award from the California Council of the American Institute of Architects. Van der Ryn has spread his ideas on green architecture through the construction of projects throughout California and the United States. He lives in Inverness, California.

• •

"Real Goods Solar Living Center," from *Design for Life*, is the architect's account of the factors that must be considered when designing a facility for sustainability. In another selection from *Design for Life*, "Integral Morphology, Geometry, and Built Form," Van der Ryn expounds his philosophy that buildings are never static but ever evolving. Here he also highlights the modular and patterned qualities of integral design.

from DESIGN FOR LIFE:
THE ARCHITECTURE OF SIM VAN DER RYN

REAL GOODS SOLAR LIVING CENTER

AFTER RETIRING FROM UC Berkeley in 1995 and making the commitment to full-time architectural practice, I didn't have to wait long for the right project to come along. Real Goods Trading Company was founded to supply back-to-the-landers in northern California with technology appropriate to a resourceful rural lifestyle. By the mid-nineteen nineties, it had grown into a national mail order company, the largest supplier of solar living products and solar electric systems in the country. Its founder and president, John Schaeffer, is a visionary and a smart businessman.

The company was outgrowing its headquarters, a cluster of anonymous metal buildings in the industrial area of Ukiah, a small city two hours north of San Francisco. John purchased a twelve-acre site in Hopland, a crossroads and a wine grape-growing town fifteen minutes south of Ukiah. The site, once agricultural, had been used as a highway department dump site. It was bordered by Highway 101, Feliz Creek, a tributary to the Russian River, which drains the northern interior to the coast, and an old logging railroad.

John's vision was to transform this ecologically wounded site into a model of ecological restoration, demonstration gardens, and outdoor people space, and as the centerpiece, build a showroom that would be a model of sustainable design practices. His brief for the project states that Real Goods wants a building that "takes less from the Earth and gives back more to people." He wanted to create a building that uses no outside energy sources, uses locally available environmentally benign materials, recycles wastes generated by its occupants, and restores the badly damaged site to full biological productivity.

Real Goods invited six architects to compete in preparing concept plans for the proposed Solar Living Center. I found John's vision statement for the project so closely aligned with my own values that I gladly accepted the invitation.

Together with David Arkin, a talented and experienced architect who had joined my firm, I spent a day on the barren site. Pulling out my ever-present watercolor kit, I sat quietly on the railroad bridge, letting the site speak to me through my eyes and hands as I sketched. The process is my form of meditation: a way to get quiet and become aware of the subtleties of place, light, colors, forms and patterns, sounds, and spaces. Watercolor painting helps me to experience an environment fully with my whole being. It's the difference between looking, which is passive involvement, and seeing, which is active engagement with place.

After painting, I started sketching. The topographic map we were given showed a slight mound at the south end of the site. The highest point, offering protection from flooding, was where the building should be. Sitting there for several hours, the highway noise became increasingly irritating. Why not scoop out part of the site to create ponds and water elements that John's brief mentioned and use the material to create a berm, or earth mound, to screen the building from the highway noise and view?

If the Center was to be the oasis that John referred to in his brief, then it should not be like most highway commercial development that insists it be visible from the road. Instead we could hide it and create a series of ecological cues announcing that something interesting was around the bend. As part of that theme, I sketched an entrance road alongside the creek corridor, which would be restored. Instead of parking being the first thing you saw, the visitor would have time to take several breaths, leave the highway behind, park in the back, and enter another reality.

Inside the rounded berm, I sketched the building as a south-facing curve. Why not make the building truly invisible and adapted to the hot summers by using a sod roof, arbors to shade the south wall, and a thick wall built into the berm on the north where the winter winds came from? Why not have the building open onto a central meeting space marked by a shallow round pond that could provide cooling in summer? To the north, I located the experimental gardens and orchards mentioned in John's program.

I went home and that weekend, David and I developed the competition drawings based on my sketches. As another meditation, I spent a day carefully doing the finished drawings and sent the package off to Real Goods. We later went up and presented it and answered questions. And then, as is common in the architecture business, we waited and then waited some more. Finally I heard from John, "Congratulations! You got the job!"

I added structural engineer Bruce King, and graduate student Adam Jackaway, a specialist in climate adaptive strategies, to the team. Real Goods added landscape designers Stephanie Kotin and Chris Tebbut and project manager Jeff Oldham. Collectively, we made the decision to reverse the usual design process, where the landscaping is the last element to be installed in a project. "Why not put in the landscape first and give it a year to get established before you start construction?" Chris exclaimed. And that's what happened. Chris and Stephanie, besides being inspired designers, are hands-on horticulturists and readers of the land. The key fact is that the site is a floodplain, and as Chris and Stephanie explained, floodplains are highly diverse ecosystems. The trees and plants they chose were all adapted to flooding conditions.

Their concept received its first test soon after they completed planting when a flood in 1995 put the site under four feet of water. All the plantings survived and, indeed, have prospered. Their landscape plan builds in various solar clocks that mark the cycle of seasons and the cardinal directions. We integrated our ideas that the site should tell a sun story, a water story, a native plant restoration story, and a food plant story. The stories are built into the design, and it's interesting to watch visitors with no prior knowledge discover for themselves what stories the place has to tell.

There were also unexpected interactions among the stories that I hadn't anticipated. As a visitor enters the center area, a large recycled redwood wine tank spills water over its top into a flow-form stream below, starting the water story. The tank is filled from the ponds at the end of the water story by a solar powered pump. When the sun is full force, the water volume is at a peak. When a cloud drifts by and obscures the sun, flow from the pump drops and the sound of water, designed to mask highway noise, diminishes. I've watched people walk by the stream when this occurs, look around them, and slowly make the connection between the sun and the water flow.

My competition sketch for the building plan started to adapt to new information and reality. The idea of a heavy earth-covered roof would require a massive structure that would interfere with Real Goods' desire for open floor space. Adam suggested a curved roof and light shelf that would bounce daylight off the curved roof for very even light distribution. We liked the idea, constructed a model, and tested it in a heliodyne, a device that simulates sun path for any location. The setup included a tiny video camera that gave us a recording of sun and shade patterns within the model for the lowest and highest sun angles—the winter and summer solstices—and also for the fall and spring equinoxes. John Schaeffer was worried that the curved roof would cost more than a flat roof. We went up to his office and ran the ten-minute time-lapse video showing the actual light inside the building. It sold him on our idea.

Our working method was collaboration. The level of integration we achieved in the building and site design was possible only by eroding the traditional professional boundaries in both design and construction. And it was more fun. Our working method related project goals to the five principles of ecological design articulated in my book:

Ecological Design:

Goal 1: Create a Climate Responsive Building
(Solutions Grow from Place)

Goal 2: Create an Educational Environment
(Make Nature Visible)

Goal 3: Design for Low Impact Construction
(Ecological Accounting Informs Design)

Goal 4: Involve Everyone and Have Fun
(Everyone Is a Designer)

INTEGRAL MORPHOLOGY, GEOMETRY, AND BUILT FORM

Integral design creates buildings and environments that are "ecomorphic"; that is, their internal structure mimics and integrates with the natural systems within which they are embedded and connected. Ecomorphism means something different than an architectural form derived directly from nature, such as the structure of a bridge resembling the structure of a bird wing, or a house looking like a nautilus shell. These are examples of biomorphism, forms taken directly from nature. Ecomorphism goes deeper, implying architectural processes and forms at many scales adapted to nature.

An ecological approach to design follows a very simple observation: Architecture is a dynamic adaptation to place, people, and pulse. This simple dictum proposes that architecture respond to these key shapers of form. Most contemporary buildings are shaped by the abstract shortrun economic programs of corporate and institutional clients and by the fashion dictates of their architects. People, the eventual users and occupants of a building, enter most building programs only as a quantitative factor, not as a qualitative cocreator, inhabitant, and change agent of built form. Short-run, narrow-focus economics dominates the design program and design process.

Buildings are not fixed entities. They are like other organisms, constantly changing due to the throughput of energy, materials, information, and context. The reason that buildings exist is people. Stewart Brand suggests that people will always find a way to change buildings that their designers thought of as fixed and immutable. An ecologic design process invites "nonprofessionals," the building's users and occupants, to be active participants in the design process. An ecologic building is designed to adapt to changing human needs, wants, preferences, and aversions.

Integrally designed communities and cities will be conceived as ecosystems that integrate natural and designed systems at similar scale levels as discussed in the last section. For example, rainwater runoff from streets and roofs is not shoved in a pipe and sent elsewhere but instead is retained on-site through cisterns, absorptive surfaces, or local retention ponds. Rather than being piped in from afar, energy is produced locally through rooftop solar devices, and carbon dioxide is absorbed by trees, green roofs, and green walls. Fractal forms become part of the urban pattern.

Another aspect of Integral built form is that its physical character and form are biophilial. The famed naturalist E. O. Wilson first articulated the concept and the term as "the innately emotional affiliation of human beings to other living organisms. Innate means hereditary and hence part of human nature." Our sense of beauty is hard-wired into us through our million years of living in nature. In the Integral epoch, we will again recognize that the source for all beauty is the natural world.

Previously, I've discussed the classes of patterns that make up the living world. Only the crystalline lattice pattern contains the grid-like cube that is the monomorphic, monotonous form that engulfs our everyday environment, creating the experience of living in a sterile geography of nowhere. If the lattice and the cube are the prototypical geometry of today's rational-mental world, then the self-similarity of the fractal will be the prototypical geometry of the Integral Era. However far you zoom in or out of a fractal system, there will always be an unending cascade of self-similar but not identical detail. It is interesting to note that other classes of natural patterns may also exhibit the fractal property of self-similarity: spirals, meanders, branching, waves, symmetry, and nets.

The discovery of fractals as a distinct class of patterns stemming from seemingly chaotic behavior was first discovered by the French mathematician Benoit Mandelbrot. Plotting the geometry of seemingly chaotic number series, he discovered that they generated a beautiful fractal configuration. An occurrence that mechanistic science wrote off as disorder and chaos turns out to be a higher, more complex level of order that is now used to describe phenomenon as diverse as the behavior of the stock market, the activity of our brains and hearts, and weather systems. Chaos represents higher order levels of dynamic change and cooperation.

James Gleick, in his landmark book, *Chaos: Making a New Science*, describes the emotional parallels between the new mathematical esthetic discovered by chaos theorists and art and architecture: "To Mandelbrot and his followers…simple shapes are inhuman. They fail to resonate with the way nature organizes itself or with the way human perception sees the world.…Why is it that the silhouette of a storm-bent leafless tree against an evening sky in winter is perceived as beautiful, but the corresponding silhouette of any multi-purpose university building is not, in spite of any efforts of the architect?…Our feeling for beauty is inspired by the harmonious arrangement of order and disorder as it occurs in natural objects."

The prototypical built form of the Integral world is the open, integrative, dynamic network in which the flows of the living world and the designed world are intricately linked together. Notice how in the integral ring diagram, nature, design, and culture are all integrally interconnected without sharp boundaries.

Cities and towns that grew organically over time in preindustrial times have many of the characteristics of fractals in that they build from a repertoire of complex similar parts, common details, shapes, materials, and levels of scale. The fractal is the prototypical built form of Integrality. I can imagine neighborhoods whose buildings and systems are built fractal-like, each piece part of an emerging whole pattern. Combined with ecomorphism, where the lines between what is nature and what is man-made are blurred, the concept becomes obvious. Green roofs that mirror the topography of the surrounding hills are one such example.

At the land planning and infrastructure scale, using fractal patterns minimizes the disruption of the already-existing fractal patterns. Tim Duane, a University of California planner, discovered that the best way to plan wildlife corridors in rural areas with conventional subdivisions was to create an intricate fractal pattern of open space. Engineers designing to control flooding are abandoning the heavy-handed, straight concrete banks in favor of fractal-like, absorbent marsh flood zones as a more effective, economical, and esthetic solution.

The geometry of the individual building won't develop fractal forms until the design process recognizes that buildings can't be designed as completed, unchanging entities. The whole idea of the single, isolated building is antithetical to Integral thinking. New design and production technology in the building products industry suggests that a move from standard linear and planar components to more intricate configurations is possible. The literal "greening" of buildings through layering vertical walls of living plants as an outer wall in front of our glass-clad cities as well as greening the roofs, could bring the fractal scale of nature to every urban high-rise occupant and provide a carbon dioxide sink in cities where we need it most.

ERNEST CALLENBACH

Ernest Callenbach was born in Williamsport, Pennsylvania. After moving to California in the 1950s, he worked for many years as an editor of books on film, art, and science for the University of California Press, including a series of guidebooks on the natural history of California. He founded and edited *Film Quarterly* and has taught at both San Francisco State University and the University of California, Berkeley. The author of several books and a frequent lecturer on environmental issues, Callenbach is best known for *Ecotopia*, his visionary novel of the future of the Pacific Northwest. Ernest Callenbach lives in Berkeley.

• •

The following excerpt from *Ecotopia* includes Callenbach's rendering of a new material for housing construction: plastic tubing. In convincing detail, he outlines the practical advantages of this material for human habitation.

from *ECOTOPIA*

SANTA CRUZ, JUNE 8. We extrude plastic sausage casings, wire, garden hose, aluminum shapes, and many other items, but the Ecotopians extrude whole rooms. They have devised machinery that produces oval-cross-section tubing, about 13 feet wide and 10 feet high; the walls are six inches thick, and there is a flat floor inside. The tubing can be made solid, or windows can be punched out along the sides. It can be bought with ends cut off square or on the diagonal. The resulting houses take many shapes—in fact I've never seen two that were alike—but you can get the general impression by imagining that jet airplane cabins could be bought by the yard and glued together into whatever shapes you had in mind.

Most Ecotopian buildings are wood, the material Ecotopians love best. But wood houses are complicated to build and thus expensive compared to these extruded houses, which are made of a plastic derived from cotton. The extruded houses also have the advantage of portability (a standard section about 12 feet long is light enough to be lifted by four men) and Ecotopians show great ingenuity in using them.

Cut off at one angle and glued together, they produce a square house; on a different angle, a hexagonal or octagonal house. You can glue sections together into an irregular zigzag shape, or make them into a long looping string, with branches or protrusions, enclosing a sort of compound—a common pattern for extended-family groups living in open country. You can build a central space out of wood or stone and attach extruded rooms onto the outer edge. You can cut doors or windows with a few minutes work. And not only can the sections be glued together by unskilled labor, their cost is very low—a room-size section costs less than a fifth of what a standard-construction room costs, including a couple of windows. This, I was told, is the astonishing result of producing housing on a truly industrial continuous-process basis, instead of by handwork.

I have just inspected one of the plants in which these extruded houses are produced. It resembles one of our carwashes. A large vat cooks the ingredients into a foam-type moldable plastic. The foam is then squirted under pressure though a huge oval slot, and hardens as it comes in contact with the air. After passing over some supporting rollers, it has window holes punched if desired, and is then sprayed inside and out with a hard-surface plastic. This has a strange neutral color and resembles a dried corn leaf—which is not surprising since it is derived from corn plants; it is washable, can be painted though few Ecotopians use paint, and modestly fits in with natural landscapes. Finally the tubing is cut off into different lengths and stored in a nearby field until needed.

The floor of the tube has troughs molded along the sides to accommodate wiring and water pipes, which are also available in standard section lengths and connect to outlets, toilets, and so on.

Ecotopians are always talking of "integrated systems," by which they mean devices that cater to several of their ecological fetishes at once. The extruded house system offers a number of examples. Probably the most startling is the bathroom. Ecotopians have put into practice an early notion of our architects, and produce entire bathrooms in one huge molded piece, proportioned to slide neatly into a section of extruded room. It contains all the usual bathroom components, including a space heater. A companion unit, a large plastic tank, is buried outside, and connected by two flexible hoses. This, it turns out, is a septic tank, which not only digests sewage but produces methane gas in the process, which in turn operates the heater! The effluent that runs out the other end is not at all repulsive, but clear and excellent for watering gardens, so that ordinarily the garden is placed adjacent to the bathroom. Sludge is removed from the tank every few years and used for fertilizer. This system may seem disgusting to some, but it has its advantages, especially in rural areas. And when you remember that gas and electric energy in Ecotopia are inordinately expensive (costing about three times what they cost us) it is clear why such an odd but thrifty idea has caught on widely. Another integrated system Ecotopians are proud of is the heat-pump solar heating device; these are especially effective with the extruded rooms, consume no fossil fuel or even water, and require only a small amount of electricity to operate their pumps.

Incidentally, one curious symptom of the high cost of energy in Ecotopia is that houses tend to be abominably ill-lit. They contain lamps of several kinds, used for reading and work purposes—though Ecotopians avoid fluorescent tubes, claiming their discontinuous emission patterns and subliminal flicker do not suit the human eye. But for ordinary socializing their houses are lit by small bulbs and often even by candles (which they produce from animal fats as our ancestors did).

Such peculiarities aside, an extruded house has a comfortable feeling once you get used to it. The fact that walls and ceiling merge into one another can make for unease at first, yet it is snug and secure too. Ecotopians decorate houses in many different modes, but those who live in extruded houses tend to use even more rugs, coverlets, blankets, and other woven objects, presumably to soften the severe geometrical lines of the structure. Sheepskin and fur rugs are also common. Because of the extremely good insulation and air seal provided by the foam shell, extruded houses are easy to heat—in fact the windows are usually kept wide open—and their inhabitants thus tend to wear little clothing indoors. (Indeed some of them are totally unconcerned about nudity—I was once greeted at the door by an Ecotopian wearing nothing at all.)

One of the pleasantest houses I have yet visited had extruded rooms arranged like spokes of a wheel around a central stone core. This provided the living, cooking and eating area, which was octagonal in shape and had a translucent dome over it. An indoor tree, perhaps 15 feet high, stood in a miniature garden under the dome. One side of the main octagon opened out toward the river from which the house stones had come. The other sides had sliding doors opening into a series of tube rooms, five of which were bedroom-study-retreat rooms, one a spacious and luxurious bathroom complete with fireplace, and one a sort of work room with a small bathroom. Plants and woven fabrics were everywhere, forming beautiful contrasts with the pale, graceful extruded shapes. In one of the bedrooms, a soft, deep-pile rug continued up the walls to window level; aside from a low bed, there was no other furniture, though a bank of cabinets lined the far end of the room. These, I discovered, are available prefabricated, like other kinds of dividers for the extruded rooms; but often people devote great artistry to making their own, with fantastically beautiful woods and intricate detail work.

Extruded houses lack the many built-in appliances of our trailers, but they are probably much more durable; some have been lived in for 15 years now. They are easily patched by the occupants. Once, to demonstrate this, an Ecotopian who was showing off his house to me took an axe and chopped a gaping hole in it! Then the family gathered round, plugged up the hole with shreds of foam, and neatly glued on a piece of surface plastic. The whole process, accompanied by much laughter, took about 10 minutes.

Like all plastics manufactured in Ecotopia, the extruded houses can be broken up and thrown into biovats, digested by micro-organisms into fertilizer sludge, and thus recycled onto the fields from whence their materials came. Oddly, the one serious problem encountered when they were first used was that they tended to blow away in high winds. But instead of our heavy, excavated foundations, they now use large adjustable corkscrew devices which anchor each corner but leave the earth surface undisturbed.

Many Ecotopians are fond of these products of housing automation. But they are very unceremonious about them, and treat them with none of the almost religious respect they extend to wood structures. If a family member dies or leaves, his room may be sliced off and recycled. When a baby is born or a new person joins a group, a new room can be glued onto the existing constellation—a long room for an adult, a short one for a child. Any self-respecting architect would shiver at such a prospect, but it does make the houses a direct expression of the life inside them.

KAREN E. STEEN

Karen E. Steen grew up in Southern California. She writes on architecture, design, urbanism, and art for *Metropolis*, the *New York Times*, and *The Guardian* of London, among other publications. Her book *Crystal Cove Cottages: Islands in Time on the California Coast* was a *Los Angeles Times* best seller. Steen lives in the San Francisco Bay Area.

• •

In "Green Architecture's Grand Experiment," excerpted below, Steen explores the connections between scientific inquiry, educational outreach, and sustainable design at the new headquarters of the California Academy of Sciences in San Francisco's Golden Gate Park.

GREEN ARCHITECTURE'S GRAND EXPERIMENT— PART 1: THE BUILDING

THE NEW CALIFORNIA Academy of Sciences, in San Francisco's Golden Gate Park, is a building of mythic proportions. At 410,000 square feet, it's expected to be the largest public building ever to attain a LEED Platinum rating. And, with a $488 million price tag, it also represents the largest fund-raising effort for a cultural institution in San Francisco history. How did this low-profile natural history museum and research facility become a half-billion-dollar marquee project by a Pritzker Prize–winning architect, not to mention a landmark in sustainable design?

According to an oft-told origin story, it all started on the roof. In late 1999, architect Renzo Piano visited the site, climbed up on top of the Academy's former building, and—there amid the canopy of trees—declared that the roof itself needed to become an exhibit of the museum. "This was a magic place in the middle of Golden Gate Park," Piano recalls. "I said, 'The roof has got to be part of the experience of the building, part of the itinerary.'"

But that was only nine years ago—the blink of an eye in the world of architecture, and even less in the world of science. If you reach further back, there's another precipitous event—appropriately enough, an event of the natural world. When the Loma Prieta earthquake struck the Bay

Area in October of 1989, the venerable museum, which dates back to 1853, sustained severe damage and was forced to close one building and retrofit several others. At first, the Academy had modest hopes: reopen the shuttered building and fix up another, the beloved Steinhart Aquarium. But then the institution decided to turn the lens of scientific inquiry upon itself, and that's when everything changed.

In 1997 one of the Academy's own scientists, Patrick Kociolek, became its interim director. A researcher accustomed to approaching problems through data, Kociolek wanted to test the hypothesis that the planned upgrade was really in the museum's best interests. "I said to the board, 'Why don't we step back and, instead of being driven by the facilities, ask ourselves: What's a natural history museum in the twenty-first century?'" he recalls. "I had no idea this naive question would lead us so far."

And so the Academy—the only museum in the country to combine a natural history collection with a planetarium and an aquarium in one building—spent a year and a half studying the role of the science museum in contemporary culture. As Kociolek, who recently left the Academy to become the director of the University of Colorado Museum of Natural History, puts it: "How do you take this Victorian-era model and concept and make it relevant?"

First, the museum analyzed 20 years of attendance data and found a dramatic but consistent decrease. Then it crunched more numbers and realized that other science museums across the country were doing even worse. To confirm some suspicions about the state of scientific knowledge in the community, it commissioned a poll with Harris Interactive. As suspected, it showed that while science is a bigger part of our lives than ever before the public's understanding of it is lower than it was a generation ago.

The bright spot in all this gloomy news came from an unlikely collaborator: Paul Ray, the demographer who helped coin the term "Cultural Creatives." In 2001 the Academy hired him to study potential visitors to the museum. Ray's data showed that science, conservation, and education about nature were important values to large groups of people around the country and crossed political, ethnic, and socioeconomical boundaries. In other words, the need and desire for science education were great, but the existing paradigm, the Victorian cabinet of curiosities, was not up to the task.

"The old model of the natural history museum is the search for eternal truths," Kociolek says, referring to traditional exhibits such as dioramas, which can remain unchanged for generations. "To me, that's the antithesis of science. Science is not this collection of facts that you put on a wall. It's a very dynamic process. It's about new hypotheses, new data." Whereas the old science had been about a lone researcher bent over his microscope, the new science was about teams collaborating to solve problems. "At the old Academy, the two most distant points were scientists' offices," Kociolek says. "The old physical plan had pushed the intellectual capital apart at a time when the program was calling for bringing the intellectual capital together."

With so many imperatives to address, it became clear that the Academy would have to do more than just fix up two buildings. The old museum wasn't going to support the new ideals—and it wasn't going to survive a continued attendance slump, either. Inspired by Mario Botta's then-new San Francisco Museum of Modern Art and the de Young Museum's decision to hire the high-profile firm Herzog & de Meuron, the Academy's trustees realized they didn't just need a new building; they needed a forward-thinking design that could carry the whole institution into the new century.

To find the architect who could meet this challenge, the Academy hired Bill Lacy, at the time the executive director of the jury for the Pritzker Architecture Prize. Lacy said he thought there were only about 40 firms in the world who could take on the scale of the project, so the Academy sent out a request for portfolios and narrowed the field of 38 respondents down to six: Toyo Ito, Moshe Safdie, Norman Foster, Richard Rogers, James Polshek, and Renzo Piano. The selection committee brought the architects to the museum site in Golden Gate Park, traveled abroad to see their many built projects, and, in late 1999, invited each of them to an interview.

The first five architects to meet with the Academy all gave the kind of polished presentations you might expect. One arrived with two slide projectors, 50 poster boards, and five staffers, "literally and figuratively surrounding the committee with an answer," as Kociolek puts it. But the final architect to interview, Renzo Piano, arrived with one associate—his daughter, Lia—and took just ten minutes to set up. When the committee members entered the room, they were surprised to see that he had no presentation materials with him. He had used the ten minutes to pull a table from the corner and rearrange all the chairs into a circle around it. Piano told them that he didn't know how he would design a new California Academy of Sciences. He would need to hear from them before he could answer that question. "If you go into a meeting and you already know everything," Piano says, "you lose the capacity to understand."

As the committee members spoke, Piano sketched ideas. He says one of the most important things he heard that day was another origin story. In 1906 the original museum on Market Street was destroyed in San Francisco's first big earthquake, and for a few years the Academy's research ship, a schooner that had just returned from the Galápagos Islands, acted as its home base. "The place that you use for research is the same place you invite people to come and enjoy and discover," Piano says with obvious admiration. The message he took from this story was that the Academy wanted to find new ways of bringing its scientists and the public back together. The other idea that came through was about building sustainably, he says. "We all thought, This thing has got to be a kind of experiment, a kind of proof that you can be wise in making a building."

After the interviews, Kociolek says, a number of the trustees wanted to hire the architect who had done the elaborate presentation. But one board member offered a different view. "She said, 'Do you want to have a lecture from that person, or do you want to have a dialogue with Renzo Piano? That person already told us the answer. Renzo Piano is waiting to talk to us about an answer.'" Her question changed the tenor of the deliberations, he says, and led the board to choose Piano to design the new museum.

One factor in the background during this decision-making process was the de Young Museum, just across the road from the Academy. The de Young had recently unveiled its architectural plans, and a public furor erupted over Herzog & de Meuron's bold design, which some San Franciscans considered an intrusion into the park. Kociolek says that Piano's collaborative approach and his experience designing projects within natural settings—like the Beyeler Museum, near Basel, and the Menil Collection, in Houston—seemed to promise not only a sensitive design but also a peaceful public process.

Which brings us back to the roof. Once he was selected, the first thing Piano knew was that he wanted the new roof to be the same height as the one he'd stood on top of: 36 feet. It was an appropriate scale for the park yet tall enough to offer a view, and it retained a vestigial memory of the old building, a local landmark. It was only later, when he learned that some program features—the planetarium and the rain-forest exhibit, for example—would need to be taller, that Piano developed the rooftop's signature hills. "The idea was: keep the roof at thirty-six feet, and every time you need more, just wave up," he says. "It's a landscape that witnesses what is underneath it."

The other big idea behind the roof—that it should be a habitat for native California plants, birds, and insects—developed more slowly, as Piano's team worked with botanists from the museum. The planted roof is not just a wildlife corridor; it also insulates the building, reducing energy consumption, and absorbs 98 percent of storm-water runoff. Meanwhile, Piano's "waves" mean that most of the building doesn't need air-conditioning: cool air from outside flows down the hills and into the building's central piazza, while hot air on the exhibit floor rises, hugging the planetarium and rain forest, and is released through automated sky-lights in the hills.

The building's sustainable features are so deeply embedded in its design that it's hard to tell where the aesthetic concept ends and the green design begins. Ironically, Piano was not known as a green architect at the time of his selection. Late in the design process, when the Academy hired the Rocky Mountain Institute to find out how much the green features would cost, it found out that Piano's design was just two points away from a LEED Platinum rating. Neither Piano nor the Academy had heard much about the U.S. Green Building Council's LEED program. They had worked not from a checklist but from a total dedication to the value of sustainability to the Academy's mission. "We decided that we would look everywhere to be green," Kociolek says. "Whether it was the planetarium, the aquarium, or the office furniture. There were no sacred cows."

This attitude—that even in a 155-year-old scientific institution nothing is sacred—may be what has allowed the Academy to make its great leap so gracefully. The old museum was made up of 11 separate buildings constructed during different eras. Now, one building integrates everything that the Academy is and does. The aquarium, planetarium, and natural history museum are no longer separate silos—there are live penguins alongside the dioramas and a coral reef surrounding the planetarium. A working lab with floor-to-ceiling windows reveals the research process to the public; scientists will even come out from behind the glass occasionally to present their work to groups of museumgoers. And, whether they are walking the exhibit floor or enjoying the view from the roof's observation deck, visitors can see and experience the park around them, reminding them—should they need reminding—of that great, green natural-science exhibit outside the Academy's walls.

GILES WORSLEY

Giles Worsley was born in 1961. After completing his Ph.D. in architectural history at the Courtauld Institute in London, Worsley worked as a writer and editor at *Country Life* magazine and as editor of the journal *Perspectives on Architecture*. In 1995 he published the seminal *Classical Architecture in Britain: The Heroic Age*, on British architecture of the seventeenth and eighteenth centuries. The author of several other books and monographs on architectural history, Worsley was architectural correspondent for the London *Daily Telegraph* from 1998 until his death in 2006.

• •

"How to Build the New World" explores the role of computer-aided design in the architecture of Frank Gehry. Worsley finds the origins of Gehry's aesthetic of chaos in the streetscapes of Los Angeles.

HOW TO BUILD THE NEW WORLD

IT WAS THE AGNOLETTI that got me worrying. They were beautifully presented on the plate, little parcels of pasta wrapping a smoked ham, ricotta mix, each individual agnoletto gently curving and undulating. But I could not help wondering what they would look like blown up a thousand times and turned into a building, a concert hall, perhaps, or an art gallery? If so, how would they differ from a building by Frank Gehry, and did that matter?

I had spent the morning in the office of the most celebrated and unconventional architect of our age, looking at the way his designs grew from tiny scrumpled balls of paper no larger than my plate of agnoletti into enormous models that were then fed into a computer to become curving, undulating buildings such as the Guggenheim Museum in Bilbao. I had also had a disjointed hour with Gehry himself. But as I sat in the restaurant in Santa Monica, mulling over the day, I was beginning to wonder whether coming to California was going to unravel the enigma of Gehry's architecture as I had hoped.

Gehry's Guggenheim Museum, which opened in 1997, was received with rare acclaim. Only the Sydney Opera House and Richard Rogers's

Pompidou Centre rival it for instant fame, and both are seen by many as flawed. Of the Guggenheim, however, it is hard to hear a bad word. The professional press drooled over it. Architects of the distinction and discrimination of Philip Johnson and Jacques Herzog (who, with Pierre de Meuron, is responsible for the new Tate Modern) celebrated it. And even the most reactionary of my friends, people you could usually rely on to dismiss any modern building, sang its praises.

But instant universal acclaim is not always proof of great architecture. Visiting the Guggenheim left me with nagging doubts about the strength and clarity of Gehry's vision. I worried that his work had a hollow heart, worries that led me to Los Angeles, the city where Gehry works and which holds the key to his aesthetic.

The Toronto-born architect changed his surname from Goldberg and settled there as a young man. "I grew up in stodgy Canadian country," he says, "and I moved here in 1947. I worked as a truck driver. We were very poor. I was 17; I did night schools. I didn't know what I wanted to be. I'd take art classes, then I'd drive. I was trained as a regular architect; you did what the client asked you to do."

Gehry [...] is short and round, with a podgy face and glasses, dressed in faded grey cords and a blue shirt. His office lies at the centre of the unpretentious converted building that houses his practice. It is a room he created himself, with lots of light from high-level windows, some enormous armchairs he designed out of cardboard—surprisingly comfortable if a little scratchy—an array of models and walls covered with laser copies of pictures, a Bellini Madonna and child, a Richard Serra sculpture, a Bosch of Christ taunted by grotesque-looking soldiers, a gentle Vermeer of an architect leaning over his desk, the charioteer from Delphi…

Their importance soon becomes clear: Gehry finds inspiration in the forms which he finds within these works. "I saw that Bosch in the Sainsbury Wing of the National Gallery. I liked it because it had a floor plan. It's a spatial organisation. Painting has been the wellspring of most of my work."

He speaks of painters with reverence: "I place painting on a very high level. It's still a kind of Mount Everest. I'd never go there. I'd never dare pick up a brush." But, interestingly, the painters he talks about, or has on his walls, are nearly all long dead.

Of painters he likes today, the only one he mentions is Ellsworth Kelly. Most of his close artistic collaborations have been with sculptors—particularly Richard Serra and Claes Oldenburg (who designed the enormous binoculars which form part of his Chiat-Day Headquarters in Venice, California)—not painters.

The same is true of architecture. Romanesque buildings and south German Baroque churches fascinate him and so do early Modern buildings. "I look at old buildings, at Erich Mendelsohn's Einstein Tower [Potsdam, 1917-21]. I speculate that if Mendelsohn were still alive today he would have done all the things I've done and I would have had to go somewhere else. Can you imagine Corbusier with a computer?" But current buildings are much less important.

Asked whether he is aware of other architects' work, he replies, "I guess in my peripheral vision. I don't go very far just to see it. I did go to Holland and made a special point to see some of Rem [Koolhaas]'s work. I made a point of going to see Danny [Libeskind]'s Jewish Museum in Berlin. I liked it a lot. I did make a point of going to see Herzog's early work because I wanted to see where he came from. I loved it, although his relentless minimalism is bothersome."

If Gehry has little time for contemporary architects, he has even less for architectural critics who try to theorize about his works: "You guys think there's all this philosophical background. There's none of that."

His key early buildings are in Los Angeles. It was Gehry's own house in Santa Monica in 1977 that first drew international attention. A conventional two-storey house in a quiet suburban street, he tore it apart, retaining the core of the old house but adding an array of corrugated iron walls, harshly angled windows and chain-link fencing.

With its prominently positioned sign "Security. Armed Response," the first reaction of someone coming from England, schooled in a hundred films about violent Los Angeles, is that this building, which resembles nothing so much as a heavily fortified police station in Northern Ireland, is a reaction to urban chaos. But looking around at the soporific streets it is clear this is an architectural statement, not a reaction to context.

It was this interest in cheap materials, chain-link fencing, corrugated iron, roughly finished timber and exploded buildings for which Gehry was initially known. There is a rawness to buildings such as his Spiller Residence in Venice, California, that works well in aggressively urban settings; a sense of transience, of materials and images caught up from the street and turned into architecture, of chaos only just contained. It is an architecture particularly suited to Los Angeles, but it seems at first sight to have little to do with the Gehry who has sprung to international stardom, whose buildings are marked not by urban aggression but by the sensuality of their shapes and materials.

From the controlled chaos of these earlier works, Gehry moved towards an interest in breaking buildings down into individual, sculptural elements, as in the Schnabel House in Brentwood, California. At the time he was inspired by the still-life paintings of the early 20th-century artist Giorgio Morandi. But increasingly he was trying to capture a sense of movement in his buildings. The work of another early 20th-century artist, Marcel Duchamp, was an influence, and so was a remarkable 10th-century Indian sculpture of Shiva as the Lord of Dance, owned by the great art collector Norton Simon, for whom Gehry designed a beach house in Malibu.

Until then Gehry's architecture had been rigorously angular, but a fascination with the image of the fish changed this. "The fish was my attack on Post-Modernism," Gehry explains. "Post-Modernism or the regurgitation of Greek temples is anthropomorphic and I said if you're going to go back, fish were here 300 million years before man so why not use fish [as a model for architecture]? That's what I said in anger. Then I started drawing the damn thing and I realised something I was looking for…It was movement in an inert medium."

Gehry's first use of the fish, at the Fishdance restaurant in Kobe, Japan, took the metaphor literally, but it was swiftly abstracted until only the essence of the curve remained. Equally important was Gehry's fascination with metal as a material: "Metal can be a wall and a roof…It allows me a lot of freedom of shape."

At the Vitra Furniture Museum on the German-Swiss border, Gehry took this interest in metal and his fascination with complex shapes and curves to create a building of great visual complexity. But he was not happy with the result. "You see that bump?" He points at a photograph of the building and at a kink in one of the curves. "That really pissed me off. I said to my guys here, 'We've got to figure out how to do that; why we got into trouble.' So that led us to the computer."

It was computers that transformed Gehry's architecture. Using a complex program called CATIA, made by the French company Dassault for designing aircraft, Gehry was able to achieve the results he sought. Computers mean that, however complex, the curves in his buildings can be accurately calculated and then fed directly to the cutting machines in steel foundries. The result is the structural complexity of Bilbao.

The process becomes clear on a tour round the office. Models are the key to Gehry's design process. Where most architects of his generation express themselves in drawing, Gehry's drawings are surprisingly crude, almost cartoonish scribbles. Instead, Gehry works out his designs in models. Simple rectangular blocks are used to work out the uses of the different spaces and their relation to each other.

With the overall massing agreed, Gehry starts ripping up paper and sticking it over the models. Once a rough design has been reached, assistants turn it into a proper model, which Gehry alters again and again until the design is finalized. The last model is scanned into the computer and transformed into construction drawings. A big project, such as the large complex Gehry has just designed for MIT in Boston, will generate 250 to 300 models.

Computers have freed Gehry of virtually all constraints in designing and constructing his buildings, and therein lies the excitement of his architecture but also the problem that lies at its core. The results are bravura buildings, and it is undoubtedly that which has caught the imagination of a public fed on a diet of dour, often incomprehensible, modernism. But in the end, is Bilbao any more than sensual space-making, origami fed into a computer and turned into solid form?

Indeed, is it any more than what the design process suggests, square boxes wrapped up with a fancy decorative cladding? One of the most disturbing realisations on visiting Bilbao is that behind the curved elevation, familiar from photographs, are boringly rectangular boxes housing the practical side of the museum.

The technology is far more advanced, but in the end is there any real difference between Gehry and the Viennese architect Friedensreich Hundertwasser, who died earlier this year, who thought the answer to modernism's problems was to make every building curved and colorful? Just because the technology is now available to make every line in a building curved, does that mean the building is better because they are? Bilbao compels because it is so unexpected. Gehry's office projects in Prague and Dusseldorf simply look mannered.

Perhaps in the end Gehry can only be understood in the context of Los Angeles. The grungy street-feel and cheap materials of his early buildings may have gone, but what seems to drive his current buildings is the same sense of a quest for an architecture of transience, movement, impermanence. Gehry was once quoted as saying that "Palladio faced a fork in the road, and he took the wrong turn. He should have recognized that there's chaos. He should have gone ahead and done what Borromini did. He would have been a pioneer."

That quotation reveals an alienation from everything that defines Western architecture. Perhaps it is not that surprising a statement from the Los Angeles architect, for whom there can be no sense of permanence or connection or order.

PAUL GOLDBERGER

Born in Passaic, New Jersey, in 1950, Paul Goldberger writes the "Sky Line" column on architecture for *The New Yorker*. In 1984 he won the Pulitzer Prize for his architecture criticism in the *New York Times*. He has won numerous other awards, including the medal of the American Institute of Architects and a Preservation Achievement Award from the New York City Landmarks Preservation Commission. Among his books are *The City Observed: New York*; *The Skyscraper*; *Up from Zero*; and *Why Architecture Matters*. Paul Goldberger lives in New York City.

• •

In "Good Vibrations," Goldberger celebrates the virtues of Frank Gehry's design for the Walt Disney Concert Hall in downtown Los Angeles. The following selection, "Sanctum on the Coast," examines the impact of Los Angeles's new Catholic cathedral on its neighborhood and city.

GOOD VIBRATIONS

FRANK GEHRY IS one of the most famous architects in the world, and the Walt Disney Concert Hall is the most important thing he has built in his home city of Los Angeles—or anywhere else in the United States, for that matter—so of course people are complaining about it. It looks like Gehry's other buildings. It's too showy. It doesn't contribute enough to the downtown L.A. environment and doesn't justify the $274 million (much of it from private funds) that it cost. These are inevitable, although probably not very significant, views. The building, which opens on October 23rd with a concert by the Los Angeles Philharmonic, has already received the kind of adulatory advance press usually reserved for blockbuster movies. In early September, however, a reporter for the *Los Angeles Times*, Scott Timberg, observed—in a piece that consisted of negative comments about the building—that "a distinct rumble of Disney Hall disenchantment has become audible." A few days later, another writer in the *Times* remarked that the hall looked like "half-torn-up cardboard boxes left out in the rain, spray-painted silver."

There are those who will never respond to Gehry's work—who feel that his intensely romantic, emotional forms are self-indulgent—and those people are missing an architectural experience of immense power and subtlety. There are also people who admire Gehry's Guggenheim Museum in Bilbao, with its swirling mass of titanium cladding, but who think that the Disney building looks too much like Bilbao's second cousin, and like Gehry's performing-arts center at Bard College, and his new business school in Cleveland. These are superficial comparisons. The façade of Disney Hall is more refined than that of the Guggenheim, and more sumptuous, even though it is made of stainless steel, a cheaper material than titanium. Gehry has not repeated himself here so much as he has expanded his architectural vocabulary. Most of Gehry's recent buildings have swooping metal forms, but their shapes are different, their proportions are different, and their relationship to their surroundings is different. Disney and Bilbao are no more similar than buildings designed a few years apart by Mies van der Rohe, or Le Corbusier.

It is ironic that Gehry is being criticized for not producing a building that will transform a dreary, lifeless downtown area, since that is what he did more successfully than any other living architect when he designed the Guggenheim in Bilbao. (The phenomenon is even referred to generally as "the Bilbao effect.") He made the first truly popular piece of avant-garde architecture in our time, and suddenly everybody else wanted one, including his own city, where he had not received a major commission until 1988, when he won a competition to design the new hall for the Los Angeles Philharmonic. Construction began a few years later but was stalled because of fund-raising problems and issues of design control, and the project ground to a halt in 1994. When the museum in Bilbao opened, in 1997, and Gehry became a household word, the largely unbuilt concert hall (it hadn't got past the foundation and the underground garage) became a major source of embarrassment: Gehry, who is now seventy-four, had lived in Los Angeles since the nineteen-forties, and the city still couldn't get a big Gehry project going. Several civic leaders joined together to resuscitate the building, Gehry updated his designs, and construction resumed in 1999.

Downtown Los Angeles has only a handful of singular pieces of architecture—Bertram Grosvenor Goodhue's Central Library of 1926, Arata Isozaki's Museum of Contemporary Art of 1986, and Rafael Moneo's Cathedral of Our Lady of the Angels, finished last year—and Disney Hall is now surely the most distinguished building in the area. It is, indeed, monumental, but it isn't fair to say that it doesn't respond to its urban context, which is, more or less, like the downtowns of many other major American cities—a lot of glass skyscrapers surrounded by a lot of freeways. Disney Hall is set on Grand Avenue, a boulevard almost as wide as a freeway, and the site has a steep grade, making it even more unfriendly to pedestrians. Still, the building has a large public garden, and the gracious, flowing staircase at the formal entrance on the corner of Grand Avenue and First Street is far more inviting than any entry to the tired old Dorothy Chandler Pavilion—the Philharmonic's former home—across the street. Gehry has placed the exhilarating stainless-steel sails that define the exterior atop a limestone base, but on the Grand Avenue façade the limestone disappears in favor of hinged glass panels that will open the building up to the street before concerts.

The outside of Disney Hall lifts the spirits of those who see it from the sidewalk or, this being Los Angeles, from the windows of their cars, and the inside is equally inspiring. The auditorium is the finest interior Gehry has ever made. It is constructed of warm Douglas fir and is relatively intimate, with only about twenty-two hundred seats, spread over terraces, balconies, and mezzanines on all sides of the stage. The hall is set within a two-layered plaster box that forms an acoustical shell and soundproofing. Gehry developed its shape with Yasuhisa Toyota, a partner in Nagata Acoustics of Tokyo, who was also his partner at Bard. The focal point, above the stage, is an enormous pipe organ whose wooden pipe enclosures create a sculpture that looks like a stack of lumber that has just exploded. The ceiling seems to be made of fabric rather than of wood, a gargantuan version of the canopy on a fourposter bed. It billows over the hall. The curved wooden walls do not meet the ceiling, and in the space between them one can glimpse white plaster walls behind the wooden forms, washed with light from hidden skylights. The hall appears to float in the larger space.

The shape of the hall and its warm, rich wood suggest a musical instrument, although I doubt that Gehry thinks in such literal terms. He is an expressionist—a romantic expressionist—who has always designed by instinct (even though he could not produce his astonishingly complex buildings without the aid of the most sophisticated computer software, a program called CATIA, used for the construction of aircraft), and what he did here was create a space that is not only acoustically suitable for listening to music but emotionally right for it.

Gehry has, clearly, studied the Berlin Philharmonie hall, which was designed in the nineteen-fifties by the German Expressionist architect Hans Scharoun. Scharoun created the first modern symphony hall in the round, an asymmetrical space with dozens of jutting terraces. It is an exciting place in which to hear an orchestra—and, until now, the only convincing new model for a concert hall—but it appears almost crude in comparison to Disney Hall. One of the best things about Scharoun's building, besides its intense, kinetic energy, is how democratic it is, and Gehry has picked up on this. There are no fancy boxes in the Disney auditorium. I moved around from the front of the orchestra to the side terraces, the mezzanines, and the balconies while listening to a rehearsal of a Mahler symphony, and I could not decide where I would rather sit. There is no obvious hierarchy, and, indeed, the upper-level seats offer a benefit that the seats closest to the musicians do not—the special pleasure of being able to take in the whole of Gehry's space.

The hall was endowed with a fifty-million-dollar gift from Lillian Disney, Walt Disney's widow. Mrs. Disney, who died in 1997, was not, initially, much of a fan of Gehry's architecture, but she was an unusual philanthropist. She didn't insist that her checkbook buy her veto power, although she did tell Gehry that she loved gardens, and he designed the bright carpet and the fabric on the seats in the hall in an intense, abstract version of a floral pattern in tribute to her. Mrs. Disney collected Delft china, and Gehry also designed a witty fountain for the outdoor plaza, a mosaic of pieces of smashed Delft.

Culture can be a potent redevelopment tool. We saw that long ago at Lincoln Center, and it is why great hopes have been placed on the role of cultural facilities at Ground Zero. But the Los Angeles Music Center has sat across the street from the site of Disney Hall for nearly forty years with almost no noticeable effect on the nearby area. It may be that restaurants, stores, and housing will rise up around Disney Hall and transform the neighborhood into the urban mecca that so many people seek, but I wouldn't bet on it, and it doesn't matter. Disney Hall is something rarer than a great urban street. It is a serene, ennobling building that will give people in this city of private places a new sense of the pleasures of public space.

SANCTUM ON THE COAST

I T IS HARD to make a landmark in Los Angeles. The city is relentlessly horizontal, and while you might think that a skyscraper would be memorable, it doesn't work that way in L.A. Big, boxy buildings stay in your line of vision longer, which is something that Rafael Moneo must have kept in mind when he was designing the new Our Lady of the Angels cathedral. It is one of the largest religious buildings constructed in the center of an American city in half a century, and one of the most ambitious. The cathedral will inevitably be compared with Frank Gehry's Walt Disney Concert Hall, which is to be finished next year. They are both eye-grabbing structures designed by famous architects and they are just a couple of blocks away from each other in downtown Los Angeles. But the new cathedral has more in common with the familiar Los Angeles megabox. It's a big, horizontal mass, like the Beverly Center, the vast shopping mall built atop a parking structure; and the Pacific Design Center, a beached whale in blue glass; and the factorylike Cedars-Sinai Medical Center. I don't say this to be disrespectful. I think Moneo has tried to take a particular kind of Los Angeles building and make it into something spiritual, although it's not a natural leap. Gehry's swooping forms are more conventionally cathedral-like. If you asked a visitor which of the new buildings was the cathedral and which was the concert hall, he would probably get it wrong.

Moneo, a sixty-five-year-old architect who is based in Madrid but has spent much of his career in the United States, is a designer of exceptional thoughtfulness and precision. Even though he almost always works in masonry, his buildings have a certain delicacy. He isn't known for dazzling new forms, but he doesn't copy the past, either. He is a modernist who strives for timelessness, and he is most comfortable working within the vocabulary that he learned when he came of age in the nineteen-sixties and seventies: crisp, hard-edged, geometric. What distinguishes Moneo is his continual push to make this kind of architecture easier on the eye, and on the psyche. His work resembles, in a way, the style called brutalism, but in Moneo's hands it isn't harsh and cold. It's gentle brutalism.

The cathedral is a three-hundred-and-thirty-three-foot-long, ninety-five-foot-high origami of warm, adobe-colored concrete, which is right for a place whose first churches were Spanish missions. The shape recalls one of those performing-arts centers that were built on college campuses in the nineteen-sixties, or a suburban church, blown up to monumental scale and produced on an exquisitely refined level.

Is that enough for a cathedral? The concrete is quite beautiful, although it may have been a mistake to set concrete panels on some sections of the building in such a way that they look like gargantuan pieces of aluminum siding. And the subordinate structures, including the cardinal's residence and the parish offices, are clad in stucco and look like ordinary commercial buildings in the San Fernando Valley. If anything about the exterior stirs the emotions, it is a two-and-a-half-acre plaza, which manages to be a true public place. The plaza has a gift shop, a café with white market umbrellas and colorful Philippe Starck plastic chairs, and an escalator that goes down to the cathedral's pricey underground parking garage. At the far end of the plaza, a wall with glass panels overlooks the Hollywood Freeway, a quirky gesture that is rather endearing. Moneo likes to compare the freeway to a river, and, with the glass wall, he figured out a way to muffle its roar.

The plaza was filled with people when I was there, many of Hispanic descent (the city's eastern neighborhoods, near downtown, are heavily Hispanic), and they were doing the kinds of urban things people so rarely do in Los Angeles—like walking around. When the Getty Center, with its immense travertine piazza, opened a few years ago in Brentwood, the haute bourgeoisie of Los Angeles got a chance to be urban pedestrians, and the cathedral is giving others the same opportunity. It's the poor man's Getty, which is not an insignificant achievement.

The architecture gets better inside the cathedral. Moneo plays with the past and is genuinely inventive at the same time. His best touch is both an homage to the traditional Gothic cathedral and a subtle, brilliant inversion of it. He has laid out the cathedral in a fairly standard way—there is a cruciform-shaped nave in the center, flanked by long, enclosed ambulatories containing several small chapels. But he placed the façade at the same end of the building as the altar, which makes for an unusual entry sequence. You don't enter the building directly into the nave, as in a traditional cathedral. A pair of somewhat pompous bronze doors designed by the sculptor Robert Graham on the left side of the façade bring you into the south ambulatory, which is a long, sloping corridor that narrows slightly as you move forward, like diminishing perspective. The ambulatory is not an open arcade, as in a Gothic cathedral, and it is largely cut off from the nave by walls. As you walk along, you occasionally glimpse the nave to your right, and, while it is possible to turn and enter the larger space, you are encouraged to keep walking to the end, at which point you turn right and enter the nave from the far end of the cathedral, facing the altar—the spot in a conventional cathedral that you would have entered in the first place.

This is great processional architecture. The dramatic experience of moving through the building has been enhanced and extended, and when you finally enter the nave it is almost worth the buildup. Moneo has made a sumptuous modern space, angled and asymmetrical but calming. It is the same adobe color as the exterior, and there is soft, even light from huge alabaster windows. Crisply modern rooms with no right angles are rarely this serene. It is the light, which appears almost to waft over the concrete, that does it. Moneo rejected stained glass as too traditional, and the Archdiocese of Los Angeles rejected it as too expensive. An astonishing twenty-seven thousand square feet of Spanish alabaster was used, but, except for certain areas in which it provides a dramatic accent (as a backdrop for a huge concrete crucifix over the altar, for instance), it is invisible. There are some wrong moves: fussy hanging chandeliers that look a little too much like the glowing-globe fixtures that were popular in modern buildings in the nineteen-sixties, and a lot of earnest, dreary representational art. Moneo had hoped to commission pieces from distinguished abstractionists like Agnes Martin and Martin Puryear, but Cardinal Roger Mahony said he wanted art that his parishioners would easily understand.

I wonder if the Cardinal didn't sell his flock short. Still, you have to take Mahony seriously as a great patron. His predecessors had been trying to build a new cathedral for nearly a century, and he got the job done in less than eight years. The genesis of the project was the Northridge earthquake in 1994, which caused structural damage to the old cathedral, St. Vibiana's, a far too small Spanish-style church near a Latino shopping district deeper in the heart of downtown. The Cardinal wanted to build on the site of St. Vibiana's, but when preservationists took the archdiocese to court, he wasted no time acquiring the much bigger site, and then sold the old church to a developer, who is converting it into a performing-arts center. The new cathedral project cost something close to two hundred million dollars, most of which came from private sources, although that didn't stop a local alternative newspaper from calling it the Taj Mahony.

I didn't sense that the parishioners saw it that way. Indeed, they seemed to have a certain pride of ownership, which is remarkable, considering how different the cathedral is from what they are accustomed to. Moneo manages to stir up a substantial degree of emotion in a giant space, which isn't easy to do. Most big things built today are secular—convention centers, sports arenas, and the like. Few really large religious buildings have been constructed in this country in the last few years, and most of them have been fundamentalist churches in the South and the Midwest that, however meaningful they may be to their congregations, seem to me spiritually akin to shopping malls. Moneo says that the modern religious buildings he likes are small—Le Corbusier's chapel at Ronchamp in eastern France, the even smaller Matisse chapel on the Côte d'Azur. In Los Angeles, he has made a valiant effort to render sacred space on a large scale, and he has done it without tricks or gimmicks.

WILLIAM GIBSON

Born in South Carolina in 1948, William Gibson is the author of *Neuromancer*, which won the Hugo, Nebula, and Philip K. Dick Awards for science fiction and in which the word "cyberspace" first appeared. He is also the author of the novels *All Tomorrow's Parties*, *Pattern Recognition*, *Count Zero*, and *Spook Country*, along with numerous short stories. The literary virtuosity of Gibson's insights into the future of technology and society has earned him the title "father of cyberpunk." William Gibson lives in Vancouver, British Columbia.

• •

The apocalyptic story "Skinner's Room" depicts the condition of a San Francisco bridge that has become a place of mass refuge from unspecified catastrophes.

SKINNER'S ROOM

I T'S HALLOWEEN AND she's found her way up into this old hotel over Geary, Tenderloin's cannibal fringe down one side and the gray shells of big stores off the other; pressing her cheek to cold glass now to spy the bridge's nearest tower—Skinner's room is there—lit with torches and carnival bulbs, far away, but still it reassures her, in here with these foreigners who've done too much of something and now one of them's making noises in the bathroom.

Someone touches her, cold finger on bare skin above the waistband of her jeans, sliding it in under her sweater and the hem of Skinner's jacket; not the touch that makes her jump so much as the abrupt awareness of how hot she is, a greenhouse sweat, zipped up behind the unbreathing horsehide of the ancient jacket, its seams and elbows sueded pale with wear, a jingle of hardware as she swings around—D-rings, zip-pulls, five-pointed stars—her thumbtip against the hole in the knife's blade, opening it, locked, ready. The blade's no longer than her little finger, shaped something like the head of a bird, its eye the hole that gives the thumb purchase. Blade and handle are brushed stainless, like the heavy clip, with its three precise machine screws, that secures it firmly to boot-top, belt, or wristband. Old, maybe older than the jacket. Japanese, Skinner says. SPYDERCO stamped above an edge of serrated razor.

The man—boy, really—blinks at her. He hasn't seen the blade, but he's felt its meaning, her deep body-verb, and his hand withdraws. He steps back unsteadily, grinning wetly and dunking the sodden end of a small cigar in a stemmed glass of some pharmaceutically clear liquid.

"I am celebrating," he says, and draws on the cigar.

"Halloween?"

It's not a noun he remembers at the moment. He just looks at her like she isn't there, then blows a blue stream of smoke up at the suite's high ceiling. Lowers the cigar. Licks his lips.

"I am living now," he says, "in this hotel, one hundred fifty days." His jacket is leather, too, but not like Skinner's. Some thin-skinned animal whose hide drapes like heavy silk, the color of tobacco. She remembers the tattered yellow wall of magazines in Skinner's room, some so old the pictures are only shades of gray, the way the city looks sometimes from the bridge. Could she find that animal there?

"This is a fine hotel." He dips the wet green end of the cigar into the glass again.

She thumbs the blade-release and closes the knife against her thigh. He blinks at the click. He's having trouble focusing. "One hundred. Fifty days."

Behind him, she sees that the others have tumbled together on the huge bed. Leather, lace, smooth pale skin. The noises from the bathroom are getting worse, but nobody seems to hear. She shivers in the jungle heat of Skinner's jacket. Slips the knife back up under her belt. She's come up here for whatever she can find, really, but what she's found is a hard desperation, a lameness of spirit, that twists her up inside, so maybe that's why she's sweating so, steaming....

Saw them all come laughing, drunk, out of two cabs; she fell into step on impulse, her dusty black horsehide fading into the glossier blacks of silk hose, leather skirts, boots with jingling spurs like jewelry, furs. Sweeping past the doormen's braided coats, their stunners, gas masks— into the tall marble lobby with its carpet and mirrors and waxed furniture, its bronze-doored elevators and urns of sand.

"One hundred fifty days," he says, and sways, lips slack and moist. "In this hotel."

She's out of here.

The bridge maintains the integrity of its span within a riot of secondary construction, a coral growth facilitated in large part by carbon-fiber compounds. Some sections of the original structure, badly rusted, have been coated with a transparent material whose tensile strength far exceeds that of the original steel; some are splined with the black and impervious carbon fiber; others are laced with makeshift ligatures of taut and rusting wire.

Secondary construction has occurred piecemeal, to no set plan, employing every imaginable technique and material; the result is amorphous and startlingly organic in appearance.

At night, illuminated by Christmas bulbs, by recycled neon, by torchlight, the bridge is a magnet for the restless, the disaffected. By day, viewed from the towers of the city, it recalls the ruin of Brighton Pier in the closing decade of the previous century—seen through some cracked kaleidoscope of vernacular style.

Lately Skinner's hip can't manage the first twenty feet of ladder, so he hasn't been down to try the new elevator the African has welded to the rivet-studded steel of the tower, but he's peered at it through the hatch in the floor. It looks like the yellow plastic basket of a lineman's cherrypicker, cogging its way up and down a greasy-toothed steel track like a miniature Swiss train, motor bolted beneath the floor of the basket. Skinner's not sure where the tower's getting its juice these days, but the lightbulb slung beside his bed dims and pulses whenever he hears that motor whine.

He admires people who build things, who add to the structure. He admires whoever it was built this room, this caulked box of ten-ply fir, perched and humming in the wind. The room's floor is a double layer of pressure-treated two-by-fours laid on edge, broken by an achingly graceful form Skinner no longer really sees: the curve of the big cable drawn up over its saddle of steel. 17,464 pencil-thick wires.

The little pop-up television on the blanket across his chest continues its dumb-show. The girl brought it for him. Stolen, probably. He never turns the sound on. The constant play of images on the liquid crystal screen is obscurely comforting, like the half-sensed movements in an aquarium: life is there. The images themselves are of no interest. He can't remember when he ceased to be able to distinguish commercials from programming. The distinction itself may no longer exist.

His room measures fifteen by fifteen feet, the plywood walls softened by perhaps a dozen coats of white latex paint. Higher reflective index than aluminum foil, he thinks. 17,464 strands per cable. Facts. Often, now, he feels himself a void through which facts tumble, facts and faces, making no connection.

His clothes hang from mismatched antique coat-hooks screwed at precise intervals along one wall. The girl's taken his jacket. Lewis Leathers. Great Portland Street. Where is that? Jacket older than she is. Looks at the pictures in *National Geographic,* crouched there with her bare white feet on the carpet he took from the broken office block in…Oakland?

Memory flickers like the liquid crystal. She brings him food. Pumps the Coleman's chipped red tank. Remember to open the window a crack. Japanese cans, heat up when you pull a tab. Questions she asks him. Who built the bridge? Everyone. No, she says, the old part, the bridge. San Francisco, he tells her. Bone of iron, grace of cable, hangs us here. How long you live here? Years. Spoons him his meal from a mess kit stamped 1952.

This is his room. His bed. Foam, topped with a sheepskin, bottom sheet over that. Blankets. Catalytic heater. Remember to open the window a crack.

The window is circular, leaded, each segment stained a different color. You can see the city through the bull's-eye of clear yellow glass at its center.

Sometimes he remembers building the room himself.

The bridge's bones, its stranded tendons, are lost within an accretion of dreams: tattoo parlors, shooting galleries, pinball arcades, dimly lit stalls stacked with damp-stained years of men's magazines, chili joints, premises of unlicensed denturists, fireworks stalls, cut bait sellers, betting shops, sushi bars, purveyors of sexual appliances, pawnbrokers, wonton counters, love hotels, hotdog stands, a tortilla factory, Chinese green-grocers, liquor stores, herbalists, chiropractors, barbers, tackle shops, and bars.

These are dreams of commerce, their locations generally corresponding to the decks originally intended for vehicular traffic. Above them, rising toward the peaks of the cable towers, lift intricate barrios, zones of more private fantasy, sheltering an unnumbered population of uncertain means and obscure occupation.

Sagging platforms of slivered wood are slung beneath the bridge's lower deck; from these, on a clear day, old men lower fishing lines. Gulls wheel and squabble over shreds of discarded bait.

The encounter in the old hotel confirms something for her. She prefers the bridge to the city.

She first came upon the bridge in fog, saw the sellers of fruits and vegetables with their goods spread out on blankets, lit by carbide lamps and guttering smudge pots. Farm people from up the coast. She'd come from that direction herself, down past the stunted pines of Little River and Mendocino, Ukiah's twisted oak hills.

She stared back into the cavern mouth, trying to make sense of what she saw. Steam rising from the pots of soup vendors' carts. Neon scavenged from the ruins of Oakland. How it ran together, blurred, melting in the fog. Surfaces of plywood, marble, corrugated plastic, polished brass, sequins, Styrofoam, tropical hardwoods, mirror, etched Victorian glass, chrome gone dull in the sea air—all the mad richness of it, its randomness—a tunnel roofed by a precarious shack town mountainside climbing toward the first of the cable towers.

She'd stood a long time, looking, and then she'd walked straight in, past a boy selling coverless yellowed paperbacks and a café where a blind old parrot sat chained on a metal perch, picking at a chicken's freshly severed foot.

Skinner surfaces from a dream of a bicycle covered with barnacles and sees that the girl is back. She's hung his leather jacket on its proper hook and squats now on her pallet of raw-edged black foam.

Bicycle. Barnacles.

Memory: a man called Fass snagged his tackle, hauled the bicycle up, trailing streamers of kelp. People laughing. Fass carried the bicycle away. Later he built a place to eat, a three-stool shanty leached far out over the void with superglue and shackles. He sold cold cooked mussels and Mexican beer. The bicycle hung above the little bar. The walls were covered with layers of picture postcards. Nights he slept curled behind the bar. One morning the place was gone, Fass with it, just a broken shackle swinging in the wind and a few splinters of timber still adhering to the galvanized iron wall of a barber shop. People came, stood at the edge, looked down at the water between the toes of their shoes.

The girl asks him if he's hungry. He says no. Asks him if he's eaten. He says no. She opens the tin food chest and sorts through cans. He watches her pump the Coleman. He says open the window a crack. The circular window pivots in its oak frame. You gotta eat, she says.

She'd like to tell the old man about going to the hotel, but she doesn't have words for how it made her feel. She feeds him soup, a spoonful at a time. Helps him to the tankless old china toilet behind the faded roses of the chintz curtain. When he's done she draws water from the roof-tank line and pours it in. Gravity does the rest. Thousands of flexible transparent lines are looped and bundled, down through the structure, pouring raw sewage into the Bay.

"Europe…" she tries to begin.

He looks up at her, mouth full of soup. She guesses his hair must've been blond once. He swallows the soup. "Europe what?" Sometimes he'll snap right into focus like this if she asks him a question, but now she's not sure what the question is.

"Paris," he says, and his eyes tell her he's lost again, "I went there. London, too. Great Portland Street." He nods, satisfied somehow. "Before the first devaluation…."

Wind sighs past the window.

She thinks about climbing out on the roof. The rungs up to the hatch there are carved out of sections of two-by-four, painted the same white as the walls. He uses one for a towel rack. Undo the bolt. You raise the hatch with your head; your eyes are level with gull shit. Nothing there, really. Flat tarpaper roof, a couple of two-by-four uprights; one flies a tattered Confederate flag, the other a faded orange windsock. Thinking about it, she loses interest.

When he's asleep again, she closes the Coleman, scrubs out the pot, washes the spoon, pours the soupy water down the toilet, wipes pot and spoon, puts them away. Pulls on her hightop sneakers, laces them up. She puts on his jacket and checks that the knife's still clipped behind her belt.

She lifts the hatch in the floor and climbs through, finding the first rungs of the ladder with her feet. She lowers the hatch closed, careful not to wake Skinner. She climbs down past the riveted face of the tower, to the waiting yellow basket of the elevator. Looking up, she sees the vast cable there, where it swoops out of the bottom of Skinner's room, vanishing through a taut and glowing wall of milky plastic film, a greenhouse; halogen bulbs throw spiky plant shadows on the plastic.

The elevator whines, creeping down the face of the tower, beside the ladder she doesn't use anymore, past a patchwork of plastic, plywood, sections of enameled steel stitched together from the skins of dead refrigerators. At the bottom of the fat-toothed track, she climbs out. She sees the man Skinner calls the African coming toward her along the catwalk, bearlike shoulders hunched in a ragged tweed overcoat. He carries a meter of some kind, a black box, dangling red and black wires tipped with alligator clips. The broken plastic frames of his glasses have been mended with silver duct tape. He smiles shyly as he edges past her, muttering something about brushes.

She rides another elevator, a bare steel cage, down to the first deck. She walks in the direction of Oakland, past racks of secondhand clothing and blankets spread with the negotiable detritus of the city. Someone is frying pork. She walks on, into the fluorescent chartreuse glare.

She meets a woman named Maria Paz.

She's always meeting people on the bridge, but only people who live here. The tourists, mostly, are scared. They don't want to talk. Nervous, you can tell by their eyes, how they walk.

She goes with Maria Paz to a coffee shop with windows on the Bay and a gray dawn. The coffee shop has the texture of an old ferry, dark dented varnish over plain heavy wood; it feels as though someone's sawn it from some tired public vessel and lashed it up on the outermost edge of the structure. Not unlikely; the wingless body of a 747 has been incorporated, nearer Oakland.

Maria Paz is older, with slate gray eyes, an elegant dark coat, tattoo of a blue swallow on the inside of her left ankle, just above the little gold chain she wears there. Maria Paz smokes Kools, one after another, lighting them with a brushed chrome Zippo she takes from her purse; each time she flicks it open, a sharp whiff of benzene cuts across the warm smells of coffee and scrambled eggs.

You can talk with the people you meet on the bridge. Because everyone's crazy there, Skinner says, and out of all that craziness you're bound to find a few who're crazy the way you are.

She sits with Maria Paz, drinks coffee, watches her smoke Kools. She tells Maria Paz about Skinner.

"How old is he?" Maria Paz asks.

"Old. I don't know."

"And he lives over the cable saddle on the first tower?"

"Yes."

"Then he's been here a long time. The tops of the towers are very special. Do you know that?"

"No.

"He's from the days when the first people came out from the cities to live on the bridge."

"Why did they do that?"

Maria Paz looks at her over the Zippo. Click. Tang of benzene. "They had nowhere else to go. They were homeless in the cities. The bridge had been closed, you see, closed to traffic, for three years."

"Traffic?"

Maria Paz laughs. "But it was a *bridge*, darling. People drove back and forth in cars, from one end to the other." She laughs again. "There were too many cars, finally, so they dug the tunnels under the Bay. Tunnels for the cars, tunnels for the maglevs. The bridge was old, in need of repair. They closed it, but then the devaluations began, the depression. There was no money for the repairs they'd planned. The bridge stood empty. And then one night, as if someone had given a signal, the homeless came. But the legend is that there *was* no signal. People simply *came*. They climbed the chainlink and the barricades at either end; they climbed in such numbers that the chainlink twisted and fell. They tumbled the concrete barricades into the Bay. They climbed the towers. Dozens died, falling to their deaths. But when dawn came, they were here, on the bridge, clinging, claiming it, and the cities, dear," she blew twin streams of smoke from her nostrils, "knew that the world was watching. They were no longer invisible, you see, the homeless people; they'd come together on this span of steel, had claimed it as their own. The cities had to be cautious then. Already the Japanese were preparing an airlift of food and medical supplies. A national embarrassment. No time for the water cannon, no. They were allowed to stay. Temporarily. The first structures were of cardboard." Maria Paz smiles.

"Skinner? You think he came then?"

"Perhaps. If he's as old as you seem to think he is. How long have you been on the bridge, dear?"

"Three months, maybe."

"I was born here," says Maria Paz.

The cities have their own pressing difficulties. This is not an easy century, the nation quite clearly in decline and the very concept of nation-states called increasingly into question. The squatters have been allowed to remain upon the bridge and have transformed it. There were, among their original numbers, entrepreneurs, natural politicians, artists, men and women of previously untapped energies and talents. While the world watched, and the cities secretly winced, the bridge people began to build, architecture as *art brut*. The representatives of global charities descended in helicopters, to be presented with lists of tools and materials. Shipments of advanced adhesives arrived from Japan. A Belgian manufacturer donated a boatload of carbon-fiber beams. Teams of expert scavengers rolled through the cities in battered flatbeds, returning to the bridge piled high with discarded building materials.

The bridge and its inhabitants became the cities' premier tourist attraction.

Hard currency, from Europe and Japan.

She walks back in the early light that filters through windows, through sheets of wind-shivered plastic. The bridge never sleeps, but this is a quiet time. A man is arranging fish on a bed of shaved ice in a wooden cart. The pavement beneath her feet is covered with gum wrappers and the flattened filters of cigarettes. A drunk is singing somewhere, overhead. Maria Paz left with a man, someone she'd been waiting for.

She thinks about the story and tries to imagine Skinner there, the night they took the bridge, young then, his leather jacket new and glossy.

She thinks about the Europeans in the hotel on Geary. Hard currency.

She reaches the first elevator, the cage, and leans back against its bars as it rises up its patched tunnel, where the private lives of her neighbors are walled away in so many tiny, handmade spaces. Stepping from the cage, she sees the African squatting in his tweed overcoat in the light cast by a caged bulb on a long yellow extension cord, the motor of his elevator spread out around him on fresh sheets of newsprint. He looks up at her apologetically.

"Adjusting the brushes," he says.

"I'll climb." She goes up the ladder. Always keep one hand and one foot on the ladder, Skinner told her, don't think about where you are and don't look down. It's a long climb, up toward the smooth sweep of cable. Skinner must've done it thousands of times, uncounted, unthinking. She reaches the top of this ladder, makes a careful transfer to the second, the short one, that leads to Skinner's room.

He's there, of course, asleep, when she scrambles up through the hatch. She tries to move as quietly as she can, but the jingle of the jacket's chrome hardware disturbs him, or reaches him in his dream, because he calls out something, his voice thick with sleep. It might be a woman's name, she thinks. It certainly isn't hers.

In Skinner's dream now they all run forward, and the police, the police are hesitating, falling back. Overhead the steady drum of the network helicopters with their lights and cameras. A light rain's falling now, as Skinner locks his cold fingers in the chainlink and starts to climb, and behind him a roar goes up, drowning the bullhorns of the police and the National Guard, and Skinner is climbing, kicking the narrow toes of his boots into chainlink, climbing as though he's gone suddenly weightless, floating up, really, rising on the crowd's roar, the ragged cheer torn from all their lungs. He's there, at the top, for one interminable instant. He jumps. He's the first. He's on the bridge, running, running toward Oakland, as the chainlink crashes behind him, his cheeks wet with the rain and tears.

And somewhere off in the night, on the Oakland side, another fence has fallen. And they meet, these two lost armies, and flow together as one, and huddle there, at the bridge's center, their arms around one another, singing ragged wordless hymns.

At dawn, the first climbers begin to scale the towers.

Skinner is with them.

She's brewing coffee on the Coleman when she sees him open his eyes.

"I thought you'd gone," he says.

"I took a walk. I'm not going anywhere. There's coffee."

He smiles, eyes sliding out of focus. "I was dreaming...."

"Dreaming what?"

"I don't remember. We were singing. In the rain...."

She brings him coffee in the heavy china cup he likes, holds it, helps him drink. "Skinner, were you here when they came from the cities? When they took the bridge?"

He looks up at her with a strange expression. His eyes widen. He coughs on the coffee, wipes his mouth with the back of his hand. "Yes," he says, "yes. In the rain. We were singing. I remember that...."

"Did you build this place, Skinner? This room? Do you remember?"

"No," he says, "no. Sometimes I don't remember....We climbed. Up. We climbed up past the helicopters. We waved at them. Some people fell. At the top. We got to the top...."

"What happened then?"

He smiles. "The sun came out. We saw the city."

MALCOLM MARGOLIN

Malcolm Margolin was born in Boston in 1940. He is the founder and publisher of Heyday, which specializes in books about California history, literature, and culture with a particular focus on California Indians. Margolin is also the founder and publisher of *News from Native California*, a quarterly magazine devoted to California Indians. He lives in Berkeley.

• •

In "Center Post for Kule Loklo," first published in *News from Native California*, Margolin describes the merging of physical and spiritual experience through the installation of a center post in a Coast Miwok dance house.

CENTER POST FOR KULE LOKLO

I T WAS MORNING, a chill still in the air. I pulled off the dirt road onto a grassy shoulder and walked into a field to join a small group of men who were stamping the ground, complaining about the cold, and waiting. A flatbed truck was warming up nearby. On the ground beside it were peavies, a chainsaw, jacks, a drawknife, shovels, bars, and come-alongs.

As we talked quietly among ourselves about the tools and the hydraulic tailgate on the truck, we were secretly sizing each other up the way men do in such a situation: who knew the most about the tools, who had had the most experience, who would eventually emerge as a leader. Anyone casually glancing our way would have assumed this was a typical work crew scene. But we were not gathered together for an ordinary logging or construction job. A mix of Indians and Anglos, we had been invited by Ester and Lanny Pinola and Bun Lucas of the Kule Loklo village to help remove an old center post from a dance house and put in a new one. Despite the modern tools, the purring of the truck motor, and the requisite "macho" noises we were making at each other, we were all aware of a religious spirit to the undertaking. The dance house was a couple of hundred yards away. Bun, Ester, Lanny, and other members of the Coast Miwok and Kashaya Pomo people had been dancing and singing in the house for the last four nights, holding a wake for the old center post that was dying, preparing a welcome for the new post that would be installed.

I had known the dance house and its old center post for about ten years, and I had long admired it. But when I first saw it, I would never have predicted the deep spiritual activity that now suffused our enterprise. Kule Loklo was not, at least in its beginnings, an authentic Indian village. It was more like a museum, set up by a group of Anglo schoolteachers to replicate a village of the "extinct" Miwok people who once lived here on the Point Reyes National Seashore in Marin County. The schoolteachers learned about Indians mostly through books, studying the ethnographies carefully, poring over the archaeological records. Then, using students and volunteers, they set about to reconstruct the village using only the old methods. The wood was shaped with obsidian tools. The ground was chipped at with wooden digging sticks, and bits of dislodged earth were scooped up with abalone shells and loaded into baskets to be carried off. It was a long and painstaking process; it took over a year just to dig out the dance house pit. Surely no California village had been built this way for well over a century. Nevertheless, bit by bit, a village grew: a dance house, a sweathouse, acorn granaries, a scattering of dwellings and shade houses. The teachers and the rangers of the National Seashore held their interpretive programs here. Busloads of schoolchildren, and on weekends family groups, descended on the village; they were taught ancient skills and ancient ways, generally by people who themselves had learned them from books only a few years before.

As the village gained prominence, however, an event occurred that the rangers and schoolteachers had never prepared themselves for. The Coast Miwok turned out not to be very "extinct" at all. Many of them still lived around Point Arena, others had married into the Pomo and were living on the Kashaya Reservation at Stewarts Point. Among them were people who still spoke the old language and who not only remembered the old ways, but in many respects still lived by them. They came to Kule Loklo to investigate what these schoolteachers and rangers were saying about them.

The initial confrontations between the teachers and the natives were at times ill-tempered, at times (at least to an outsider) quite comic. The situation had all the makings of a bitter fight, a long-term grudge, a power struggle, even—at times—a fiasco. But that is not what happened. Gradually, the Indian community felt itself more and more drawn toward the village. Perhaps, they admitted, they had something to learn from these people who had studied the literature and researched their past so devotedly. The teachers and rangers, for their part, came to realize that perhaps they were not well equipped emotionally and spiritually to interpret Indian culture.

Over a few years the Indians became integrated into the programs, until finally they took them over entirely. Under the direction of Ester and Lanny Pinola and with the help of Bun Lucas, Lorraine Laiwa, Gladys Gonzalez, and others, they began to run the interpretive programs and make the decisions. As time passed and the Indian presence grew stronger, they began to use the village for feasts and dances, infusing the buildings with spirit and belief. The schoolteachers had created a stage setting; the drama was now in the hands of the Indians. Kule Loklo was no longer just a museum. It had come alive.

The old center post had seen all these changes. Thousands of schoolchildren and visitors had passed around it, and the center post had heard the respectful voices of those whose hearts were open, as well as the nervous snickerings of those who did not yet understand. It had witnessed—and lent strength to—the prayers and ceremonies of recent years. A month or so before our gathering, vandals had broken into the dance house and set fire to its base, scarring and weakening it. In the previous four nights it had been thanked with dances and songs, and perhaps its spirit was put to rest.

We entered the dance house through a low, northeast-facing entranceway. We had to stoop low, and during the rest of the day I would repeatedly whack my head—a useful, if painful, lesson about humility that was literally drummed into me again and again. A narrow, sloping passageway led to the interior. It was dark and comfortable within, about 32 feet in diameter, and dug about four feet into the ground. The walls below ground level were banked with stone. The earth-covered roof, with a smoke hole near the center, was held up by the center post, by four other posts around it, and by twelve shorter posts that stood closer to the edge. There were various interpretations about what the posts signified. Some Indian people, combining ancient beliefs with their conversion to Mormonism, felt that the center post was Jesus; the four middle posts were God, the Resurrection, Repentance, and the Witness; and the twelve posts around the edge represented the twelve apostles. Others, holding more traditional views, referred to the spiritual significance of the number four and the four directions. Interpretations varied, but one thing was obvious. These posts were not randomly or carelessly placed. They were here for a sacred reason. And as we pulled the shovels and digging bars into the dance house, we knew that we had entered sacred space.

The old center post had been dug four feet into the ground, and it was interlocked with the roof above us. To get it out, we first dug a deep trench from the entranceway toward the center post, so that we could slide its base along the trench and eventually out the door. There were several hours of digging. Bars chipped away at the hard floor, shovels plunged into the earth. I was secretly glad that Indians were running the show this time, not schoolteachers; otherwise, we might have been using digging sticks.

As we worked, I had the curious sense of this event running on two channels. On one channel was the physical work: a crew of men sweating, grunting, giving orders, "spelling" each other, even swearing. Then we would pause and switch to the other channel, the spiritual, as Ben Lucas said a variety of prayers, thanked the crew, and talked to the old center post. "The spirit is here among us," said Bun, and, deeply quiet, we could all feel it—not just in the prayers, but in the air, in the wood, in the ground. We then returned for a while to the grunting, sweating, and giving or taking orders as we deepened the trench and tried to detach the top of the post from the roof. We were finally ready to pull the center post entirely loose and carry it outside to where a funeral pyre had been prepared. We stopped for a final prayer. Spoken by Bun in Pomo, it was filled with deep ritual sighs and real tears that spread among all of us. At the end of the prayer, Bun gave forth with four prolonged howls. In all my life I do not think that I have ever heard a more unearthly, beautiful, moving sound. I call them "howls" for lack of a better word, but they were really something else— the sound a mountain might make, or a large tree, or the earth itself. This,

Bun explained later, was the cry Earthmaker had made at the creation of the world. With this cry, the sense that I had had of two separate channels ended. As we bid the old center post farewell, pulled it down, and marched it to the funeral pyre, the physical and spiritual worlds merged. Like the warp and woof of a textile, they were now inextricably woven together in our aching muscles, with those howls reverberating deep within us.

D. J. WALDIE

D. J. Waldie was born in 1948 in the Los Angeles suburb of Lakewood, and he continues to reside there, in his childhood home. His *Holy Land: A Suburban Memoir* is both a journalistic examination of his hometown and a personal meditation on his life there. The longtime public information officer for the city of Lakewood, Waldie is also a contributing writer to *Los Angeles* magazine and has written for both the *Los Angeles Times* and the *New York Times*. His other books are *Real City: Downtown Los Angeles Inside/Out, Where We Are Now: Notes from Los Angeles,* and *Close to Home: An American Album.* D. J. Waldie has received a fellowship from the National Endowment for the Arts, the William Allen White Memorial Medal, and the nonfiction Book Prize of The Commonwealth Club of California.

• •

In the following excerpt from *Holy Land*, Waldie dissects the construction of houses in Lakewood to peer into the character of his family and his community.

from *HOLY LAND: A SUBURBAN MEMOIR*

THE HOUSES IN my neighborhood touch the ground lightly. There is no basement.

Foundations are hardly more than a foot deep. It took a bucket excavator only fifteen minutes to dig each one.

Carpenters followed and nailed up three-foot foundation forms as quickly as possible.

Workmen poured the concrete quickly, too. The crews poured 2,113 foundations in a hundred days. For every ten houses, they wasted enough concrete for the foundation of an eleventh.

The raised foundation of each house leaves an eighteen-inch crawl space beneath the floor.

My father went under there occasionally, to move an electrical outlet without the benefit of a city building permit.

The crawl space is partly lighted by vents in the foundation. From association, the pale wood of the joists beneath the floor has become the same gray color as the dirt.

The attic is different. At the ridge board, where the rafters join, there is just enough space for a grown man to stand slightly hunched.

My father rigged a light there, over the attic hatch in the hallway ceiling. Before you climb into the attic, you can turn the light on by reaching up and pulling a string tied to the socket chain.

In this light, the wood seems new. It still smells of sawn lumber.

My parents filled the attic with things we used every year, but only once a year—the aluminum Christmas tree, ornaments and lights, plastic houses for the train set, winter clothes, and vacation luggage.

The attic held things that were no longer used—my father's Navy uniforms, the love letters my mother sent him during the war, and the notebook he kept when he belonged to a Catholic religious order.

Despite the light, the attic is threatening to walk in, because only a few loose planks lie across the joists. A bad step will put your foot through a bedroom ceiling.

My house is largely a void.

The emptiness is not just in the span of the rooms or in the attic and foundation spaces. All the walls are hollow, too.

Houses in Southern California are built as sketchily as possible, while still able to shed rain. Walls are a thin, cement skin over absence.

Roofs are important here, but only when it rains. The rest is for modesty.

The outside walls are stucco, a mixture of sand and Portland cement.

The exterior coat is about an eighth-inch thick, with a ratio of four parts of sand to one part of cement.

The middle coat is three-eighths of an inch. The ratio of sand to cement is five to one.

The first layer of stucco—three-eighths of an inch of four parts of sand to one part cement—was quickly troweled over chicken wire. The wire was furred a quarter-inch from tarpaper sheets nailed to the outside edge of the studs.

The surface of a stucco house clings to this network of light wire and not to the wood frame. The wire intersections support the stucco over the empty span of the walls.

The brittle exterior of these houses is a little more than an inch thick.

The houses on my block have been painted so often that the grains of sand in the surface of the stucco have begun to disappear.

Behind the layers of stucco and tar paper are the vertical studs, pine two-by-fours sixteen inches apart. Spanning these are wooden members called fire blocks.

The fire blocks are not for support; they separate pockets of dead air inside the finished wall.

Fire blocks prevent the empty vertical space between each pair of studs from becoming a chimney that would carry a fire to the rafters and bring the house down.

Frame houses are based on a rough balance. The wood frame resists gravity's downward thrust of the heavy roof; the rafters nailed to the roof's ridge board brace the walls from falling outward.

Playing hide-and-seek once, just at sunset, I stood in the doorway of the darkened bedroom I shared with my older brother, knees actually knocking in fear.

My house was built by a real estate development company in 1942. The company built eleven hundred houses on land Clark Bonner had sold them.

The company built the houses for workers at the Douglas Aircraft plant.

My house was bought by a guard at the federal prison on Terminal Island in Long Beach.

When my parents bought the house from him in 1946, it was landscaped with a row of palm trees along the driveway. There was a rock garden behind the house.

The pile of rocks was higher than the wood fence around the yard. Whitewashed boulders from the San Gabriel River edged the front walk.

The guard had used men from the prison to plant the palm trees and build the rock garden.

It took my father months to remove the palms, which eventually would have towered over the house. He took down the rock garden and carried the boulders to the county dump in the trunk of his car.

The guard left behind several pieces of furniture, made by prisoners from scrap lumber.

My parents had to keep the furniture when they bought the house. They couldn't afford to replace it.

The furniture was in the room my brother and I shared. I still have some of the pieces.

ABOUT THE EDITOR

DAVID CHU was born in New York City and raised in Northern California. He received a bachelor's degree in medieval studies from Brown University and a master's degree in religion from Harvard University Extension School. He has worked at libraries, bookstores, and book publishers. Over the years he has enjoyed visiting great buildings and public spaces in California and throughout the United States. He currently works as a freelance copyeditor.

A California Legacy Book

Santa Clara University and Heyday Books are pleased to publish the California Legacy series, vibrant and relevant writings drawn from California's past and present.

Santa Clara University—founded in 1851 on the site of the eighth of California's original twenty-one missions—is the oldest institution of higher learning in the state. A Jesuit institution, it is particularly aware of its contribution to California's cultural heritage and its responsibility to preserve and celebrate that heritage.

Heyday Books, founded in 1974, specializes in critically acclaimed books on California literature, history, natural history, and ethnic studies.

Books in the California Legacy series appear as anthologies, single author collections, reprints of important books, and original works. Taken together, these volumes bring readers a new perspective on California's cultural life, a perspective that honors diversity and finds great pleasure in the eloquence of human expression.

Series Editor: Terry Beers

Publisher: Malcolm Margolin

Advisory Committee: Stephen Becker, William Deverell, Charles Faulhaber, David Fine, Steven Gilbar, Ron Hansen, Gerald Haslam, Robert Hass, Jack Hicks, Timothy Hodson, Jeanne Wakatsuki Houston, Maxine Hong Kingston, Frank LaPena, Ursula K. Le Guin, Jeff Lustig, Ishmael Reed, Alan Rosenus, Robert Senkewicz, Gary Snyder, Kevin Starr, Richard Walker, Alice Waters, Jennifer Watts, Al Young.

Thanks to the English Department at Santa Clara University and to Regis McKenna for their support of the California Legacy series.

For more on California Legacy titles, events, or other information, please visit www.californialegacy.org.

Other California Legacy Books

Califauna: A Literary Field Guide
Edited by Terry Beers and Emily Elrod

California Poetry: From the Gold Rush to the Present
Edited by Dana Gioia, Chryss Yost, and Jack Hicks

Death Valley in '49
William Lewis Manly

Eldorado: Adventures in the Path of Empire
Bayard Taylor

Essential Bierce
Edited with an Introduction by John R. Dunlap

Essential Mary Austin
Edited with an Introduction by Kevin Hearle

Essential Muir
Edited with an Introduction by Fred D. White

Essential Saroyan
Edited with an Introduction by William E. Justice

Inlandia: A Literary Journey through California's Inland Empire
Edited by Gayle Wattawa with an Introduction by Susan Straight

Lands of Promise and Despair: Chronicles of Early California, 1535–1846
Edited by Rose Marie Beebe and Robert M. Senkewicz

No Place for a Puritan: The Literature of California's Deserts
Edited by Ruth Nolan

Under the Fifth Sun: Latino Literature in California
Edited by Rick Heide

Unfolding Beauty: Celebrating California's Landscapes
Edited with an Introduction by Terry Beers

Wallace Stegner's West
Edited with an Introduction by Page Stegner

HEYDAY
into California

About Heyday

Heyday is an independent, nonprofit publisher and unique cultural institution. We promote widespread awareness and celebration of California's many cultures, landscapes, and boundary-breaking ideas. Through our well-crafted books, public events, and innovative outreach programs we are building a vibrant community of readers, writers, and thinkers.

Thank You

It takes the collective effort of many to create a thriving literary culture. We are thankful to all the thoughtful people we have the privilege to engage with. Cheers to our writers, artists, editors, storytellers, designers, printers, bookstores, critics, cultural organizations, readers, and book lovers everywhere!

We are especially grateful for the generous funding we've received for our publications and programs during the past year from foundations and hundreds of individual donors. Major supporters include:

Anonymous; Audubon California; Barona Band of Mission Indians; B.C.W. Trust III; S. D. Bechtel, Jr. Foundation; Barbara and Fred Berensmeier; Berkeley Civic Arts Program and Civic Arts Commission; Joan Berman; Lewis and Sheana Butler; Butler Koshland Fund; California State Coastal Conservancy; California State Library; California Wildlife Foundation; Joanne Campbell; Keith Campbell Foundation; Candelaria Fund; John and Nancy Cassidy Family Foundation, through Silicon Valley Community Foundation; Christensen Fund; Creative Work Fund; The Community Action Fund; Community Futures Collective; Compton Foundation, Inc.; Lawrence Crooks; Ida Rae Egli; Donald and Janice Elliott, in honor of David Elliott, through Silicon Valley Community Foundation; Evergreen Foundation; Federated Indians of Graton Rancheria; Mark and Tracy Ferron; Furthur Foundation; George Gamble; Wallace Alexander Gerbode Foundation; Richard & Rhoda Goldman Fund; Evelyn & Walter Haas, Jr. Fund; Walter & Elise Haas Fund; James and Coke Hallowell; Sandra and Chuck Hobson; James Irvine Foundation; JiJi Foundation; Marty and Pamela Krasney; Robert and Karen Kustel, in honor of Bruce Kelley; Guy Lampard and Suzanne Badenhoop; LEF Foundation; Michael McCone; Moore Family Foundation; National Endowment for the Arts; National Park Service; Organize Training Center; David and Lucile Packard Foundation; Patagonia; Pease Family Fund, in honor of Bruce Kelley; Resources Legacy Fund; Alan Rosenus; Rosie the Riveter/WWII Home Front NHP; San Francisco Foundation; San Manuel Band of Mission Indians; Deborah Sanchez; Savory Thymes; Hans Schoepflin; Contee and Maggie Seely; James B. Swinerton; Swinerton Family Fund; Taproot Foundation; Thendara Foundation; TomKat Charitable Trust; Lisa Van Cleef and Mark Gunson; Marion Weber; John Wiley & Sons; Peter Booth Wiley; and Yocha Dehe Wintun Nation.

Getting Involved

To learn more about our publications, events, membership club, and other ways you can participate, please visit: www.heydaybooks.com.